D0484682

the series on school reform

Patricia A. Wasley	Ann Lieberman	Joseph P. McDonald
University of Washington	Carnegie Foundation for the Advancement of Teaching	New York University

SERIES EDITORS

(Continued)

the series on school reform, *continued*

Managing to Change

How Schools Can Survive (and Sometimes Thrive) in Turbulent Times

THOMAS HATCH

TEACHERS COLLEGE PRESS

Teachers College, Columbia University
New York and London

Published by Teachers College Press, 1234 Amsterdam Avenue, New York, NY 10027

Library of Congress Cataloging-in-Publication Data

Hatch, Thomas.
  Managing to change : how schools can survive (and sometimes thrive) in turbulent times / Thomas Hatch.
    p. cm. – (Series on school reform)
  Includes bibliographical references and index.
  ISBN 978-0-8077-4966-1 (pbk.)–ISBN 978-0-8077-4967-8 (hardcover)
  1. School improvement programs–United States. 2. Educational change–United States. I. Title.
  LB2822.82.H4 2009
  371.2'07–dc22

                                                                            2008053401

ISBN 978-0-8077-4966-1 (paper)
ISBN 978-0-8077-4967-8 (hardcover)

Printed on acid-free paper
Manufactured in the United States of America

16   15   14   13   12   11   10   09   8   7   6   5   4   3   2   1

Contents

Acknowledgments

Work on this book spanned a number of years and reflects the contributions of many groups and individuals. While I take responsibility for the ideas presented here, I want to acknowledge their contributions and the deep debt I owe to all of them. A conversation with Ray Bacchetti, in particular, helped launch this work, which later benefited from the generous support of the William and Flora Hewlett Foundation and the Spencer Foundation. I carried out the research and work related to this book as a staff member at the Carnegie Foundation for the Advancement of Teaching and as a faculty member at Teachers College, Columbia University, and at the National Center for Restructuring, Education, Schools and Teaching (NCREST). Many members of those organizations–including Lee Shulman, John Barcroft, Pat Hutchings, and Jacqueline Ancess–provided me with both the time and support that made this work possible. In addition, a number of colleagues participated directly in the research related to this book, and for their contributions I would like to thank Shannon K'Doah Range, Noel White, Karen Herbert, Melinda Martin Beltran, Melissa Eiler-White, Jonah Liebert, Lisa Beck, and Annis Brown. Meredith Honig, in particular, collaborated with me in developing some of the initial ideas related to capacity and coherence that served as a basis for the book. The research and writing of the book also benefited from the comments of several anonymous reviewers and from conversations with Ann Lieberman, Joe McDonald, Susan Liddicoat, and Karen Hammerness, all of whom read drafts and provided crucial feedback that helped advance the work. Lisa Beck helped prepare several of the figures and statistics on California. Ruby Kerawalla, Felicia Smart-Williams, and Grazyna Hulacka and the staff at NCREST also provided support throughout the research and writing process. I also sincerely appreciate the efforts of Marie Ellen Larcada who helped shepherd this book through the publication process.

The work in this book also grows directly out of the experiences I had working on a number of educational reform projects early in my career. Those experiences presented me with truly unusual opportunities to learn about many different aspects of schools and schooling. Those experiences would not have been possible without the sustained support of Howard Gardner and my colleagues at Project Zero, the Mather Afterschool Program, the ATLAS Communities Project, and the ATLAS Seminar. Through those experiences, I was also able to work and learn alongside a number of individuals–including Allan Collins, William Damon, David Perkins, James Comer, Ted Sizer, and Janet Whitla–who generously shared their perspectives with me, but were always willing to help me develop my own point of view. Through my work at Project Zero, I also had a chance to meet and learn from Ernesto Cortes, Jr., Christine Stevens, Joe Higgs, and the many other members of the Alliance Schools. Their approach has had a significant impact on my thinking, especially on the ideas related to community involvement discussed in the later chapters of this book.

I am also particularly thankful for the opportunities that I have had over the years to talk about issues of school improvement with many of the educators and researchers whose work I refer to throughout these pages. They not only returned e-mails, they met with me after classes and during conferences, and they provided advice and feedback on many of the papers and presentations in which I tried out some of these ideas. Michael Fullan, in particular, served as a discussant on a paper that provided an initial outline of some of these ideas. Initial work on the issues discussed in this book appeared in *American Educational Research Journal, Phi Delta Kappan, Education Week, American Journal of Education, Educational Researcher,* and *The New Educator.*

This work truly would not have been possible without the time and effort of the many teachers, principals, administrators, and members of school reform organizations who have graciously participated in my research. I owe a special debt to the leaders of the schools described in this book. They welcomed me into their schools, introduced me to their colleagues and parents, and participated in countless interviews themselves. In addition, they have continued to provide advice and feedback throughout the publication process.

While it goes without saying, I could not have carried out any of this work without the constant encouragement of my parents, which I continue to feel every day. Finally, I cannot imagine doing this work without the support of Karen Hammerness. Karen willingly talked with me about these ideas as they developed, read numerous versions of this manuscript, and made sure that I could complete this work while she juggled the demands of her own work and research. This book is for her, and for Hannah, Clara, and Stella.

Introduction

Altering context is not up to others; all of us can, to a certain extent, change the immediate context around us–and this starts us down the pathway of transformation.

–Michael Fullan (2003, p. 29)

The twentieth century began with the efforts of the leading educators at the time to create what they believed would be the "one best system" (Tyack, 1974), but it ended with concerns about whether there was any educational system at all. As the twenty-first century unfolds, a host of ideas for new kinds of schools and school systems have emerged as alternatives to the common school of Horace Mann; we now have charter schools, small schools, magnet schools, and home schools. We still have school boards, superintendents, and principals, but we also have a variety of parent councils, school-based management schemes, teacher-led schools, and voucher plans to help free schools from the prevailing bureaucracy and create the flexibility, consensus, or competition that various advocates believe will lead to improved performance and a faster pace of change.

Amidst these developments we have debated the purposes of schooling, argued about the nature of intelligence, and wondered whether or not schools really have gotten worse. We have struggled to integrate the schools and questioned to what extent integration has really been achieved. We've fought curriculum wars, reading wars, and math wars; battled over standards; and pitted progressives against traditionalists. We've gone back to basics, searched for alternatives, and then gone back to basics again.

In the end, some improvements in education have been made, but few people seem satisfied with the results so far. Even with sustained attention to educational reform since the publication of *A Nation at Risk* (National Commission on Excellence in Education, 1983), the accomplishments of individual schools, remarkable people, and outstanding programs continue to be overshadowed by the inability to improve learning opportunities for many

1

students or to change the system as a whole. On the one hand, the broad general agreements about what will contribute to improvements in individual schools—such as consensus around goals and missions, strong leadership from principals and superintendents, and parent involvement—have failed to provide the specific guidance needed for significant changes on a wide scale. On the other hand, the efforts to scale up promising programs have not addressed the basic conditions that make it difficult for many different schools to improve.

This book begins with the assumption that the conditions and quality of schooling can be improved, but cannot be improved on a large scale simply by raising standards, aligning policies, changing curricula, implementing improvement programs, mandating new tests, and demanding that schools become more accountable. Policy makers cannot make all policies "coherent" or supply each school with all the resources that school needs (McLaughlin, 1990). Instead, I argue that schools have to help create the conditions they need to be successful. In short, schools that demonstrate the *capacity* to make improvements are neither totally dependent nor completely independent of the demands, pressures, resources, and opportunities that exist around them. They are intimately tied to their environments, and they can shape as well as respond to external demands and pressures (Fullan, 1999; Hargreaves & Fullan, 1998; Stoll, 1999).

In order to address what it takes for schools to shape and respond to constantly changing external demands and pressures, this book describes a small number of key organizational practices that can serve as the focus for improvement efforts. The discussion of these practices raises fundamental questions about some of the taken-for-granted assumptions about educational reform including the role of the principal and other school leaders, the need for schools to identify specific outcomes and closely monitor their performance, the value of short-term rewards and sanctions, and the promise of external support and technical assistance for "low-performing" schools. In the end, these strategies may only benefit a small number of schools—schools that already have the capacity to use resources and external assistance effectively. Unfortunately, the low-performing schools many of these practices and polices seek to help lack this capacity (see for example, Mintrop, 2003). Furthermore, many strategies that focus on low-performing schools fail to address the fundamental conditions that limit the capacity of all schools to make improvements (Malen, Croninger, Muncey, & Redmond-Jones, 2002) and that lead to the inevitable failure of many efforts to replicate and scale up model programs and isolated successes. Even well-intentioned reform efforts may perpetuate some of the current inequities by helping to give successful schools a competitive advantage over others. By seriously reexamining what it takes for schools to make improvements and by learning how educators can help more schools to strategically manage the demands in the external environment, this book seeks to enable school members and those who work with them to create the conditions for their own success.

THE BASIS FOR THIS BOOK

The argument I make in this book grows from several sources: my reading of the literature on school reform; my own personal experiences working with schools and reform organizations; a survey I conducted of the reforms and improvement programs in which schools in several districts were engaged in the late 1990s; and the data I collected over a period of four years (2001–2005) from six schools in the San Francisco Bay Area.

In my reading, works by researchers including Seymour Sarason, Larry Cuban, David Tyack, David Cohen, Richard Elmore, Michael Fullan, Andy Hargreaves, Milbrey McLaughlin and Joan Talbert, and countless reform evaluations make three things clear: (1) Reform is difficult work; (2) too often reformers repeat the mistakes of previous eras; and (3) while optimism is essential for inspiration and motivation, unrealistic expectations often mean that reformers underestimate what needs to be done and how long it might take to make improvements. The work of these researchers demonstrates that as much as some may want to create a high-quality educational system that is powerful and efficient and governed by data and logic, for better or worse, we actually have a hodgepodge of institutions, groups, and individuals; a variety of often conflicting beliefs and values; and a "system" filled with the kinds of politics, emotions, and outcomes that can overwhelm data, reason, and good intentions (Cohen, 1995; Fuhrman, 1993).

My own experiences as a researcher and practitioner have reinforced both the difficulties of making large-scale changes and the hope that can come when small-scale changes begin to appear. In the 1980s, as a graduate student working at Harvard Project Zero with Howard Gardner–who developed the theory of multiple intelligences (Gardner, 1983)– I had the opportunity to work in several different early childhood and elementary classrooms where teachers' perceptions of "unsuccessful" students changed radically when they saw those same students as engaged, persistent, and highly accomplished in activities involving spatial, musical, interpersonal, linguistic, logical-mathematical, or bodily-kinesthetic intelligences rarely tapped by the regular curriculum. At the same time, I also saw how much easier it was for schools and professional development programs to claim that they were taking multiple intelligences into account than it was for them to address students' intellectual strengths and interests in substantive, sustained ways.

Subsequently, I helped to develop an after-school program for third, fourth, and fifth graders that brought together the theory of multiple intelligences with the work of psychologists William Damon (1990), David Perkins (1992), and Allan Collins (1989) on social development, collaborative learning, thinking skills, and cognitive apprenticeship. That project gave us an opportunity to create a program from scratch—outside of the usual constraints of the school day—and I could see the transformation of students who became engaged in long-term projects, plays, and community service activities. At the same time, I grew frustrated by the inability to transfer those results and foster equally impressive improvements in the students' work during the regular school day and in their performances on traditional academic measures.

Building on that experience, in the early 1990s, I had an opportunity as a member of the ATLAS Communities Project to participate in the development of a comprehensive approach to educational reform that addressed many different aspects of the regular school day. ATLAS began as a collaboration of four of the most prominent organizations involved in school reform at the time: the Coalition of Essential Schools, the School Development Program, the Education Development Center, and Harvard Project Zero. ATLAS sought to bring together the expertise and resources of these organizations to create "pathways" of elementary, middle, and secondary schools around the country. ATLAS was one of the original design teams sponsored by the New American Schools Development Corporation (NASDC). In seeking comprehensive, "break-the-mold" school designs, NASDC helped to fuel growing interest in the idea that in order to make changes in one aspect of education it was necessary to make changes in all aspects at once (Hatch, 2001c).

While my work on ATLAS gave me a chance to learn about the wealth of expertise and resources that these four organizations had developed, I also experienced firsthand how difficult it can be to bring together many different ideas and resources in one coherent approach to school reform. For one thing, the materials and approaches that each organization developed reflected different assumptions and theories about how students learn, how schools should work, and how organizations change (Hatch, 1998a). Furthermore, even with the combined resources and expertise of four of the best known organizations involved in educational reform, many questions about how to support improvements in schools and in students' learning remained unaddressed (Hatch & White, 2002).

My work on ATLAS also demonstrated that even a plethora of good ideas and programs can end up contributing to the fragmentation and overload that many teachers and administrators feel. In fact, in every school I visited as a member of ATLAS, I seemed to run into colleagues from other reform organizations who were trying to get those same teachers and principals to put another program in place.

As a consequence, I started to ask about the experiences of the teachers, principals, and reform colleagues I encountered, and I found that they too were working in schools where far too much was going on with far too little coordination. But I knew that the people and schools that I came in contact with were an unusual group. Perhaps this was just an isolated phenomenon restricted to a small number of schools? To explore the issue further, I carried out a survey in a school district in the San Francisco Bay Area that I referred to as "Meadowlark." (Throughout this book I have used pseudonyms for the names of districts and schools and for all individuals associated with them.) The survey asked all principals in the district to report on the number of improvement programs that were at work in their schools. The results showed that more than half of the schools that responded (77%) were involved in three or more different reform programs like ATLAS, Success for All, Accelerated Schools, or others. A subsequent survey in three comparison districts revealed similar results (Hatch, 2002).

To explore this phenomenon further, I interviewed principals of some of the schools in the Meadowlark District and developed a case study of Charleston High School, a school where a number of reform initiatives were underway. (The results of the surveys along with the case study are briefly summarized in Chapter 1.) For the most part, the experiences of the people in those schools resonated with my own, and I began to hear surprising and specific details about the ways in which practitioners felt that the multiple reform initiatives intended to help them were actually hampering their work. Although these initiatives were supposed to bring new resources and support that could help these schools improve their performance, it became clearer and clearer that many of the schools could not take advantage of this support or these resources and use them effectively. In short, these schools lacked the capacity to make improvements.

In order to learn more about what it takes for schools to make improvements, I set out to study a small number of schools from a number of other districts in the Bay Area that had maintained relatively good reputations over long periods of time. Of course, any number of factors could affect the performances of these schools. Therefore, I sought to identify schools that differed in several ways. First, I looked for schools that were either high-performing or low-performing, but had consistently worked on making some changes and improvements in their structures and operations. Second, I looked for schools with different kinds of student populations, with students from different income levels and from different backgrounds. Third, I sought schools in different kinds of districts: some that could be considered higher functioning and more supportive and others that provided a less supportive or more problematic context. Fourth, reflecting my belief in the value of many different kinds of instructional approaches, I looked for schools with distinct and different instructional philosophies—some more progressive, others more back-to-basics. Interestingly, it was very difficult to find schools with any pronounced instructional philosophy at all. When I spoke to educators in districts throughout this area or reviewed information about local schools, only a small number of schools with distinct instructional approaches could be identified. Most schools simply adopted or adapted whatever curriculum their districts endorsed at the time. As a result, the schools that had the kinds of distinctive and contrasting instructional approaches I looked for were all "schools of choice," with participation determined primarily by application and lottery.

Eventually, I focused on six schools: two K–5 elementary schools–Dewey and Peninsula–in a small suburban district with families with a high median income; two K–8 schools–Emerson and City–in a medium-sized urban district with a much wider range of income levels and lower median income; Horizons, a charter high school, established in 1998 in the same urban district as Emerson and City; and Manzanilla, a low-performing K-5 bilingual school that had a good reputation with parents, teachers, and school reformers despite being in a neighboring troubled urban district.

Both Emerson and Dewey were launched in the 1970s with an open classroom or progressive instructional approach; City and Peninsula were established at about the same time to reflect a more conventional or back-to-basics approach. All four schools have maintained good reputations among many parents and local educators since their founding. Nonetheless, their tests scores in recent years vary, ranging from a low at Emerson, where less than half of the students received scores of "proficient" or above in English and mathematics, to a high at Peninsula, which consistently had some of the highest test scores in the state.

Horizons's instructional approach did not fit neatly into "progressive" or "back-to-basic" categories. In some ways, it embraced aspects of both philosophies as it developed a college-preparatory curriculum that focused on addressing the learning differences of all students. Although the school was located in the same urban community as City and Emerson, as a charter school it did not report directly to the surrounding district and operated more independently than the other schools.

In contrast, Manzanilla, in a neighboring urban district, was subject to extensive district and state regulation as both a bilingual school and a low-performing school. Although California's Proposition 227, passed in 1998, mandated instruction in English, an overwhelming number of the school's Hispanic families signed waivers allowing the school to maintain its bilingual program. In terms of instruction, Manzanilla placed a heavy emphasis on reading and literacy, implemented a writer's workshop approach, and established mixed-age classes. The school also carried out a smaller "Sheltered English Program" for students whose parents did not sign a waiver. That pro-

---

Focus Schools (2001–05)

Urban

City

Principal: Julianne Fredericksen (later Bernice Lao)
K–8, 600 students: 25% English Language Learners (ELL); 46% Free and
Reduced Lunch (FRL); 73% Asian; 65% proficient or above in English;
71% proficient or above in math
Three Rs approach; emphasis on academics and homework

Emerson

Lead Teacher: Toni Simon (previously Diane Kirsch)
K–8, 303 students: 34% ELL; 61% FRL; 38% Hispanic, 24% Asian; 39%
proficient or above in English; 44% proficient or above in math
Mixed-age classes; project-based instruction; community involvement;
consensus-based decision making (with a staff-selected, rotating,
Lead Teacher)

Manzanilla

Principal: Melora Vasquez
K–5, 360 students: 76% ELL; 88% FRL; 92% Hispanic; 4% proficient or
above in English; 27% proficient or above in math
Low performing school; bilingual instruction; mixed-age classes; inquiry-
based professional development; shared decision making

Horizons

Principal and later Executive Director: Paul Archer
9–12, 430 students: 5% ELL; 25% FRL; 15% African American, 14%,
Asian; 22% Hispanic; 94% passing California High School Exit Exam
in English; 88% passing in math
College-preparatory curriculum with an emphasis on individualized
instruction to meet the needs of students with different learning needs

---

gram conducted instruction entirely in English and more closely mirrored
the district's standard curriculum.

In the end, I found that all six of these schools—regardless of the test scores
their students achieved, the instructional philosophies they pursued, or how
much district regulation they faced—experienced numerous problems, some
of which they addressed and some that they never did. This book grew out
of my effort to understand where these problems came from and what both

---

Focus Schools (2001–05), Continued

Suburban

Peninsula

Principal: David Summers
K–5, 360 students: 11% ELL; 3% FRL; 57% Asian; 27% White; 89%
    proficient or above in English; 89% proficient in math
Structured approach; emphasis on academic rigor and homework; no
    team or collaborative teaching; no parents in classroom

Dewey

Principal: Charlene Moore
K–5, 430 students: 19% LEP; 5% FRL; 63% White; 78% proficient or
    above in English; 79% proficient or above in math
Emphasis on whole child; mixed-age classes; project-based instruction

---

higher and lower performing schools might be able to do make the improvements that could address those problems more effectively.

Ultimately, the experiences of the schools I studied, my reading of the literature, and my own work in the field, suggest that in the United States we have not established the conditions that can enable all—or even many—schools to be great; but, whatever the conditions, every school, including those described in this book, can be better.

AIMS OF THE BOOK

While I believe the work and practices described in this book can help schools create the conditions for their own success, I do not expect readers to derive lessons that they can simply put in place in their own contexts. Such an implementation effort runs counter to my argument that researchers, reformers, policy makers, and others too often have laid their ideas and proposals onto schools without adequately taking into account the capacity of schools to carry out those ideas.

Pursuing and putting in place the ideas advanced in this book should only be done after carefully considering the work and initiatives that are already underway at a school, the resources and demands in the surrounding community, and the constantly developing research base on organizational change inside and outside education. As this work developed, for example,

I noted frequent connections between the experiences of these schools and the experiences of many businesses and other organizations described by researchers like James March, Jim Collins (2001, 2005), Rosabeth Moss Kanter (2004), and Michael Porter (1998). Their work in particular serves as rich ground for considering the dynamics of organizational change and for questioning and exploring the issues and practices described in this book.

In turn, building on these ideas will likely take many different forms, with no single program or set of strategies equally effective in all schools or contexts. In other words, the "managing" I discuss in this book is not an exact science. It is more akin to the efforts to deal with the ebb and flow that characterizes the activities and performances of a team than the efforts to control hierarchically organized personnel "by the book." Correspondingly, this book offers hypotheses for readers to consider and to judge against the available data, their personal experiences, what their common sense and reason suggest, their beliefs about the ways that schools should work, and their sense of imagination of what might be possible if we finally address the difficult and changing conditions in which schools operate.

DESIGN AND OUTLINE OF THE BOOK

In preparing this book, I have drawn on a wide range of ideas and research that I hope readers will explore further. Therefore, I have used a series of sidebars to provide some facts and figures and brief summaries of related readings and research, many of which can be found online. In order to make it easier for readers to locate these resources, I have constructed a Web-based reference page that includes these citations and the hyperlinks that were available at the time of this book's publication. You can find that page at: http://www.tc.edu/ncrest/hatch/managingtochange.

The book is intended to help educators and those interested in education around the country to understand what it takes for schools in their communities to make improvements. At the same time, the descriptions and sidebars in the first two chapters of the book go into some detail on the specific educational context in California and the conditions encountered by the schools I studied. In addition to its size, changing demographics, and diversity, California has pursued a particularly wide range of different educational initiatives, sometimes veering between more progressive and more traditional approaches. (For more on the educational context in California see Cohen & Hill, 2001; Loeb, Bryk, & Hanushek, 2007; Wilson, 2003.) Focusing on California highlights what schools have to do to contend with a turbulent environment—one in which conditions change relatively rapidly and often unpredictably.

The book itself is organized in three parts. Part I provides background and context on the challenges of improving schools, with Chapter 1 describing the problems and paradoxes of school capacity and Chapter 2 exploring the changing conditions and conflicting demands that many schools face. Part II opens with a brief overview of the key practices that enable schools to manage the external environment and to make improvements over time. The following four chapters then describe each of these key practices and provide illustrations and examples from the six schools. Part III begins with a recap of the view of capacity put forward in the book and explores the implications for future reform efforts, with the final two chapters addressing what school members, community members, and policy makers need to do at both a local and a national level in order to develop the conditions that can support educational improvements on a broader scale.

In the end, I suggest that educators need to shift their focus from the short-term implementation of particular policies and improvement initiatives to long-term investments that will build the capacity of schools to strategically manage the environment. Reformers cannot change what's going on inside schools without thinking seriously about how to help schools deal with the limited resources and conflicting demands in the surrounding environment.

PART I

CAPACITY, CHANGE, AND IMPROVEMENT

Despite the fact that change and improvement are often used synonomously, there is no direct relationship between them. In fact, changes can be positive, negative, or neutral (Elmore, 2002). Nonetheless, developing the capacity to make improvements depends on how organizations deal with changes of all kinds. Four aspects of change are particularly important for organizations like schools to take into account in their improvement efforts.

1. *There are no hard and fast rules about what "counts" as change.* Changes range from minor and usually inconsequential shifts (as in "he changed his clothes") to dramatic transformations ("she changed the course of history"). Reflecting this range, the same reforms and change efforts that leaders see as major transformations intended to improve an organization can be seen by staff and others as the same old thing: unlikely to cause real change and provide solutions, and just as likely to cause problems.

2. *Change is a natural process that is always underway.* Change occurs all the time as people mature, populations grow and shift, cultures flourish and decline, economies expand and contract, climates evolve, and technologies develop.

3. *Change cannot be controlled.* Although many leaders treat organizational change as an intentional process–a project that can be planned, carried out, and completed–many of these naturally occurring changes cannot be directed, and any effort to make changes, particularly in organizations like schools, has to take into account the unplanned and the unpredictable going on at the same time. As the well-known Rand Change Agent Study of four federally funded projects to support innovative practices in public schools demonstrated, the nature of change in education is a product of local factors largely beyond the control of higher-level policy makers (McLaughlin, 1990).

4. *Change is a multidimensional phenomenon.* Change is often imagined as a one-dimensional cause and effect, but changes in one context, one arena, or for one purpose quickly merge into changes in others. Furthermore, no intentional effort to make changes is immune to change itself, resulting in

adaptations that are difficult to predict from the outset. In *Tinkering Toward Utopia* (1995), David Tyack and Larry Cuban highlight this aspect of change by showing that while educational reforms are designed to change schools, in fact, schools change reforms. Tyack and Cuban point out that established structures and dominant practices (what they call the "grammar of schooling") and the realities of the time, resources, and personnel available naturally force changes and adaptations in the reforms that policy makers and other educational leaders pursue. In other words, there are constant and often unpredictable interactions between the planned and unplanned changes underway at any given time.

Within this context, schools focus too often on initiating changes of their own or trying to resist changes demanded by others. Given the complex, subjective, and uncontrollable nature of change, schools need to develop the capacity to manage change: to influence changing conditions wherever possible and to take advantage of the changes underway to facilitate work and maximize performance. In this view, reform efforts have to take into account work already underway and they cannot be planned entirely in advance; they can only be set in motion and guided. As Fullan (1993) puts it: "Ready, fire, aim."

While educators cannot plan change efforts entirely in advance, they can prepare. In particular, they can make an effort to understand current circumstances and the local context and try to assess what it will really take to make improvements. In Chapter 1, I describe the context in which school reform efforts in the United States in general and in one district in California are being carried out at the beginning of the twenty-first century. I provide an overview of recent perspectives on school capacity and offer a view that emphasizes that a school's capacity to make improvements is bound up with the ability to manage the changes that are always underway. In Chapter 2, I lay the groundwork for the specific discussion of the practices schools can use to manage changes by illustrating the effects that changing conditions can have on schools, focusing specifically on the experiences of the schools in the San Francisco Bay Area.

Chapter 1

It Takes Capacity
to Build Capacity

"We have too much to do and too many scattered ideas," one principal in the Meadowlark School District in the San Francisco Bay Area once told me. "It seems like we have eight major initiatives and 25 subsets of those." From the perspective of a Meadowlark associate superintendent, this problem is not unique. As he put it, "Our principals are going crazy." The result, he explained, is that frustration and anger at the school level have never been higher. When attempting to garner new funds or develop new programs, over and over again he hears from principals and teachers, "We don't want anything else. We're over our heads."

Many schools and teachers appear to be caught in this double bind where they need the money and resources that come with new programs and initiatives, but cannot take advantage of them without adding to their workload. "[Principals] need the money so they can hire people on their staff to do things," the associate superintendent continued, but "they can't use the money to pay teachers in the afternoon to do teaming and to do professional development activities, because the teachers don't have time. They're too burned out trying to keep on top of what they're expected to do." These laments reflect a new reality that has grown along with a spate of reform efforts since the publication of *A Nation at Risk* in 1983 by the National Commission on Excellence in Education: Schools operate in an environment where they have to deal with a dizzying and constantly changing array of new initiatives. Rather than a problem that can be solved by policy makers and administrators who seek to streamline "the system," these multiple and often conflicting demands reflect the now "normal" conditions schools have to learn how to manage.

MULTIPLE REFORM EFFORTS IN ONE DISTRICT: AN EXAMPLE

The mere mention of a few of the major initiatives that Meadowlark has been involved in since the 1990s provides a sense of the growing, and constantly changing, demands that schools have to face year in and year out. At the beginning of the 1990s, the district had to deal with the development of new state curriculum frameworks and plans for related assessments in language arts, mathematics, and several other subjects; in the mid-1990s the district had to endure public ideological battles over the curriculum in California that helped to scuttle the development of the new assessments; and at the end of the 1990s, the district had to contend with the passage of California's Public Schools Accountability Act (PSAA), which created a system of rewards and incentives designed to encourage schools to improve their performance on tests like the SAT-9 that were inconsistent with the newly implemented framework. In addition, in 1996 the state's class-size reduction program required many elementary schools in the district to reorganize staffing and space; in 1997 Proposition 227 required most schools to eliminate their bilingual programs; and in 1999 many schools had to establish tutoring and reading academies as part of the governor's 1999 education reform initiatives.

In the midst of trying to respond to these kinds of state initiatives, in 1996 Meadowlark also adopted a 5-year strategic plan that addressed the improvement of student achievement, diversity awareness, community involvement, professional development, district management, and school facilities. As part of that plan and in response to calls for higher standards around the country, the district strengthened graduation requirements in mathematics, science, and foreign languages (in order to correspond with entrance requirements for the University of California system), put in place exit exams in a number of subjects, and added a requirement for high school students to complete 40 hours of community service before they graduated. The district and schools also increased tutoring, summer school, and student support programs in response to these increased standards (Hatch, 2001b).

On top of these state and district initiatives, many schools in the district also worked with one or more external partners. These individuals, groups, and organizations offered a variety of services and technical assistance, such as support for the implementation of whole-school improvement efforts as well as the implementation of initiatives designed to improve student performance in subject areas like language arts, mathematics, or science, or on other collaborative projects. These included nationally known programs like Success for All, Accelerated Schools, and Reading Recovery, as well as regionally or locally based initiatives like the Bay Area School Reform Collaborative (BASRC, created in response to the Annenberg Challenge) and Joint Venture Silicon Valley (JVSC, an initiative of community and business leaders to encourage systemic change in local education in the 1990s). In fact, in the survey I carried out in Meadowlark in 1998–99, more than half of the schools reported that they were already working with three or more of these kinds of improvement programs and 15% reported that they were involved with six or more different groups.

A Sample of Major State Policy Changes Affecting Schools in California from 1996–2001

Class-Size Reduction K–3

In the 1996–97 school year elementary schools were required to reduce the size of K–3 classes to no more than 20 students per teacher. It took 3 years to fully implement this program and resulted in increased teacher-supply challenges (Perry & Teague, 2001).

Academic Content Standards (ELS, Math, Science, History/SS)

In 1997–98, the State Board of Education began to adopt content standards in English/language arts, history/social studies, mathematics, and science.

Pupil Promotion and Retention

In 1998 the California Legislature passed AB 1626, which required school districts to develop official policies for the promotion and retention of K–8 students. This legislation was designed to put an end to "social promotion" by establishing guidelines for promotion based on the state testing system.

Proposition 227

In June 1998 Proposition 227 was passed, requiring that all public school classes be taught exclusively in English. The law stipulates that schools are permitted to provide non-English classes if more than 20 parents at a grade level request a waiver.

Public School Accountability Act (PSAA)

In April 1999 the Public Schools Accountability Act was passed into law and required that the Academic Performance Index (API) measure the performance of schools and that every school be given an annual growth target for improving their API. The act also decreed that high-performing schools and staff would be awarded bonuses for meeting or exceeding API targets (Perry, Miller, Carlos, Teague, & Frey, 2001).

The Immediate Intervention/Underperforming Schools Program (II/USP)

II/USP was a major component of the PSAA legislation. The program established intervention programs for schools that failed meet the API growth targets. The guidelines stipulated that schools considered "underperforming" would receive funds for school improvement, would need to contract with outside providers, and could be taken over by the state if they failed to improve (Perry et al., 2001).

Since the year 2000, the constant changes in policies have continued. The passage of the No Child Left Behind (NCLB) legislation in 2002, in particular, increased the press of demands and requirements from the federal level. As a consequence, among other things, the district has also had to deal with the testing requirements and related sanctions and rewards of both California's Public School Accountability Act and NCLB.

Multiple Reforms at Charleston High

When a new principal arrived at Charleston High School in the Meadowlark School District in 1996, she found at least eight different initiatives underway at the school and what seemed like "25 subsets of those." The school's involvement with several of these improvement programs began in response to significant pressure to improve that grew out of what one administrator called a "miserable failure" to use state funds to create a science magnet program. Fearing that the state might demand the money back, the school, with the support of the district, sought to develop a schoolwide instructional approach that focused on environmental science. To do so, they built upon the work of the Bay Area Coalition of Essential Schools and Second to None (a school-to-work program). Through these initiatives they established a strong integrated curriculum for freshman and sophomores, and began to gain some recognition within the district for being a Coalition school with a focused science curriculum.

About that same time, the creation of Joint Venture Silicon Valley and the Bay Area School Reform Collaborative established more opportunities for schools like Charleston to get support and resources to pursue a variety of other reform initiatives. As one district administrator put it, "You didn't want to say no to these opportunities, because they were things you should be doing." Charleston did not say no, and applied for and received funding from BASRC to create demonstrations and exhibitions of students' work. As part of a Joint Venture initiative they began to develop a coordinated science curriculum with the elementary and middle schools that many of their students attended. In addition, in order to help improve their success rate with students who needed extra academic support, Charleston also implemented the AVID program, which focused on helping students who might not ordinarily attend college excel in school and continue their education at the college level.

Of course Charleston's involvement with these programs constituted only a small part of its work at any given time. The school also had to deal with numerous district and state improvement efforts that included implementation of new professional development programs, curricula, graduation requirements, tests, and assessments. In addition to the plans and reports the school had to submit to each of its support providers, every year, Charleston was also required by the district to complete a desegregation plan, a GATE plan for gifted and talented students, a plan for bilingual students and students with limited proficiency in English, a plan for their vocational initiative, and a staff development plan.

MULTIPLE REFORMS FOR ALL

Schools in California and in the Meadowlark School District are not the only ones who face the challenges of responding to a wide range of local, state, and national reform programs, policies, and initiatives. As Michael Fullan described it,

> the biggest problem facing schools is fragmentation and overload. It is worse for schools than for business firms. Both are facing turbulent, uncertain environments, but only schools are suffering the additional burden of having a torrent of unwanted, uncoordinated policies and innovations raining down on them from external hierarchical bureaucracies. (Fullan, 1999)

In fact, schools in districts all across the United States have been embroiled in several different approaches to educational reform at the same time. Some districts experimented with charter schools and voucher programs while promoting school-based management and increasing incentives for improvements in student performance (Hill & Celio, 1998). Others, as Frederick Hess (1999) discovered in a study of 57 different districts, pursued as many as eleven "significant initiatives" in basic areas such as scheduling, curriculum, assessment, professional development, and school management at the same time.

Compounding the problem, the recognition of the difficulty of making changes in one aspect of a school at a time—curriculum or professional development or parent involvement or management practices or assessment—fueled an interest in developing comprehensive reform efforts and helped create incentives for schools to implement a wide range of improvement initiatives simultaneously (Elmore, 1990; Fullan, 1993; Murphy, 1991). This movement crystallized in the Comprehensive School Reform Demonstration Program (CSRD) launched in 1998. In that program, the federal government set aside $145 million for qualifying schools to get at least $50,000 to work with "research-based" improvement programs or to develop their own "comprehensive" approach to improvement.

The growing interest in comprehensive reform was accompanied by substantial growth in the number of improvement programs like those at work in Meadowlark. In fact, 76% (48) of the 63 improvement programs listed in a *Catalog of School Reform Models* in 2001 (Northwest Regional Education Laboratory, 2001) were created since 1980 (with only one in existence before 1960). As in Meadowlark, many of these improvement programs were at work in schools at the same time. In my comparison surveys of principals in one other urban district in California and two districts in Texas, 68% of the responding schools were engaged with three or more improvement programs, and 23% with six or more. In one district, 18% of schools were working with nine or more different programs simultaneously.

In many ways the systemic reform efforts launched at the end of the twentieth century were designed to combat this fragmentation and to produce greater alignment and consistency among policies and practices at the state, district, and school levels. Ironically, however, the efforts intended to reduce fragmentation themselves launched a spate of reform efforts at many different levels of the educational system. Thus, following the development and adoption of standards, curriculum frameworks, and new testing policies in many states, concerns about the slow pace of improvement contributed to the impetus for NCLB at the federal level and the institution of another whole layer of testing, accountability, and teacher certification requirements that states have to meet in order to qualify for funding.

Of course the more policies, programs, and initiatives there are at work (and the more difficult they are to understand), the more time, energy, and resources schools have to expend in order to coordinate them. However, there are many reasons why schools might not expend as much effort as they need to in order to coordinate initiatives. In fact, schools may actually have many incentives for adopting new initiatives without expending the time or resources to implement them effectively (Hess, 1999; Popkewitz, Tachnick, & Wehlage, 1982). For one thing, school, district, education, and community leaders receive considerable rewards (often in both funding and publicity) for bringing in new initiatives and demonstrating short-term success, while the rewards for maintaining programs and sustaining accomplishments over the long haul pale in comparison. Second, the frequent turnover among superintendents and principals and the pressures for each of these new leaders to "do something" places an emphasis on starting new initiatives, not sustaining them. Third, funding cycles for many reform efforts often last less than 3 years, leaving even schools and districts with stable leadership in constant need of finding or inventing new initiatives in order to get needed funds and resources. As a result, rather than contributing to substantial improvements, multiple reforms initiatives like those that have been underway for the last 20 years can also function as an endless cycle of initiatives that sap the strength of schools and undermine the spirit of their communities.

THE REALITIES OF WORKING IN A TURBULENT ENVIRONMENT

While systemic and comprehensive reform efforts may contribute to the challenges of coordinating multiple reform initiatives, ultimately, the problems of fragmentation and overload experienced by schools may be a natural consequence of a "system" in which schools, districts, and improvement programs all face conflicting demands from diverse constituencies, constant changes in personnel and policies, and significant limits on the time, resources, and funding available.

From this perspective, schools operate in a turbulent environment where many demands and conditions constantly change. In a turbulent environment, it is particularly difficult to anticipate, predict, or prepare for the future. Organizations have to respond and react to changes in their immediate circumstances, which in turn discourage them from doing the long-term planning and development crucial to their survival. As Jim Collins (2001) and others point out, in the business world learning how to adapt to a changing environment is a key ingredient in developing a successful organization. By remaining aware of the changes in their business environment and planning for future possibilities, companies can maintain their advantage over

---

Why Businesses (and Schools) Have to Manage the External Environment

James March (1991), a noted researcher who has studied organizations, organizational learning, and organizational decision making for years, suggests that one of the key challenges for all organizations and business organizations in particular is to continue to explore and develop new practices at the same time that they maintain practices that have been successful in the past. Countless businesses fail either because they stick to their "core" business without adapting to the changes in the economy, technology, and customer base, or because they invest heavily in risky new ventures without tending to the basic business that can keep them going in the short term.

The challenge is to find the right balance between what March calls "exploiting" current practices and "exploring" new ideas that may lead to success in the future. A failure to find such a balance and an overemphasis on establishing or maintaining success in the short term can contribute to the demise of even successful organizations and to the stagnation of entire industries.

Many of the same factors that make it difficult for schools to improve—particularly a turbulent environment and significant turnover in personnel—can affect an organization's ability to balance exploitation and exploration. These factors influence the extent to which organizations can free up resources to focus on the research and development of new practices as well as the extent to which organizations can collect and distribute the knowledge and expertise needed to develop and sustain innovations. In addition, March argues that excessive short-term feedback (particularly when high stakes are attached) can discourage organizations from taking the risks that may be required to learn how to adapt to a changing environment. As a consequence, from March's viewpoint, organizations not only need to make changes in their own operations, they also need to take into account the external conditions that can discourage them from making those changes.

competitors when possible or develop new "core" businesses and find a new "niche" when necessary. If businesses do not adapt to changing conditions, however, they may lose customers, lose access to the personnel or resources they need, and find their operations constrained and their profit margins eroded. Even if these problems do not force businesses to close, the failure to adapt to changing conditions means that businesses will have a difficult time maintaining efficient operations and will miss key opportunities to make improvements.

Just like businesses and other kinds of organizations, schools have to learn to deal with the fact that many aspects of their operating environment–policies, leadership, funders, funding priorities, and the like–change relatively rapidly. Schools have to develop the capacity to find resources and manage the conflicting demands and requirements around them. They have to create the conditions that allow them to make improvements and to sustain their performance over time.

Rethinking the Capacity for Successful School Improvement

What does it take for schools to make improvements and sustain them over the long haul? Answering this question depends on reexamining conventional assumptions about school capacity. Many of the common connotations of the term *capacity* apply in considerations of school performance and school reform. They conjure up images of schools as empty containers waiting to be filled, factories able to reach their performance targets, and collections of individuals able to engage in certain activities or achieve certain goals.

Many discussions of capacity in education, however, take the view that *capacity* is a measurable amount of power or productivity that depends on the

---

Capacity (*n.*)

1. The ability to receive, hold, or absorb.
2. A measure of this ability; volume.
3. The maximum amount that can be contained: *a trunk filled to capacity.*
4. The maximum or optimum amount of production: *factories operating below capacity.*
5. The ability to learn or retain knowledge.
6. The ability to do something; faculty, aptitude.
7. The quality of being suitable for or receptive to specified treatment: *the capacity of elastic to be stretched.*
8. The position in which one functions; role: *his capacity as host.*

(*The American Heritage Dictionary,* 2006)

money, resources, or qualified personnel inside a school. This approach treats schools like reservoirs that have not been filled up with "enough" money and resources (Cohen & Ball, 1999).

Repeated failures of school reform efforts of all kinds, however, have contributed to the development of more sophisticated conceptions of *school capacity* that make it clear that simply *having* resources does not mean that those resources will be *used* well (see for example Malen & King Rice, 2004). Reflecting this idea, many recent examinations. define *school capacity* as the amount of effort needed to reach a particular goal (Newman, Smith, Allensworth, & Bryk, 2001). Influenced by the development of systemic and standards-based reform efforts in the 1990s, recent discussions of school capacity focus particularly on what it takes to enable all students to reach high standards—sometimes defined in terms of higher standards in many different content areas, sometimes as high levels of achievement on standardized tests in reading and mathematics (O'Day, Goertz, & Floden, 1995). Thus a school is said to have "low capacity" if it requires new investments of resources, time, energy, new personnel, and professional development programs or if it has to make major changes in structures or routines in order to enable all students to meet performance standards. In contrast, a school is said to have "high capacity" if it does not have to make significant new investments or changes to enable its students to meet those standards.

Whether or not schools have the capacity to meet their performance outcomes depends on a complex interaction between the skills and experiences of the people in those schools, the kinds of tasks those people are asked to carry out, and the quantity and quality of the resources available to complete those tasks. For example, in their conception of "instructional capacity," David Cohen and Deborah Ball (1999) argue that whether or not a school has "high" or "low" capacity depends on the relationship between three components:

- The understandings, experiences, and attitudes of the *teachers*
- The understandings, experiences, and attitudes of the *students*
- The *content* (the type and quality of the instructional materials, technologies, and tasks)

From this perspective, instructional capacity is not fixed; instead capacity reflects the relationship between all three. Thus students may show few learning gains with one teacher using a particular set of math materials or a new reading program, but that same group of students might make more significant gains with another teacher or another set of materials or program. Similarly, a teacher who is ineffective with one group of students in one content area, might achieve impressive results with a different class or in another content area. As Cohen and Ball put it, "Change in students, teachers, or materials has the potential to change the relations of teachers, students, and materials, and hence affect instructional capacity" (p. 4). Thus in this view building capacity for improving instruction depends on changing the interaction between teachers, students, and content. As Richard Elmore (2002) argues, if school reform efforts do not ultimately address these three elements, constituting what he refers to as the "core of instruction," then meaningful and lasting improvements in students' performance cannot take place.

To influence the "core of instruction," however, reformers have to face a fundamental paradox: Improving instruction and enabling all students to learn to high levels means many schools need to make significant changes in their curriculum, assessments, professional development structures, staffing arrangements, schedules, and many other aspects of their instructional and organizational practices all at once. Unfortunately, many schools that lack the capacity to meet their instructional goals also lack the capacity to make these kinds of significant changes in classroom and organizational practices.

In fact, even though many low-performing schools may need resources and technical assistance, the support these schools receive can end up causing problems as well as solving them. The assistance schools receive often requires them to hold more meetings, create more professional development opportunities, take on more roles and responsibilities, and expend more time, energy, and resources than these already struggling schools have available. In other words, reform efforts themselves create a whole set of demands that many schools, particularly low-performing schools, do not have the capacity to meet.

Looked at in this way, schools are less like containers waiting to be filled or factories that could meet demands if they performed up to their capacity; schools are more like elastic—rubber bands that only have the capacity to be stretched so far. From this perspective, there is little reformers can do for schools except try to figure out how much "help" schools can take before they snap.

Instead of treating schools as containers waiting to be filled or elastic stretched too far, policy makers and reformers have to figure out how to enable schools to develop the means and mechanisms to act as autonomous agents that have the ability to use resources, training, and other support effectively in order to improve instruction. In this book, I argue that this ability—what I call the "capacity to make improvements"—is a necessary (though not a sufficient) condition for schools seeking to build instructional capacity: If schools do not have the ability to make improvements in many aspects of their operations, they are unlikely to be able to improve instruction and meet higher learning goals. In turn, I suggest that in order to make improvements schools have to be able to act on and take advantage of the people and organizations on the "outside," not just the resources and personnel who happen to be "inside" the organization at any given time.

From Increasing Supply to Managing Resources and Demands

An analogy to strategies for building the capacity of municipal water systems presents one way to think about these different views of organizational capacity. The systems of reservoirs and dams constructed early in the twentieth century in the United States were designed to provide water for rapidly growing populations. Initial efforts to increase capacity focused on increasing the amount of water available for delivery. From this perspective, the capacity of the system could be measured by the amount of water held at any one time, and it could be increased by putting larger amounts of water into reservoirs, expanding the size of those already in place, and building new reservoirs.

As the population grew, the problems associated with building more dams and reservoirs, including the economic and ecological costs, made it clear that increasing the amount of water available could not be the only means of building water capacity. In response, strategies for building water capacity expanded to include efforts to manage the demand for water. In this approach, the amount of water available is only a part of the equation for determining water capacity; capacity is a function of the resources available (in this case water) and the demand that exists at a given time. Thus those responsible for the water system began devoting time, resources, and attention to developing appliances and other devices that required less water and to educating the public about the benefits of conservation. By managing the demand for water in this manner, they reduced the need for the construction of new dams and reservoirs and increased the capacity of an overburdened system.

Currently, in order to ascertain the capacity of their systems over time, water managers have had to learn how to balance the supply of water with the demand for it, and in the process they have had to learn how to take into account a wide range of factors, including shifts in weather patterns, ecological changes, influences of new technologies, and the impact of changing demographics. If they fail to address these factors, they will be unable to determine how to manage the supply and demand for water or to ensure that the water system has the capacity required to serve the public over the long term.

While vast differences exist between water systems and educational systems, drawing an analogy between the two suggests that it may be useful to look at capacity as a function of the resources available and the demand that exists at any given time. Just as it was for municipal water systems early in the twentieth century, the demands on schools at the beginning of the twenty-first century far outstrip the resources needed to meet them. Schools have to deal with limited funds, inadequate facilities, antiquated materials, and a paucity of high-quality professional development and teacher preparation programs. These conditions could be improved, but they are unlikely to change dramatically soon: policy makers cannot simply turn on a spigot and produce more money, new facilities, or improved professional development and teacher preparation programs. While hoping for better conditions in the future, schools have to figure out how to deal with the conditions they have.

Capacity as a Function of the Relationship Between Schools and the Surrounding Environment

Viewing a school's capacity to make improvements as a function of the resources available and the demands that exist at any given time highlights several key aspects of school capacity that are often ignored. First, the resources and features "inside" the school on their own do not determine a school's capacity. School capacity depends on the relationship between the school and the people, organizations, and institutions in the surrounding environment (Jennings, 2008, Stoll, 1999; Stoll & Earl, 2003).

Second, although the development of school capacity seems to depend on the addition of resources or the development of mechanisms within a school, schools can also deal with issues of capacity by trying to shape the demands that are placed upon them. Thus in this formulation capacity reflects both a school's ability to receive and implement certain policies and practices and its ability to act on and influence the surrounding environment: Changing the demands placed on a school will change the resources and the amount of effort that the school needs to achieve its goals. Increasing demands for performance—raising standards, for example—may mean that some schools that were meeting previous demands will have to get new resources, put in place new structures, or engage in other efforts to increase their performance. At the same time, in some cases schools and their supporters also might argue that new performance demands (like those imposed by NCLB for example) are unreasonable and instead might strive to show how they could or are already meeting what they consider to be more appropriate goals. In other words, goals and expectations are not set in stone and no single constituency (policy makers, parents, educators, and so on) controls them; goals and expectations are social and cultural constructions—subject to influence and negotiation—and how they are determined has profound implications for views of a school's capacity to make improvements.

Third, while research often focuses on the capacity required for schools to demonstrate certain levels of student performance, schools face a host of demands that they have to have the capacity to meet. These include explicit demands (in the form of regulations, contracts, policies, and so on) from the district, the state, support providers, and others to implement certain practices. They also face demands from board members, educators, community members, and the general public to conform to their expectations and operate in certain ways. Thus managing demands entails not only managing demands for performance but also managing demands for compliance and conformity that may affect schools' ability to meet their performance goals.

Complicating matters further, what some may see as demands for increasing performance, others may view as demands for conformity. Thus, on the one hand, advocates may believe that NCLB "raises the bar" in ways that will require schools to improve their performance in reaching the learning needs of all students. On the other hand, many critics see NCLB as increasing demands for schools to conform to traditional, skill-based forms of teaching that they feel do not meet the learning needs of all students. Given this complexity, those schools that have the capacity to enter into the local or national discussions of what counts as "high performance" may have a distinct advantage over others.

Fourth, this view of school capacity accentuates the fact that capacity has a temporal dimension. Policies and practices that aim to ensure that the supply of high-quality instructional practices meets the demand for improved performance at a given time may be quite different from policies and practices that seek to ensure that a certain level of performance can be maintained over a significant period of time. In particular, those polices and practices that seek to support a school's capacity over time have to go beyond examinations of internal resources and other characteristics to take into account changing external conditions.

All in all, a school's capacity to make improvements depends on the ability to take into account and influence the supply of resources and the demands placed upon it and to make appropriate organizational adjustments and changes over the long haul. Developing this capacity sets the stage for making improvements in instruction. However, as the experiences of numerous schools demonstrate—including those discussed in this book—the ability to make some improvements and sustain them over time does not in and of itself guarantee that those schools will either demonstrate high levels of student performance or go on to make substantial improvements in student outcomes. Ultimately, schools have to use the capacity to make improvements in their operations to develop and carry out instructional practices that meet the needs of all students.

The Challenges of Meeting Demands for Performance and Conformity

Theorists have struggled for decades to explain why organizations in many sectors, including schools, can survive even without performing as well or as efficiently as they should. The thinking goes that in pursuing their own interests, people and organizations should act rationally to improve their performance. Yet examples abound in which entire sectors of organizations maintain the same practices and structures despite poor performance or adopt structures and practices that have no positive impact on "the bottom line."

One explanation for this phenomenon comes out of the work of researchers who study the development of institutions and patterns of organizational structure and behavior in different areas such as government, business, and education (Rowan & Miskel, 1999). Meyer and Rowan (1977), for example, argue that modern bureaucratic organizations gain resources and legitimacy by conforming to "rationalized myths" about the most appropriate and effective means of reaching their goals. As a consequence, particularly when there are few clear, agreed upon indicators of performance, many organizations can survive by conforming to expectations and acting in ways that make it look like they are operating appropriately. As Rowan and Miskel (1999) put it:

> A logic of confidence and good faith develops in organizations as administrators deliberately ignore and discount information about technical activities and outcomes in order to maintain the appearance that things are working as they should be even if they aren't. (p. 363)

The separation between work to improve performance and work to maintain legitimacy is particularly pronounced in organizations like schools where the "technical" activities that lead to improved performance are "loosely coupled" (Bidwell, 1965; Weick, 1976) with the institutional structures—governance, staffing arrangements, budgets, and so on—that determine whether or not these organizations are viewed as operating in appropriate ways. In schools, this loose coupling promotes a division of labor in which individual teachers working in isolated classrooms are responsible for the technical activities of instruction, while school and district administrators are responsible for carrying out managerial responsibilities and for making sure that schools look like they are doing what they are supposed to do (Elmore, 2000). While some see this loose coupling in schools as an advantage because managers and administrators can "buffer" or protect teachers from unwarranted demands, fads, and politically motivated intrusions that might interfere with their ability to do their work, others see it as a prime reason why it is so difficult to promote systematic changes in instruction. Many standards-based reform efforts, in particular, are designed to help tighten the connections between the work of teachers and administrators and to focus the work of schools around instruction and improving performance.

Chapter 2

Changing Conditions, Changing Times

Ideally, schools will benefit from strong, stable leadership; a surplus of highly experienced personnel; a consistent, coordinated set of policies and regulations; and patient, long-term support from politicians, funders, and the general public. For the most part, however, schools do not enjoy such supportive conditions. Instead, schools try to get by even though principals and superintendents come and go, the supply of teachers varies, policies conflict, and support wavers. Rather than problems that schools can resolve, these issues reflect the normal conditions that schools have to deal with every day: they are symptoms of work in a turbulent environment.

PREDICTABLE PROBLEMS FOR ALL SCHOOLS

The experiences of the six schools I studied in the San Francisco Bay Area–City, Emerson, Peninsula, Dewey, Horizons, and Manzanilla–illustrate what it takes for schools to deal with turbulent conditions and make some improvements over time. At some times, all of these schools–both those that are higher performing and those that are lower performing–exhibited some of the hallmarks associated with successful schools: strong principals, clear missions that members of the school community "bought into"; well-prepared and highly skilled and committed faculty members; and significant support from parents. The fact that all the schools were "schools of choice" with student participation determined by application and lottery is also consistent with the belief that student and parent motivation may also be key factors in school success.

Like other alternative schools in the United States, however, these schools of choice do not necessarily face fewer problems or experience less pressure than "regular" public schools; nor are such alternative schools necessarily more likely to demonstrate higher levels of performance. In fact, regardless of how their students performed on standardized tests or how much support they received from their districts, a closer look at all six of these schools reveals that they experienced a host of problems and had to figure out how

27

**What Is an Alternative School
and What Difference Does It Make?**

A variety of alternative schools have emerged over the last 50 years in the United States. In the 1960s the increased attention to the inequitable education that poor and minority students were receiving in public schools helped to launch a number of alternative schools, including "magnet" schools, often designed with a particular theme or focus and usually intended to support desegregation by encouraging students from different neighborhoods to attend or to reflect a particular instructional philosophy, like the open schools that were based on child-centered educational approaches. Alternative schools also have been created to serve particular populations, such as students who have dropped out or who have not been able to make it in the regular system. In the 1990s charter schools, small schools, and other schools of choice began to be added to the mix in some (usually large, urban) districts around the country.

Despite the proliferation of these alternative schools, research about the effects of the different options remains mixed. To date, there is little evidence to support the claim that it is easier to create and carry out different and innovative organizational and instructional practices in alternative schools than in regular public schools; and for every study that seems to indicate improvements in academic performance in some alternative schools, there seem to be others that indicate that regular schools do as well or better (Ballou, Goldring, & Liu, 2006; Lange & Sletten, 2002). According to The National Working Commission on Choice in K–12 Education (2003), classes in alternative schools that students have chosen to attend "could be better taught, more supportive, and more motivating than those in their regular public school. They could be about the same. They could be worse" (p. 23).

to make changes both large and small without losing their distinctiveness or their reputations.

Emerson, for example, maintained its progressive instructional approach, mixed-age classes, and consensus-based and teacher-led governance structure since its founding in the 1970s. However, it also experienced periods of considerable internal turmoil. In particular, the staff had to resolve major conflicts around the "project approach" that emerged as a cornerstone of the school's instructional philosophy in the 1990s. Up until that time, with a relatively small and stable staff, staff members spent relatively little time working together on matters of instruction. Diane Kirsch, a former lead teacher at the school, explained:

People still cared about kids and there was a sense of community and of family and of really knowing kids. . . . And there were always multiage classrooms, but it reached a point where people taught whatever they were teaching and people really didn't have a clue as to what was going on in other people's classrooms.

Once they recognized the problem, the staff decided to work together to develop a more common instructional approach. Although the whole staff ultimately agreed to conduct all of their instruction through projects, the amount of work turned out to be overwhelming. "People almost died," Kirsch lamented. "I mean it was almost a mass exodus [at the end of the year]. . . . It was a nightmare." Things got worse when one of their most veteran and respected teachers threatened to leave if they did not make some changes. According to Kirsch, "Everything we had done could have been lost," and they had to come up with a new solution. Ultimately, the staff developed a compromise arrangement in which the students spent 9 weeks with their homeroom teacher in conventional, classroom instruction, followed by 9-week period in which students chose to participate in projects offered by any teacher within their developmental team (K–2, 3–5, or 6–8).

At Dewey, schisms within the faculty have also undermined the school's child-centered instructional approach at times and threatened the school's survival. When Charlene Moore, the school's fourth principal since its founding, arrived at the school, the school still had a general reputation as a successful, progressive school within the wealthy suburban community. Nonetheless, the waiting list for the school was not always filled, and in some instances the district assigned to Dewey some "overflow" students who came from other neighborhood schools and who knew relatively little about the school's approach. One board member even told Moore that she was wondering if the school should retain its alternative status. As Moore put it, "This was bad news. This was really bad news. . . . I realized, 'Oh, my God, we are in trouble. If we don't do something, all we will be is a regular school with multigrade classrooms.'"

At Peninsula and City, the two more traditional schools with test scores among the highest in their districts, the challenges were of a different order and often revolved around the principals. At Peninsula, tensions between parents and the school contributed to considerable turnover in leadership, including five different principals over an 8-year period. Sylvia Swanson, a parent who had children at the school throughout that time, explained that the first of those five principals was autocratic and that the parents' attitude toward her was "either you endure with [the principal] because there are good teachers or you go to the neighborhood school." After that principal left, the school went through two principals quickly, and then the fourth lasted several contentious years. As Swanson reported, "He was one people either loved or hated," and he was a central player in a variety of issues that raised concerns among many parents. In particular, a number of parents viewed him as "financially irresponsible." In one instance, some parents wondered if he was mishandling funds because the school ran out of supplies like construction paper that teachers needed for their work. Another parent explained, "There are a lot of parents [in this affluent community] who are really strong on finance, and they wanted a big say in the school, and they used the principal's inexperience with finance to basically bash him over the head." Faced with vocal concerns from some parents, the fourth principal was removed, and a fifth principal, David Summers, was appointed to the school in 2000–01 with the job of healing some of the divisions that had arisen in previous years.

City also had to endure long-standing tensions between administrators and teachers. A veteran teacher, James Anderson, reported that at one point the school gained a reputation for "throwing out" principals as two principals came and went in 2 short years. "The traditional teachers here weren't going to buy into what they [the new principals] wanted to do," Anderson said. While Julianne Fredericksen, the next principal, stayed for some time with much more success, she had to deal with the fact that many of the veteran faculty objected to initiatives she tried to put forward and the union building committee frequently lodged complaints against her.

As a relatively new school (established in 1998), Horizons experienced the typical challenges that come with trying to launch a charter school. Finding facilities proved particularly difficult, and the whole staff had to juggle the significant demands that come with developing an innovative instructional program while inventing organizational practices and routines, creating discipline policies, and dealing with the many practical issues associated with starting a new school. The school already experienced some of the usual turnover in teachers early on and faced typical leadership challenges as the founding principal, Paul Archer, began to work with a state network of charter schools and spent more and more time outside the school and less and less time with faculty on the "inside."

Reflecting the demands of working in a deeply troubled district and meeting the needs of a community with high levels of poverty, Manzanilla faced a constantly shifting roster of superintendents, district administrators, and district mandates, and dealt with numerous constraints on its budgets and resources. At times, these problems exacerbated differences between teachers who worked in the bilingual program (with Hispanic students) and those who taught in the "Sheltered English Program" (with largely African American and Asian students) and created enormous stress among the staff and members of the whole community who were never sure exactly what the next year would bring.

Charter Schools

Charter schools are publicly funded schools usually governed by a group or organization authorized by a contract or charter with the state. The charter exempts the school from some state or local rules and regulations. Although the rules differ in different states, a school's charter is reviewed (typically every 3 to 5 years) and can be revoked if guidelines on curriculum and management are not followed or standards are not met.

- In 1991 Minnesota passed the first charter school law.
- By 1995, 19 states had signed laws allowing for the creation of charter schools.
- By 2004–05, 40 states and the District of Columbia allowed charter schools.
- In 2007 there were 4,147 charter schools serving 1.2 million students across the country (National Center for Education Statistics, 2008; US Charter Schools, 2008).

CHANGING DEMOGRAPHICS, SHIFTING POLICIES, AND THE RAVAGES OF TIME

Many of the problems that schools like these experience reflect changes in the external environment from which few schools are immune. Five factors, in particular, contribute to the crises and problems that affect a school's ability to operate effectively and to maintain a common and coherent instructional program and a strong professional community:

- Shifts in enrollment levels and associated district-directed efforts to consolidate old facilities or find new facilities
- Changes in student populations
- Changes in funding
- Changes in policies
- The passage of time that brings with it changes in staff and changes in the popularity of predominant instructional approaches and other educational practices

Changing Enrollments and Changing Locations

All districts and schools have to deal with issues of space and size and problems associated with the usual decay in facilities. In many cases, however, district efforts to respond to these normal issues and the natural ebb and flow of student enrollments create crises with which schools and their staff members, students, and families have to contend. Emerson, Dewey, and Peninsula all faced threats of closure or have experienced moves to new buildings (or both); and Emerson, Manzanilla, and Horizons have all had to deal with the challenges and constant negotiations that come with sharing space with other schools and programs.

At Emerson, in the 1980s, dropping enrollments throughout the district led district administrators to try to close the school on several occasions. While the school successfully fought those efforts, the district forced the school to relocate to two floors of a building on the other side of the district in a much more disadvantaged section of the city. Adding to the complications, the school had to share their new space with another district program and that "colocation" resulted in constant battles over how to accommodate the growing numbers of students who either applied to the school or were assigned by the district. As Diane Kirsch reported, "We were on the third floor, and we had two rooms on the second floor, and we were sharing with a program that didn't want us there." Unfortunately for Emerson, a high-ranking official in the administrators' union ran the other program in the building, and he used his connections to block Emerson from acquiring more space, despite the fact that their numbers were growing. "He had empty rooms that he refused to give to us," Kirsch explained, "so it was really a very contentious situation." Beyond the stress and the time required to try to negotiate solutions, the uncertainties around space meant that the staff was constantly making adjustments to their classroom assignments.

Over a period of almost 10 years, staff and parents at Emerson lobbied to get either more space or a new building. Several times members of the

---

Changing Student Enrollments

Student enrollment in the United States increased 26% between 1985 and 2007 with record levels of enrollment projected for every year at least through 2016 (National Center for Education Statistics, 2007). Echoing that increase, the public school student population in California grew by over 1 million students from 1993–2005 from about 5,267,00 students to over 6,322,000 students, with those new students more likely to be low-income, English learners, and Hispanic (California Educational Demographics Unit, 2008; Carroll, Krop, Arkes, Morrison, & Flanagan, 2005). By 2006, however, overall student enrollment in California had leveled off and had even begun to decline in some areas. That shift largely reflected decreases in elementary enrollment while high school enrollment was projected to continue to increase in many areas for the next few years (Ed-Data, 2008).

school were convinced that they had an agreement only to see it fall through when the superintendent or administrators with whom they had worked out the agreements left the district. Finally, California's passage of class-size reduction forced the district to give the school more space in order to meet the lower teacher-student ratio requirements. Even then, the conditions in the building were far from conducive for work and learning. "It was the most depressing place you could walk into," Kirsch lamented. "Paint was just peeling off the walls in the cafeteria, lead-based paint. It was horrible." Once they were finally able to convince the district to make the necessary repairs in the late 1990s, the facilities issues subsided to the normal level of needed maintenance, limited storage, and overcrowding that face most schools.

As is the case with many charter schools, Horizons also faced numerous struggles over facilities during its short history. The school was originally given space on one floor of a district building that housed another high school. They learned of their placement at this location only 2 days before the start of classes for their first year. As they expanded their enrollment and added grade levels each year of operation, Horizons came to need a building of their own. The district was moving out of a building downtown, and it seemed as if it would work for Horizons. (According to Paul Archer, the founding principal and now Executive Director, the building had "seismic issues," but they "didn't have many other options.") Unfortunately, Horizons found themselves in competition for that space with an arts magnet school that had been in a temporary building. They lost the battle. "When they [the members of the arts magnet school] heard that we were going in," Archer told us, "they just went bananas. And they lobbied incredibly effectively before the Board not to let us in there." At that point, Horizons had nowhere else to go, but through what Archer called "serendipity" the opportunity to

---

Facts About California's Students

- California is one of the most racially and ethnically diverse states in the United States, and students in California are more diverse than California's total population.
- Nearly one in every ten Californians is a recent immigrant.
- Approximately 25% of public school students are English language learners.
- Approximately 50% of students qualify for free or reduced price meals (Ed-Data, 2008).
- Approximately "one of every five children in California lives in a family whose income is below federally established poverty thresholds" (Carroll et al., 2005, p. xxvi).

Facts About School Facilities

A 1999 survey by the National Center for Education Statistics found:
- Three quarters of schools in the United States required repairs, renovations, or modernizations.
- One in four schools (enrolling approximately 11 million students) are in buildings in "less than adequate conditions" with 3–5 million students enrolled in a school building that was in "poor condition or needed to be replaced because it was nonoperational or showed significantly substandard performance" (NCES, 1999, p. iv).
- Overall, about half of public schools were underenrolled; approximately one quarter were within 5 percent of capacity; and about one quarter were overcrowded.
- Schools with a minority enrollment of more than 50% were more likely to be seriously overcrowded than schools with a minority enrollment of 5% or less.
- Total cost of repairing or replacing buildings was estimated to exceed 127 billion dollars, with schools in need of repair requiring, on average, over 2.2 million dollars.

In California:
- 43% of schools had an inadequate building, and 70% had a building with at least one inadequate building feature.
- 33% of all students were enrolled in an overcrowded school or one in need of significant modernization (California Legislative Analysts Office, 2001).
- Construction needs from 2002 to 2007 were estimated at $23 billion (Carroll et al., 2005).

---

move to their current building "came up at the 11th hour."

Manzanilla's crisis came about almost by accident as the school and parents sought to take advantage of a district program in the early 2000s to create small schools. Concerned about the performance of their students in middle schools, a group of staff and parents from the school decided to apply to create a school that would serve their students in 6th, 7th, and 8th grades. The district granted the request to create Manzanilla Middle School and agreed to find another building or location for it since there was no room at Manzanilla. However, the following year, with considerable budget problems and space issues, the district could not provide another building. Instead, the district put portables on the elementary school playground and performed some renovations, but that meant that the elementary school lost both classroom space and their space for recess and recreation. Beyond the disruptions of construction, the loss of their playground, and overcrowding (not to mention a persistent "rodent problem" and a number of break-ins), the reduction in enrollment at the elementary school contributed to reductions in the teaching staff at the elementary level. Not surprisingly, serious tensions arose between the members of the middle school and the elementary school. Even some of the elementary teachers who supported the development of the middle school grew concerned that they or their colleagues would be fired or transferred to other schools.

Dropping enrollments in the 1980s meant that Dewey and Peninsula, in a wealthy suburb, had to deal with threats of closure as well. As Charlene Moore, the current principal at Dewey and a longtime employee in the district, described the situation: "The district was trying to find a way to get rid of the alternative schools" because that would have been easier than closing any neighborhood schools. As a consequence, both Dewey and Peninsula were moved to new sites (Dewey to a larger building that required more students and teachers), and both schools were told that they had to maintain full enrollment. "I honestly believe that the district thought they would die," Moore explained. Despite the moves, the schools did manage to maintain, and, in Dewey's case, increase, their enrollment. In fact, Peninsula, which even at that time was well known for high academic achievement, began drawing students from the neighborhood school near their new location, a school that was one of the most diverse in the district and did not have as good an academic reputation. While the reasons were never made clear, the district chose to move Peninsula again several years later.

For these schools, the normal fluctuations in enrollment and the related and predictable problems with space and facilities created pressures that demanded a response. They consumed considerable amounts of time and attention from administrators and others who had to negotiate with district officials, muster support, and sometimes mount full-scale campaigns to preserve their student populations, protect their core staff, and maintain their instructional approaches. Nonetheless, in some instances, these challenges and crises helped galvanize school communities and, eventually, enabled them to move to better facilities that created new opportunities for organization and instruction.

Changing Student Populations

Beyond issues with facilities, changing student populations affect the work of teachers and the curriculum and instruction in schools in more direct ways as well. District decisions about increasing or decreasing student populations of schools, for example, lead to reductions or expansions in staff that can have significant effects on morale and teachers' sense of professional commu-

---

Growing Diversity of the Student Population

In addition to getting larger, the prekindergarten to 12th-grade student population in the United States has also grown substantially more diverse. From 1972 to 2006 the percentage of public school students considered to be part of a racial or ethnic minority group increased from 22% to 43%. This increase largely reflected growth in the percentage of Hispanic students from 6% of public school enrollment in 1972 to 20% in 2006. Although enrollment of minority students generally increased in all regions, the distribution of minority students in public schools differed by region, with the largest minority enrollments in the South and West. In the West, by 2006 minority students made up 55% of public school enrollment, compared with 45% for White students (National Center for Education Statistics, 2008).

---

nity. Last-minute fluctuations in students assigned to schools can also require the schools to make hiring decisions at the beginning of the school year that are both hasty and late or accept teachers the district might assign. In turn, hasty and late hiring means that schools cannot always do the recruiting and vetting of candidates to find those who best fit with their school; many of the most qualified and desirable candidates have already taken jobs elsewhere (Lui & Johnson, 2006); and those who are hired have less time to get to know the school community and get prepared for the year.

These kinds of changes in the student population at Emerson spawned a series of problems that came to a head in 1997. For the most part, the school maintained a relatively small student enrollment and retained a stable veteran staff throughout its early years. In 1997 growing enrollment in the district, as well as the school's growing popularity, led the district to give the school 25 more middle school students. In order to accommodate these new students and reduce class sizes as required by the state, the school had to hire a total of five new teachers that year (including one hired at the last minute to accommodate the newly assigned middle school students).

A larger school might have been able to absorb those new teachers more easily, but adding five new teachers to a staff of nine meant that the school quickly had to figure out how to bring the newcomers up to speed on the school's unique instructional approach and how to adapt their organizational practices to a much larger staff. To deal with the challenges, the school developed a more differentiated governance structure that included the adoption of developmental-level meetings (which, in turn, made it more complicated to make decisions previously decided by consensus in meetings of the whole staff). In addition, while the school had received a grant the year before to develop assessments to deepen their project-based approach, the staff had to put much of that work on hold. Instead, the veterans had to spend time figuring out how to develop more explicit means of sharing what they had already learned about projects with the new staff.

In addition to changes in the size of the student population, changes in the backgrounds, income levels, and diversity of student populations can also have a substantial effect on schools (see Figure 2.1). While City did not have to contend with the same crises around facilities that the other schools faced, the changing nature of the student population precipitated efforts to change the schools' instructional approach in the mid-1990s. Julianne Fredericksen, the principal at the time, reported that many of the teachers were

> outstanding teachers for children that learned a certain way, but they weren't outstanding teachers for children who learned in ways that were not real traditional. . . . our African American students and

Figure 2.1. Changing Demographics in California Public Schools: Percentage of Enrollment by Ethnicity

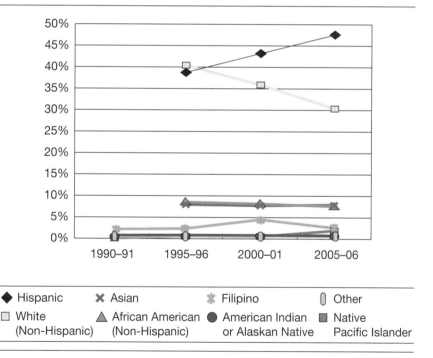

Note: Statistics for this chart were obtained from data from the California Educational Demographics Unit, 2006.

those with different learning styles, their needs were not always met and addressed.

She suggested that the school's approach needed to change with the times and become more responsive to the changing population and needs of its students:

> In the old days, City was an alternative school in the sense that if [the students] didn't do it the "City way" [the teachers] could say, "well, we're an alternative school and goodbye you're out of here." The world's not that way now. And we work with families and the students that come, and although every family applies to get into City (and not all get in), once you're in, you're in. And it was hard for a lot of the teachers to accept the fact that they couldn't go by the old rules.

As a consequence, Fredericksen launched initiatives to increase the number of teachers who possessed certification in working with students for whom English was a second language and, over time, created opportunities for the school to explore more differentiated approaches to curriculum.

Manzanilla shifted from being a school with a large percentage of African American students to one with a largely Hispanic population. That change in student population at Manzanilla went hand in hand with the development of the Spanish bilingual program. However, the growing popularity of the bilingual program meant that the school had to add more and more bilingual classrooms and cut down on the number of classes available for what they called the Sheltered English Program, in which instruction was entirely in English and most of the students were African American or Asian. (For example, with only 60 slots available for kindergarten registration in 2002–03, 56 of the first 60 students to register wanted to be in the bilingual program.) These changes in the demographics of the students registering at the school created tensions within the school as "sheltered" teachers worried they would be pushed out of the school and felt more and more like second-class citizens as the agenda of meetings became dominated by the concerns of the larger bilingual program. These changes in the student population also created tensions within the neighborhood as African American parents feared that opportunities to meet their children's needs were being lost or ignored. As a consequence, the staff at the school had to spend considerable time thinking about the mission and identity of the school. Should they become a "Spanish-only" school, or should they seek a more diverse student body that better reflected the families in the neighborhood?

At Emerson, the effects of the growing diversity of the student population throughout the district was exacerbated by the changing pool of students that came with their relocation. Because they were relocated from a well-off neighborhood to a much poorer neighborhood, they found that many of their wealthier students no longer wanted to make the trip. Those changes in the student population in turn required adjustments in the curriculum and the approaches of the teachers.

Like good businesses, schools like these need to keep abreast of the needs and expectations of changing populations, and they can target their goods and services to markets they would like to serve. But in contrast to good businesses, schools have almost no resources or capacity to predict changes in their environment, and they have to rely on others at the district level to help them to recognize and respond to these changes. Yet, with different priorities and facing different demands, districts and schools do not always see eye to eye. As a consequence, schools have to figure out how to anticipate and deal with changes in student demographics, and they have to deal with their district's response to those changes as well.

Funding for California Schools

The poor performance and often shaky financial condition of schools in even well-off communities calls into question the fundamental adequacy of our school finance system across the board. (Carroll et al., 2005, p. v)

California's public schools are funded primarily by state funds, and approximately 40% of the state budget is appropriated for K–12 education. Yet, while California has spent well above the national average in police and fire protection, health care and hospitals, public welfare, and corrections, the state has remained below average in per capita expenditure in K–12 education (EdSource, 2004).

California has steadily increased its spending on schools from 1996 to 2001, and the 2001–02 school year brought the state closer to the national average than it had been in over a decade; but state finance problems in the following years caused California to lose the ground it had gained in money spent per student (Carrol et al., 2005; EdSource, 2004).

In 2007–08, the governor cut the current budget for K–12 schools and community colleges by 557 million dollars and the California Department of Education reported a grim outlook for 2008–09 with the governor's budget proposing 4.8 billion dollars in cuts. (California Department of Education, 2008a)

Changing Funding

Schools also have to deal with a cluster of related factors—including the strength of the economy, the development of new policies, and evolving beliefs and assumptions about education—that can come together to have a dramatic effect on budgets, curriculum, and relationships among educators, parents, and policy makers.

Growth in the economy may mean more resources, but it may also mean new policies and new initiatives. While these new policies and initiatives can create new opportunities and can offer hope and support to schools, they also can bring new people and new work that has to be coordinated with work already going on. For example, in the 1990s, many schools in California benefited from a spate of new policies and the development of new reform organizations and new initiatives that accompanied the economic expansion and "Internet bubble." In particular, schools throughout districts in the Bay Area, including schools like Emerson and Manzanilla, encountered new opportunities to partner with organizations like the Bay Area School Reform Collaborative (BASRC) Partners in School Innovation, the Bay Area Coalition of Equitable Schools, and others. These initiatives not only brought in funds that the schools could control, they also brought them in contact with education experts from these and other organizations who began working closely with them to help them make improvements.

Just as quickly as some of these programs and supports appeared, however, the following severe downturn in the economy when the bubble burst also meant that schools had to find ways to maintain their work and momentum while they lost funding, curtailed initiatives, and had to cut staff positions. At Manzanilla, for example, the budget allocation from the district and other external sources over which they had discretion dropped from $700,000 in 2003 to around $400,000 in 2004. As Tom Michaels, a teacher in a mixed third/fourth-grade classroom and a member of the budget committee, reported at the time, "[Last year] there was more money to work with and you could imagine filling the needs of different kids that had not previously had those needs met. Last year, we added a whole slew of intervention teachers, and this year they are the first thing to be cut." (Ironically, the budget squeeze also meant that Manzanilla had to eliminate the spring retreat at which the staff at this democratically run school usually discussed and voted on the budget.)

Economic woes and related budget cuts can also have a debilitating snowball effect on schools. Just the uncertainty around the budget and the possibility of cuts can frustrate planning efforts and expose tensions around staffing issues and resource allocation that can undermine improvement efforts and poison the atmosphere. As Mark Simmons, a 2nd-year teacher and a member of the budget committee at Horizons explained it, when the economy is bad, "we know we're going to lose all this money, but we don't know how much." These uncertainties are particularly problematic when it comes to staffing. Although the education code in California required schools to offer contracts to teachers by March, the schools often did not know how much money they would be allocated until the budget passed later in the year. As a result, Simmons said, some schools have to tell their teachers, "Sorry, you don't have a job next year, but come back in June when we actually have our dollars and cents and we'll talk."

With students on a waiting list to get in and some control over how many students to admit, a charter school like Horizons has more flexibility than many others in responding to these budget fluctuations: If they admit more students, they get more revenue. But their decisions about what to do have significant ramifications: If they admit more students, then they also have to increase class sizes in order to maintain their current staff. Adding to the difficulties, budget fluctuations constantly force the school to debate priorities that can lead to significant conflicts among the members. For example, staff at Horizons have to weigh their commitment to college preparation for all and the potential value of adding AP classes in some subjects, for some students.

Compounding the budget problems for schools that rely on grants and other external sources, when times are bad for schools, they are often bad for many grant makers and support providers as well. As a consequence, when California cut the state education budget, both Manzanilla and Emerson also lost some of the support staff from their partner organizations like BASRC; and they lost some of the funding from those organizations that previously allowed them to launch and maintain some of their signature initiatives around professional development and instruction.

These budget problems affected the preparation and professional development of teachers overall and some of the specific programs that these schools relied on. For example, in the late 1990s California made considerable investments in developing programs to recruit and retain teachers and significantly increased the number of credentialed teachers; but by 2003 many of the state's primary professional development programs had seen their budgets cut entirely or reduced by as much as 50%, and the university and college programs dedicated to preparing most of the state's new teachers also faced significant budget reductions (Shields et al., 2003).

Changing Policies

Regardless of changes in the economy, political developments can also contribute to significant policy shifts. Among recent changes that have swept across the country, efforts to reduce class-size have had a particularly profound impact on many schools. In California, the mandate to reduce class size in the lower grades implemented in the mid-1990s meant that many schools had to find new classroom spaces, shift teachers into the lower grades, hire new teachers, or in some cases deal with the loss of effective teachers who suddenly found opportunities to work in other schools. The impact of class-size reduction on a school's ability to develop and maintain coherent instructional programs and strong professional communities differed from school to school. Thus at City the need to hire new teachers to meet the state demands gave Julianne Fredericksen the opportunity to bring in faculty who had been trained to work with students from different backgrounds and with different language and learning needs. But the principal at Dewey, Charlene Moore, described the advent of class-size reduction as "almost the death of Dewey," because it required the hiring of so many new teachers who were relatively unfamiliar with the "Dewey way."

While class-size reduction affected all elementary schools, Proposition 227—effectively limiting bilingual instruction—had a particularly dramatic impact on schools like Manzanilla with large numbers of students whose first language was not English. A ballot initiative that passed in California in 1998 (receiving 61% of the vote), Proposition 227 sought to replace bilingual instruction that might go on for several years with "structured English immersion" classes that would move students quickly into mainstream classes taught in English. However, Proposition 227 included a provision allowing schools to offer bilingual instruction if at least 20 parents at a grade level signed waivers. Staff at Manzanilla, who felt a strong commitment to the idea that students' native culture and language should be valued and supported, sought to maintain their bilingual program even as they tried to improve it and improve the rates at which students "transitioned" into full instruction in English. In order to maintain their bilingual program, however, school staff had to work every year to inform parents about their options and their rights, and the school's ability to maintain the program depended on the willingness of parents at every grade level to sign the required waivers.

In recent years, spurred by systemic reform efforts, interest in aligning many aspects of the educational system, and growing concerns about accountability, many states have also made changes in their assessments, standards, and textbook adoptions. In California, in particular, schools have had to deal with the rise and fall of support for alternative assessments and broader "world-class standards" in many subjects, and then a move back toward more traditional instructional approaches, and a narrower focus on math and reading. The development of many new state accountability systems over the past 15 years, along with the more recent introduction of No Child Left Behind at a national level, has meant that schools have also had to deal with a changing roster of tests and systems of rewards and sanctions (see Figure 2.2). One description of the accountability policies in California

Figure 2.2. Timeline of Assessments: California Public Schools

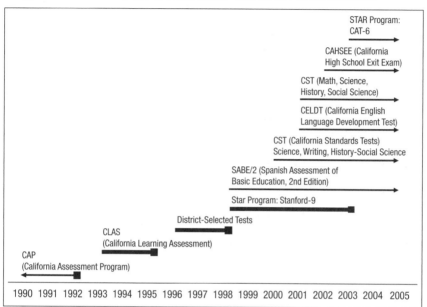

Note: Data for this chart were obtained from Ed-Data, 2004; EdSource, n.d.; EdSource, 2008; Perry, Miller, Carlo, Teague, & Frey, 2001.

in 2007–08 stated: "In a relatively short amount of time, California has gone from no statewide accountability system to two separate, high-profile systems that measure and report school progress in different ways" (EdSource, 2008a, ¶ 16).

At the same time that many schools have had to deal with a constantly changing roster of policies at the district, state, and federal levels, they also have had to deal with the fact that many of these policies are in conflict. To some extent these conflicts reflect the constant "swinging of the pendulum" between different views of education; but these conflicts also result from the complexity of the system and the number of different actors involved. Thus, in California as in many other states, differences in the demands of the state accountability system and those of NCLB can send conflicting messages when the same school that makes strong growth on California's Academic Performance Index may fail to make "adequate yearly progress" toward the growth targets established by NCLB. Or a school that demonstrates adequate yearly progress according to NCLB's criteria may end up being sanctioned by the state for not meeting state expectations for growth in its Academic Performance Index. Adding to other inequities, low-performing schools and schools

---

The Shifting Control of Education Funding in California

In the late 1970s, on average, 60% of the funding for K–12 public schools came from local taxes; the state provided about 34%; and 6% came from federal sources. Ninety percent of these funds were designated as general purpose or unrestricted.

In 2004–05, on average, 67% of the funding for K–12 schools came from the state; 22% from local sources; 9% from the federal government, and 2% from the state lottery. Of the 67% from the state, 40% is restricted for state-specified purposes through categorical programs and other designations. These included 233 different categorical programs, an increase from 57 categorical programs in 1993 (Timar, 2006).

---

in economically disadvantaged communities (like Manzanilla) that depend on significant amounts of federal funding need to focus on demonstrating adequate yearly progress according to NCLB's criteria. But schools (like Dewey and Peninsula) that do not qualify for the same federal funds face few of those financial rewards or incentives for focusing on either improving their Academic Performance Index or demonstrating adequate yearly progress.

These conflicts and complexities can lead administrators and staff to make largely symbolic changes in their practice as they wait for the next policy to come along and for the pendulum to swing back in a more favorable direction. When asked if the state and district tests and standards would ever be aligned, one district administrator in the Bay Area joked, "Will it all mesh? Yeah. Then they'll change it. We all know that."

On top of all these other changes, in California court decisions and the passage of Proposition 13 (limiting the amount of local tax increases that could be used to pay for public education) in 1978 contributed to a dramatic shift in control over school financing:

> Since the early 1970s, traditional patterns of school governance in California have changed dramatically. The presumption of local control, a system of governance based on local electoral accountability–the system in place for the previous 150 years–has been superseded by a system of state control. Decisions that used to be matters of local discretion among them, decisions about resource allocation, curriculum, student assessment, and student promotion and graduation–are now matters of state policy. (Timar, 2006, p. 3)

Not surprisingly under these conditions, one study reported that many policy makers and administrators throughout the California education system felt that revenue fluctuations were common, that changes in student assessment and curriculum contributed to frustration and mistrust, and that the amount of legislation has both increased and become more prescriptive (Brewer & Smith, 2007).

Changing Times

Even in the absence of new policies, however, the simple passage of time brings with it evolution in societal expectations for education, shifting endorsements for different instructional approaches, and corresponding changes in preparation and professional development. Combined with the challenges of turnover and fluctuating needs for new staff, these changing times can contribute to the development of different generations of teachers within the same school who have different styles, goals, and values.

Even at Peninsula, where all the teachers pursued the school's traditional academic approach, David Summers, the principal, could see some tensions:

There are some teachers who were here toward the very beginning of the school being established and they're very regimented in their teaching and they're very direct in their approach to teaching. And there are other teachers who utilize to a certain degree cooperative learning and a more open discovery learning. And there's some conflict within the staff about how that works.

At Dewey, the problems Moore encountered when she arrived as principal were even more pronounced. She quickly identified what she described as "two camps": The "new guard"—teachers who were relatively new to the school—and the "old guard"—teachers who had been at the school for a number of years. From the "new guard," she heard things like "Dewey is what you want it to be. . . . You get the opportunity to be creative and do whatever it is that works for you." From the old guard, who were firmly committed to Dewey's original child-centered approach, she heard things like, "After a while, I thought I would just close my door and do my own thing." Particularly alarming to Moore, these divisions were even apparent to many parents who were concerned that their children would not experience the "Dewey way," until they reached fourth grade, taught by some of the school's most veteran teachers.

Schools that strive to maintain a particular approach, therefore, have to contend with the possibility that their approach may fall out of favor. Thus, in the mid-1990s staff and parents at Peninsula found themselves contending with new, more "progressive" math standards and corresponding textbooks that conflicted with their more traditional approach. As a consequence, they expended considerable time and effort fighting those new standards. By the turn of the century and the launching of NCLB, however, those more progressive ideas had fallen out of favor, and the members of Peninsula found that the academic approach that they thought distinguished them from many other schools was now being adopted all around them. The members of Dewey had the opposite experience: While they found the shifts to more progressive approaches to math were consistent with their child-centered instructional philosophy, the shift back to basics at the turn of the century meant that they had to work much harder to defend and maintain their approach.

While many policy changes may reflect changing expectations among the public in general, changes in the composition, values, and goals of parents can also have a direct and significant impact on a school's ability to maintain a particular instructional approach. The changing demographics of the student body at City, for example, brought some parents with new ideas and demands for differentiated instruction that they felt might be better suited to their children. Even if Horizons continues to attract parents committed to a college preparatory curriculum that takes learning differences into account, those committed and knowledgeable parents also mean that the school constantly faces pressure to keep up with and provide the "latest" innovations in these arenas.

CHANGE AS A GIVEN, NOT A PROBLEM

On the one hand, one can look at the problems that many schools experience as isolated incidents, irregularities in normally tranquil and effective operations. On the other hand, one can see these as the natural manifestation of the stresses and strains that always exist in schools, exacerbated by the pressures of a changing and turbulent environment. In the latter sense, the crises are predictable and regular; they are part of the normal operations of both effective and struggling schools. For schools, the challenge is not to avoid entirely the impact of a changing environment, but to learn how to deal with the inevitable problems that arise.

PART II

KEY PRACTICES FOR MANAGING CHANGE

Dealing with the normal problems that come with a turbulent environment takes more than money, expertise, or hard work. The capacity to adapt to changing conditions and make some improvements over time depends on the ability of schools to carry out four key practices for managing both work inside the school and managing relationships outside the school:

- *Developing shared understanding.* Developing a shared understanding of missions, goals, and key organizational practices provides a basis for distributing leadership and enabling many members of the school community to make decisions and act in coordinated and consistent ways.
- *Dealing with hiring and turnover.* Like the "great" companies studied by Jim Collins (2001), schools need to be able to hire the "right" people and find ways to get those people into the right roles whether or not those schools have the bureaucratic authority to hire, fire, or make job assignments.
- *Creating a productive work environment.* Carefully orchestrating time, space, and staffing—allowing for both individual flexibility and collaborative work—fosters the development of common purposes, the sharing of expertise, and the promotion of interdependence and trust among members.
- *Managing the external environment.* Getting "insiders" out of the school and "outsiders" in builds relationships between school staff and parents, community members, district administrators, reform organizations, and others. Those relationships in turn give staff members opportunities to learn about and influence what's going on outside the school and to reshape demands when necessary. Turning those relationships into networks of allies who will provide support in times of crisis enables schools to create conditions more conducive to their success.

Figure II.1. Key Internal and External Practices that Enable Schools to Make and Sustain Improvements

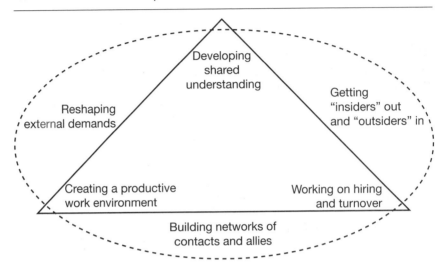

These "internal" and "external" practices are closely intertwined (see Figure II.1). The internal practices–developing a mission, hiring appropriate staff, and creating a productive work environment–equip school staff with the knowledge, expertise, and authority they need to work productively outside the school. In turn, the ability of these schools to develop external relationships, influence work on the "outside," and reshape external demands makes it easier for them to sustain their mission, attract qualified staff, and create a productive work environment.

As Rosabeth Moss Kanter (2004) shows in *Confidence: How Winning Streaks and Losing Streaks Begin and End,* this kind of circular relationship helps to explain why particularly successful organizations are able to achieve one success after another while others seem to be stuck in permanent slumps. She argues that developing confidence in advance of "victory" attracts the investments and resources–money, talent, support, attention, and effort–that make victory and sustained high performance possible. Rather than describing confidence as a personal quality or internal characteristic of an organization, however, Kanter illustrates how confidence grows from having a system that attracts and develops people, builds bonds among them, gathers external support, and takes advantage of historical, economic, and organizational forces.

In schools, this circular relationship between internal and external practices helps to explain why it takes capacity to build capacity and why it is so hard to help schools that do not already have some capacity to manage external demands (Elmore, 2002; Fullan, 2003; Hatch, 2001c).

The focus on these internal and external practices also helps to explain why some schools are not particularly successful even though they exhibit some of the well-known features of successful schools—such as strong principals, professional community among teachers, and parent involvement—and why some schools can be effective even if they do not display these features. These features are symptoms of schools that have the capacity to be successful; these factors may help schools to monitor goals, manage turnover, and create a productive work environment, but they do not guarantee that these key practices will be carried out effectively. Ultimately, how schools fulfill the functions reflected in these internal and external practices is more important than whether or not schools display the features often associated with success. From this perspective, efforts to put in place strong principals, build teacher community or get parents involved will not necessarily build capacity. Instead, schools should treat capacity building as a constant process in which they have to manage goals, deal with turnover, attend to the work environment, and shape the external demands and expectations needed to support their efforts (Honig & Hatch, 2004).

Chapter 3

Developing Commmon Purposes and Shared Understanding

The belief in the power and importance of a clear "mission" or "vision" for an organization remains so widespread both in education and the business world in general that questioning it seems ludicrous. Yet reviewing what has been written in recent years also reveals no widespread agreement on what counts as the most effective mission or the best way to go about creating one. As a result, numerous questions remain:

What Makes a Difference in Organizational Missions?

Books and articles provide no simple consensus on what an organizational mission should provide. Some highlight one factor, some highlight another:

- A key purpose for the organization OR
- Clear goals OR
- An inspiring vision OR
- A description of the values and culture of the organization OR
- Some combination of any of the above.

There is also no consensus on how a mission should be built. Some urge leaders to

- Articulate a mission and build "buy-in" for it OR
- Build it collaboratively through a formal process with a representative group of stakeholders OR
- Build it collaboratively and formally with all stakeholders OR
- Build it informally through regular conversations OR
- Derive it from the analysis of performance data and identification of strengths and weaknesses OR
- Do some or all of the above.

What matters most: A shared understanding and sense of purpose has to be sufficiently widely held and specific to guide the actions and decision making of the members of an organization.

- How clear and how specific should a mission be?
- How well and how widely understood does a mission have to be to be effective?
- Does a mission have to be created collaboratively or can strong leaders get others to buy into their vision?
- Is there a difference between a mission and a vision?

Answering these questions means shifting the focus from the mission or vision itself to the function that a mission or vision serves. Most schools (and many other organizations) have missions written down somewhere, but what really matters is how schools use their missions and mission-building activities to help them cultivate, monitor, and maintain shared understanding of the school's purposes and key practices. With a shared understanding, members of the organization know what they are supposed to do and why, and they can work together productively by making mutually reinforcing and coordinated decisions even when they are acting independently. Furthermore, with a shared understanding, leaders can delegate and distribute responsibilities more effectively because members of the organization can take the initiative and act in ways that are consistent with the aims and best interests of the organization. While shared understanding among an organization's members always needs to fulfill these central functions, the content, depth, and breadth of that understanding, and the nature and timing of the work needed to develop and maintain that understanding, differ from case to case.

WHAT SHOULD SHARED UNDERSTANDING INVOLVE?

There is no single answer to what kind of mission, purpose, or goals might be best for an organization. In fact, developing a common mission or vision is just one way to build shared understanding among members of an organization. Thus schools can build a shared understanding of goals, histories, standards, strategies, philosophies, or signature structures and practices (like mixed-age classes, the use of uniforms, a focus on a foreign language, or an emphasis on traditional curricula) without ever discussing the "mission" or creating a specific mission or vision statement. In short, each of these "products"–mission statements, visions, goals, strategies practices–can serve as tools that help build and sustain common understanding.

A Distinct Organizational Identity

Although many different goals, strategies, and practices can serve as the basis for shared understanding, the value of having shared understanding depends in part on the extent to which it provides a sense of identity that

---

Shared Understanding in Business and the Social Sectors

In *Good to Great* (2001) and *Good to Great and the Social Sectors* (2005), Jim Collins argues that great companies pursue what he calls a "hedgehog concept"—a simple clear conception of how to attain long-term results—and use it to guide all aspects of their operations. (He uses the word *hedgehog* to bring to mind the animal's simple, successful, and ingenious strategy of rolling into a ball to avoid predators.) Collins suggests that great organizations embrace hedgehog concepts that reflect a deep understanding of

1. What they are passionate about
2. What they can be the best in the field at
3. What drives their economic engine (if they are a business) or how to generate needed resources (if they are an organization in the social sector)

---

helps members to understand how their organization differs from others. That sense of identity, in turn, can encourage individuals to feel a sense of commitment to the organization and its purpose. Dewey's commitment to child-centered education and Emerson's community-based philosophy and commitment to a project-based approach, for example, are evident in their printed materials and echoes of them can be heard in conversations with both teachers and parents. But these ideas also come to life in the accompanying structures of mixed-age classes, hands-on and personalized learning in classrooms, and, at Emerson, a teacher-leadership structure and consensus-based decision making. Taken together, these philosophies, structures, and practices communicate key differences between these schools and many others around them; they provide staff and parents with a reason to choose to go to these schools (or a reason to go somewhere else); and they serve as useful heuristics that define the parameters of school activities, rather than governing them specifically.

In the end, the specific mission, approach, or signature practices schools adopt may not matter as much as the extent to which those organizational features distinguish the school from others in the surrounding environment. For schools like Emerson and Dewey, the fact that they have a specific history—including identifiable founders and an explicit reason for the school's establishment in the first place—provides characters and a plot for an organizational story that many members can share and recite.

As Howard Gardner (1995) points out, effective leaders can use that story (or develop one) as a key means of motivating and organizing people. But organizational histories, in a sense, can also tell themselves. Thus members do not need to rely on strong or charismatic leaders; they can share memorable events and characters with one another and with newcomers as well. At Horizons, for example, many different members of the school community refer to the "founding mothers": two parents whose interest in finding a school that met their children's needs helped to launch the school's development. That phrase encapsulates the school's founding story, its rationale, its unconventional character, as well as the passion and commitment that runs throughout its work. Simply by using that phrase members indicate that they have joined a family that distinguishes their organization from others. In contrast, schools that look and sound the same (or were simply created to serve a growing population) do not provide much intellectual and organizational basis for developing allegiance, loyalty, or direction for work and behavior. Instead, those schools need to rely on other factors—such as their academic or athletic performance—in order to stand out from the crowd.

As a consequence of this relational quality between schools, changing times and changing circumstances can mean that the value of a mission, approach, and signature practices changes even if the organizational features of a school stay the same. Peninsula's traditional academic approach, for example, helped to distinguish it for many years from other schools in the area that adopted more progressive instructional approaches. As the educational climate changed, however, and as more back-to-basics approaches in reading and mathematics began to take hold in California and around the country, staff at Peninsula began to worry that, as Pamela Green, a veteran Peninsula teacher put it, "everybody's beginning to look more like us." In response to the changing times (and the difficulties with previous school leaders), principal David Summers launched an effort to revisit the school's core values and practices in 2000. That process resulted in the elaboration of the school's guiding principles and reaffirmed many of the key ideas and practices. These included a primary emphasis on academic, problem-solving, and critical thinking skills; the explicit adoption of limits on the number of assemblies and field trips; and specific homework expectations for each grade, K–5. In addition, the school reinforced its commitment to having one teacher in charge of all activities in each classroom, which meant that the school did not use teaching assistants or allow parents in classrooms after kindergarten. Green explained:

> So whether I was teaching at Peninsula or I was teaching at any other school in the district, you wouldn't see a great big difference in my classroom as far as how I taught than you would at another school. What you see in my classroom, which you wouldn't see in other places, is I don't have an aide for instance. You don't have parents in the classroom. So it's pretty much *mano a mano* with the kids, which has upsides and obviously downsides."

In some cases, just maintaining a public perception of difference may be enough for schools to retain their individual character. At Peninsula, even outsiders' somewhat misguided perceptions of the school may have helped staff recognize that they were doing something unusual. When people from the area "find out I work at Peninsula," Green went on,

> either they give you this really funny look or they'll come in your classroom and say, "But you have art on the walls." "Yeah." "Your kids are sitting in groups." "Yeah." It's like they think we're in the early 1900s where everybody is hitting [kids] on the back of the hand with the ruler, and everybody is sitting in these nice, neat little straight lines.

Thus this distinctive history—whether it is fact or fiction—is a scarce resource that many public schools lack; as a consequence, it makes schools like Peninsula stand out (even among other high-performing schools) and serves as a source for loyalty and attachment to the organization.

Guidance for Collective and Individual Activity

Beyond a general sense of distinctiveness, organizations depend on shared understanding among members to provide some guidance for organizational decisions around budgeting, resource allocation, and hiring, as well as for individual decisions about how people should behave. Unfortunately, a distinctive overarching mission, an inspiring set of goals, and signature structures and practices may not provide specific enough guidance to ensure that the organization and the individuals in it are working in the most effective, consistent, and coordinated ways. At Peninsula, being "different" did not, in and of itself, help leaders make decisions that were consistent with the history of the organization or the expectations of staff, nor did it help staff know what to do beyond focusing on academics, providing homework, and limiting assemblies and field trips.

As a consequence, schools have to depend on both shared understanding both of general organizational approaches and practices and also of what to do in the classroom with students. In addition to an organizational identity, this kind of shared understanding of teaching and learning provides what Fred Newmann and colleagues have called "instructional coherence" (Newmann et al., 2001). Instructional coherence reflects the extent to which instruction throughout a school focuses on common goals and curriculum frameworks and uses common strategies for instruction and assessment.

Richard Elmore and his colleagues argue that instructional coherence cannot be imposed from the outside (Abelman & Elmore, 1999; Elmore,

---

Organizational Identity and the Organizational Saga

Burton Clark (1970), a sociologist who studied institutions of higher education as well as other kinds of institutions, refers to the long-standing characteristics that determine the distinctiveness of an organization as forming an institutional or "organizational saga":

> An institutional saga may be found in many forms, through mottoes, traditions, and ethos. It might consist of long-standing practices or unique roles played by an institution, or even in the images held in the minds (and hearts) of students, faculty, and alumni. Sagas can provide a sense of romance and even mystery that turn a cold organization into a beloved social institution, capturing the allegiance of its members and even defining the identity of its communities. (p. 235)

2002). In fact, they suggest that schools need to have a high level of agreement around norms, values and expectations (what they call "internal accountability") in order to respond effectively to policy makers' demands to improve performance and meet higher standards (what they refer to as "external accountability"). From this perspective, these external demands may lead to superficial responses–like producing detailed documents and plans that delineate outcomes and align them with curriculum and assessments– that make schools *look* more coherent. Simply aligning different structures within a school, however, is not the same thing as enabling staff to develop a common understanding of what to do in the classroom. In other words, instructional coherence, at least in part, is a state of mind; it reflects an understanding of how the school is supposed to work and how the individuals within it can work to accomplish common goals. Simply telling schools that they should develop that understanding does not give them the capacity to do it.

At the same time, schools–particularly those that already have strong internal relationships or some shared understanding–can use a variety of approaches and tools (like curriculum alignment) that, under the right circumstances, can help build or reinforce a sense of instructional coherence and internal accountability. At City, principal Bernice Lao, who joined the school in 2002, worked with the staff to establish a matrix that delineated the key skills to be taught at each grade level in each of the core subjects. In turn, she and the staff used a series of district assessments to track progress on those skills and to make related adjustments in both instruction and the budget to address what they learned. At Emerson and Manzanilla, as concerns about the achievement gap between students of different backgrounds grew both locally and nationwide, staff at both schools coupled a careful look at students' performances on a variety of measures with collaborative inquiries

---

Instructional Coherence

According to Newmann, Smith, Allensworth, and Bryk (2001), strong instructional coherence derives from

- A common instructional framework that guides curriculum, teaching, assessment, and learning climate (providing specific expectations for student learning, with specific strategies and materials to guide teaching and assessment)
- Staff working conditions that support implementation of the framework
- Allocation of resources such as funding, materials, time, and staff assignments to advance the school's common instructional framework and to avoid diffuse, scattered improvement efforts

They suggest that instructional coherence benefits students by promoting the integration of learning experiences and connecting those experiences over time. These connections can make learning experiences clearer, more meaningful, and more motivating.

---

in which the teachers explored why those gaps existed at their schools and what they could do about them. Dewey, in contrast, focused much less time on the examination of test-score data and much more time on developing an understanding of one another's child-centered instructional practices and studying related developments in psychology and education. In these cases, the tools and strategies that each staff used mattered far less than the informal and formal conversations, meetings, and activities that enabled the members of the school community to ascertain whether or not they were on the same page and headed in the right direction and what to do to build their understanding if they were not.

HOW SPECIFIC DOES SHARED UNDERSTANDING NEED TO BE?

No single answer explains how clear and how common an understanding of the mission, goals, and instructional practices needs to be to guide the organization and the individuals in it. On the one hand, missions and goals have to be specific or tight enough to provide some basis for making decisions and to provide a foundation for the development of new initiatives and practices that can then serve as a focus for collective work. On the other hand, understanding of the organization's goals and practices also has to be loose enough to allow for some variation and some tolerance for differences of opinion around key issues of teaching and learning.

Internal and External Accountability

Richard Elmore and Charles Abelman (Abelman & Elmore, 1999; Elmore, 2002) argue that external incentives, rewards and sanctions, on their own, cannot produce effective improvement processes in schools. A school's response to external pressures "is contingent on the capacity of the individual school or school district to receive the message the incentive carries, to translate it into a concrete and effective course of action, and to execute that action." (Elmore, 2002, p. 21)

From this standpoint, schools need to develop some instructional coherence and internal accountability before external accountability systems can work effectively. Schools with weaker internal accountability are more like to produce superficial, fragmented, and incoherent responses; schools with strong internal accountability are more likely to respond in productive and coordinated ways. In turn, strong internal accountability depends on the belief that school staff can have a positive impact on student learning and the knowledge and skills staff members need to act on those beliefs.

Schools that reflect a tight approach to building and maintaining a common understanding—like City under Bernice Lao—articulate specific performance goals, adopt specific strategies for reaching those goals, and frequently assess how members are doing in carrying out those strategies and meeting those goals. In the process, however, leaders have to carefully calibrate how much to "tighten," and they have to expect to spend considerable time renegotiating the balance between individual and collective activity established previously. If the mission and goals are too tight—if they do not allow room for people with somewhat different points of view to operate and act independently—then the organization will have to spend considerable effort in monitoring the behavior of members and making sure that they are acting in ways that are consistent with the organization's goals and mission.

While organizations that opt for loose understanding may not have to invest as much energy and effort in making sure that all organization members are acting in exactly the same ways, they run the risk that there will be little organizational basis for hiring, guiding behavior, or coordinating activities. This is what Charlene Moore found when she arrived at Dewey as principal. Although the mission was "written everywhere," there were few mechanisms for connecting staff or fostering a common understanding of what it meant to be part of a child-centered school. "Nobody gave [the mission] to anyone to read," Moore lamented. "So the [new faculty] didn't know. They said, well it's just a place, a nice place where you can be creative as a teacher and do your thing." In the course of individual conversations that Moore held with each member of the faculty, one relatively new teacher even told her, "When I came to this school, nobody told me what it was. I had no clue it was an alternative school, and everybody kept telling me, the parents kept coming in and asking me for the 'Dewey way,' and I said, 'What the hell are they talking about?'"

While both tight and loose missions each have benefits, there may be a tension between them that is related to the size of the organization and the number of stakeholders an organization seeks to engage. In small organizations where members have frequent contact and conversations with one another, general understandings may suffice, and simply "managing by walking around" may reveal how well organization members understand key goals and practices. At the same time, specifying a mission, goals, or vision too narrowly may make it hard to find people who share exactly the "right" mind-set. Large organizations may benefit from the fact that broad-general, understandings enable many people to feel that the organization reflects their views and values; but their size also makes it harder to monitor how well a mission is understood and whether some groups or individuals inside the organization are losing their common focus.

How many people in an organization have to be on the same page may depend not only on the size of the organization but also how closely connected their responsibilities are. Organizations where each member depends on others to get their job done require more specificity and more widely held understanding; organizations that can operate effectively even without much coordination can get by with a more general understanding, held by fewer people.

HOW SHOULD A SHARED UNDERSTANDING BE BUILT?

Unfortunately, common understandings among members of an organization can be fragile. Even in an organization that has established a common understanding, time will naturally take a toll. In schools, the demands of hiring new staff and responding to changing student populations and the demands of dealing with changing policies, budgets, and public expectations serves as a potent mix that can cause missions to drift, individuals to grow apart, and connections to unravel. As a result, schools need ways of recognizing when missions have drifted too far or common understandings have been lost, and then they have to spend time and resources finding ways to bring the members of the organization back together.

Recognizing Many Paths to a Common Place

Just as there is no single element common to the missions of all success-ful organizations, there is no one way to develop or reestablish a common identity and sense of purpose or a shared understanding of practice. For example, schools can take a technical approach, like the one Lao undertook, that specifies and aligns goals, strategies, and outcomes and closely monitors them. Schools can also take a democratic approach in which they engage diverse stakeholders and work collaboratively to develop a vision and make decisions that reflect the interests of all involved. Schools can also take what can be called a "buy-in" approach in which a strong leader or a small group of individuals develop a vision and organizational plan and then get other members of the organization to agree to it. Technical approaches rely on a belief in rationality, that the work itself, along with the data, will help make it clear to everyone what needs to be done. In contrast, democratic approaches are rooted in a belief that different people have different values and deserve an equal chance to be heard. Buy-in approaches reflect the belief that there may be some individuals with special expertise, abilities, or motivation who are likely to be more capable and effective than others in making decisions and developing plans.

Whatever approach or combination of approaches organizations take, the work can be done more or less effectively: either in ways that promote wider understanding or in ways that try to impose that understanding onto organization members. The goals and monitoring strategies of technical ap-proaches can be developed and carried out in close collaboration with the members of an organization (and other stakeholders) or simply announced by leaders. Goals developed collectively can be implemented collaboratively and reflectively or inflicted on members without further explanation or dis-cussion. Individual leaders and strong leadership groups can develop buy-in by "walking around" and engaging organization members in dialogue and discussion or by relying on one-way edicts and directives. The "right" ap-proach for an organization depends on the history and values of the organi-zation, the working styles and expectations of members, and the demands and circumstances the organization faces; but in any case the ultimate goal has to be developing common understanding not just faithfully adopting or implementing someone else's goals or plans.

At City, while Bernice Lao sought to put in place a more technical ap-proach by using a matrix to align instructional goals, curriculum frameworks, and assessments, she did so gradually, trying to involve the staff and parents in each step of the process. "I walked into a high-performing school with an outgoing principal who was a strong principal," she reported. "And so part of my first year was to learn the school structure, processes, culture, meet the people–to make sure that I really had a good understanding of what is this school about." However, she also took advantage of opportunities to introduce the matrix and to begin the process of creating greater alignment. When the district stopped scoring an integrated writing assessment the school used for benchmarks in fourth and seventh grades, Lao brought the scoring in-house. She discussed it with the fourth- and seventh-grade teachers first, and then decided to engage the whole school in the process:

> I used one of our faculty meetings to train everybody to score [the assessments]. I took it to the parent group, explained the circumstance, put a call out for volunteers to be trained and to help score. There was a schoolwide professional development day that was given to us. We built that in as one of the activities.

In the process, she turned what had been an activity for fourth- and seventh-grade teachers into an opportunity for collaboration and joint reflection on how well the whole school was doing in meeting an important goal.

At both Emerson and Dewey, when staff felt that they were losing the common understanding of their mission and practices, they embarked on a democratic and collaborative process. At Dewey, that process was clearly laid out and led by principal Charlene Moore, but the work they did and the decisions they made were democratic. She began by establishing a committee to rearticulate the "Dewey way." She selected equal numbers of faculty and parents to serve on the committee; and then the committee gathered everything that had been written about the school, solicited input from a number of those inside and outside the school, and used all of these materials, as Moore explained, "to see if we can come up with some easy way of saying what Dewey is all about." All of this took almost 2 years, and they emerged with a short brochure and concise description of the school.

At Emerson, as with all major decision making at the school, they discussed and planned the process together, launching what one teacher termed the "goals thing" in 1989. Given the district's periodic efforts to shut them down, the teacher turnover they were experiencing at the time, and a changing student population, the faculty was concerned about how to improve their curriculum and ensure (and demonstrate) that their students were making adequate progress. They began by examining the school's history; then they looked at where they wanted the school to be in 10 years and what their goals for those 10 years should be. With a smaller staff than Dewey, however, they chose to carry out those meetings at a series of retreats and at other times when all staff could be present.

Finding Reasons and Resources for Coming Back Together

Whatever paths organizations take, staff members have to figure out how to fit this additional work and many meetings into already full days and busy schedules. The willingness to make the commitment to that work comes in part from the recognition of a need for reexamination felt throughout the community. However, recognizing too many problems can sap energy and motivation because members either don't know where to start or fear that improvement efforts will be futile. As a consequence, organizations have to walk a fine line in trying to help members identify some common concerns that they can productively address in a reasonable amount of time without raising alarms that promote despair.

At the same time, members of schools performing adequately without too many obvious signs of trouble may lack the motivation for change; in these contexts it may be easier to bring some problems to the surface while also building on the positive aspects of organizational performance at the same time. Thus, at Dewey, Moore helped the whole community to see that even though the school was performing relatively well, it was not fulfilling its mission or carrying out the philosophy that justified its existence. She surfaced the need for a major reexamination of the school's philosophy through her individual conversations and subsequent reports back to the school community. She shared what she heard from both faculty and parents at a faculty meeting early in her tenure, saying "Guys, I want you to hear what [people] are saying to me. . . . I'm new to this thing, okay? Help me out. I'm being told this. What does it mean?"

Schools that never establish a distinct focus or a sense of instructional coherence may have a harder time building up a public perception that something needs to be done because they have never experienced what it's like to have a shared understanding to guide them. For many schools, an isolated, disconnected state is normal and expected, not a cause for another major improvement initiative. Schools like Dewey and Emerson also benefit from the fact that they are not starting from scratch. They might not have significant reserves of time and money to dedicate to the process, but they can draw on their founding principles, their histories, and former members for support if they start losing their way.

Established principles and histories provide a common starting point and can be used as touchstones or guidelines that can keep conversations focused. At Emerson, for example, they did not start with a blank slate but began their examination process by looking at the founding tenets of the school and considered to what extent those tenets remained powerful and relevant. That work included a series of retreats with activities like a "fishbowl discussion" (McDonald, Mohr, Dichter, & McDonald, 2007), in which some of the veteran teachers sat in a circle surrounded by the rest of the staff and talked about their memories of the school's founding and subsequent development. At Dewey, they looked at the history of the school by having the founding principal return to talk about the school's origins and having a well-liked retired teacher who was a founding member of the school observe in classrooms and talk, with the newer faculty, about their teaching.

Both schools also looked outside their walls to find parents, partner organizations, and other community volunteers who could help them. At Dewey, Moore asked a parent who worked at a nearby high-tech company and was an excellent facilitator to head the committee for "rearticulating the Dewey way" so that Moore could be an equal participant. Similarly, Emerson benefited from the support of members of Partners for School Innovations. In addition to providing the schools with classroom help from Americorps volunteers, consultants from Partners, who had extensive experience in organizational change in both the business world and education, also served as facilitators, thus allowing all members of the school staff and the governing boards to participate as equals.

Establishing Mechanisms for Communication and Reflection

Despite all the work that can go into determining goals or deciding on courses of action, the specific outcomes may matter far less than the relationships developed and the mechanisms and structures established to sustain future work. Although the reexaminations at Dewey and Emerson began with a focus on the mission and goals, the rearticulation of the mission that was put on Web sites and in the brochure was not the most important product of the deliberations. "Every time I see this," Moore rolled her eyes as she held up a small brochure, "I wonder, 'why did it take us 2 years to do this?'" Like the discussions of student work that enveloped all members of the City staff, the most important products of the collaborative examinations of Dewey's and Emerson's goals and practices were the conversations those deliberations spawned as well as the opportunities created for members of the community to work together on a regular basis to monitor and assess their collective work and to make decisions about whether or not they needed to tighten their shared understanding of their goals and responsibilities.

Correspondingly, at Dewey, following the development of the brochure, the exercise of establishing a common statement of philosophy was largely put aside, but the work of discussing school goals, activities, and future directions continued in a number of ways. "The group thought the task was done when we did the brochure. Oh, no. . . ." Moore said shaking her head. Instead of simply dissolving the group, she asked several of the members to form a community relations committee that continued to meet on an ad hoc basis and served as what Moore called "the gadflies for the Dewey phi-losophy." Moore also established two other committees to help her address issues related to the "culture" of the school. One group that Moore referred to as the "the historians, the old guard," met weekly on Friday afternoons. "When they come to me and say, 'Well, we always did that at Dewey,' they have to tell me why," Moore explained. She saw their charge as keeping the history alive so that when they leave, "the history remains." In order to en-sure that history lived on even as these veterans departed, Moore gradually added newer teachers to the group. Moore created a second advisory group by bringing leaders of the PTA and the school site council together twice a month (before their meetings) to discuss new ideas and recent develop-ments. All three groups Moore established served as "sounding boards" for her ideas and helped her to distribute the responsibility for reflecting on and maintaining the school's culture and work environment.

Similarly, at Emerson, one of the most significant results of their meet-ings to examine their goals and mission was the decision to develop their schoolwide project-based approach and to establish a variety of meeting and organizational structures to support it. Developing a schoolwide approach to project-based instruction, as Diane Kirsch, the lead teacher at the time explained,

> brought up all of these specific questions that we had to answer. . .
> "how will I know what's going on in your classroom, or that students
> are going to be getting what they need?" So we ended up having to
> develop different kinds of structures for communication, for teachers
> working together, for work being much more explicit.

One of the structures they developed was the formation of developmental teams so that K–2, 3–5, and 6–8 teachers worked together, with team meet-ings taking place every week. In fact, before they began working on their project-based approach, the faculty held a weekly staff meeting that usually involved discussions of issues like field trips, social events, and school be-havior. But as they began to develop their instructional projects, faculty es-tablished an extensive meeting structure that grew to include a number of different meetings focused on teaching and learning. In addition, the joint work on project-based learning also led to a series of collaborative initiatives like an effort to develop common assessments and rubrics across classes.

Picking the Right Time

The strategy and means for establishing or reestablishing common pur-pose and shared understanding also depends on timing—where the organization is in its history and development. Reflecting the recursive challenges of managing change, without structures and mechanisms for exchanging ideas and information in place, developing common purposes and shared understanding can be particularly difficult. Under these circumstances, repeated efforts to articulate or revise a mission may simply demonstrate to organization members that they lack a shared understanding and suggest that attempts to produce one are futile. Ironically, such mission-building efforts may also fail in situations where schools do have some of these mechanisms in place and have a long-standing mission. The common bond or identity may breed a sense of complacency that overshadows any efforts to motivate new initiatives, let alone launch a reexamination of core principles and practices.

In these situations, drawing on other key practices–like focusing on hiring and turnover or revitalizing the work environment–may make more sense. Bringing in new personnel, for example, who share some values and assumptions can help to seed new ideas among the staff, and creating new relationships and opportunities to develop new expertise can establish a foundation for tightening the organization and motivating collaborative work. When Lao's predecessor Julianne Fredericksen arrived at City, she also found a high-performing school, but the veteran faculty were set in their ways, unwilling to make adjustments to their instructional approaches or to learn some of the new techniques for working with diverse learners. Recognizing that engaging this veteran faculty–who had already resisted the new initiatives of several previous principals–in reflecting on their goals and purposes was unlikely to produce significant changes, Fredericksen focused instead on managing hiring and turnover. She turned her attention to hiring new teachers who had experience working with diverse students and supported a wide range of professional development initiatives to help staff learn new skills, including instructional strategies for students whose primary language was not English. Once Fredericksen had successfully made some changes in the composition and skills of the staff, she was able to launch a schoolwide process to revisit and revise the school's mission and provide a public affirmation and demonstration of the school's new approach.

Once organizations like City have established a mission, however, launching too many major reevaluations or visioning exercises may cause more problems than they solve. In these cases, new superintendents and new principals have to figure out how to adapt their ideas to the organization, rather than the other way around. In that sense, leaders like Moore at Dewey, are in a better position to launch major new initiatives and put their own stamp on a school than those like Lao who enter schools that have made some changes and function relatively well. With a high-performing school without recognized problems, Lao had to build on already established groups and meeting times and make the matrix work part of regular responsibilities.

SUMMING UP

While a clear mission may be useful for many schools, it is just one tool that organizations can use to help build a common understanding of their goals, philosophy, and practices. Tight missions may work for some organizations at some times, and loose missions might work at others. What really makes a difference are the activities that organization members engage in that help them to develop some shared understanding and to recognize when that understanding is not clear enough or is not as widely shared as it needs to be.

In the end, what matters most may be whether a school has a set of instructional practices, an educational philosophy, a content area, or vocational focus that it is known for and that gives it an organizational identity that helps to distinguish it from others. When a school is distinct from others, there is a basis for people to join and align themselves with the organization and its approach and practices or to decide that they do not belong and that they or their children would fit better somewhere else.

If having a distinct organizational identity can help foster a productive, shared understanding among members, then schools that parents have to choose or "opt into" may well have an advantage over regular public schools. Schools of choice, like City, Dewey, and Emerson, have to distinguish themselves from others or else there is no basis for parents to send their children. However, schools within the regular public system can distinguish themselves in any number of ways, including through their performance, the adoption of policies like school uniforms, or an emphasis on the arts or sciences. But in creating a distinct organizational identity, public schools in general may be at a disadvantage when relatively little is known about the history of the school. Private schools and alternative schools can often return to stories of their founding, the principles on which they were based, and the individuals who were selected by those communities to lead them at different points in time. But many public schools were started simply because more schools were needed, and most are expected to deliver the same kind of instruction and activities that other students are getting. For many schools, the strongest sense of history comes from the performance of their athletic teams and the division and state titles they have acquired in different sports. Without a sense of history or purpose that distinguishes them from others, many schools may not have the same basis or foundation for creating and maintaining or re-creating an organizational identity that schools of choice like those in this study have.

Whether a school is a school of choice or a regular public school, simply being distinct—requiring uniforms or focusing on the arts, for example—is unlikely to help unless these distinctive aspects enable members of the organization to develop some instructional coherence and to learn what kinds of behavior, decisions, and activities are consistent with the identity of the organization. As Jaqueline Ancess and David Allen (2006) point out in their examination of "theme" schools in New York City, a vocational or thematic focus may be marginal to the school's primary activities; they cite the example of the Academy for Public Safety (APS), which began with a focus on law enforcement careers, but now simply offers courses related to these careers as electives for juniors and seniors. Furthermore, they argue that many schools are "nominal" theme schools–theme schools in name only–where an original focus on the arts or specific vocations may simply have disappeared over time. Only when schools have a theme or focus which can truly be said to be integrated throughout the organization and its activities is it likely to serve as the basis for the kind of shared understanding needed to drive collective activity.

Chapter 4

Working on Hiring and Turnover

Although mission building often gets more attention, managing hiring and turnover provides another avenue for schools to develop shared understanding and to make improvements. Hiring teachers whose ideas and approaches seem to "fit" with those of the existing staff and with the general expectations of the school community helps minimize conflicts and facilitates collective work and organizational learning. Conversely, when staff members get worn down or performance slips, bringing in "new blood" can create new energy, foster the development of new expertise, and stimulate innovation.

CHALLENGES OF STAFFING: TWO PERSPECTIVES

Too often, however, discussions of staffing stall on questions of control: Do schools and school leaders have the authority they need to hire the candidates they want? In reality, who has the bureaucratic authority to hire and fire makes relatively little difference if potential applicants do not have the values or expertise schools want or if the schools do not have the power to distinguish between applicants who are likely to meet their performance demands and those who do not.

As a consequence, staffing reflects challenges and opportunities at both national and local levels (see Figure 4.1). On the one hand, individual schools depend on the efforts of policy makers and others to stimulate and support the development of a strong national labor pool. On the other hand, whatever the economic conditions and quality of the national labor force, individual schools need to be able find and recruit the "right" candidates. Schools need to be able to make informed hiring decisions, and then they need to make sure that those hired are put into appropriate roles.

The National Problem: Creating a Strong Labor Force

On a national level, the work of researchers and policy makers reflects three different strategies for creating a strong teacher labor force: recruitment strategies for getting qualified and potentially effective teachers into the labor market, distribution strategies for addressing problems and inequities in the

Figure 4.1. The Challenges of Staffing

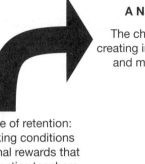

A National Perspective

The challenge of recruitment: creating incentives for job entrants and minimizing entry barriers

The challenge of retention: creating working conditions and professional rewards that encourage effective teachers to stay and work in all schools

The challenge of distribution: creating hiring procedures, incentives, and organizational structures that support the equitable assignment of teachers

A Local Perspective

The challenge of recruitment: establishing and maintaining a pool of appropriate candidates

The challenge of turnover: maintaining a balance between local experience and new ideas and expertise

The challenge of hiring: developing hiring procedures that facilitate a "match" between candidates available and jobs required

---

Key Facts and Figures on School Staffing

- In 2006 there were 3,954,000 prekindergarten–12 teachers in the United States with 4,330,000 teaching jobs projected by 2016 (Bureau of Labor Statistics, 2008).
- Data from 2003–04 shows that high-poverty schools are more likely than low-poverty schools to be staffed by teachers with less than 4 years of experience, who lack an advanced degree, and/or lack a full state teaching credential. High-poverty schools also tend to be staffed by teachers who are paid, on average, less than teachers in low-poverty schools (Goldhaber, 2008).
- According to analyses of the Schools and Staffing Survey conducted in 1999–2000, almost one third of teachers were in transition, either joining a new school at the beginning of the year (534,861) or leaving at the end (539,778) (Ingersoll, 2003b).
- Of teachers in transition, over half of the new hires (302,629) and almost half of those who left (287,370) were teachers changing schools (Ingersoll, 2003b).
- While the overall turnover rate was about 15% in 2000–01, the turnover rate in low-poverty schools was about 12%; it was about 16% in rural high-poverty schools; and about 22% in urban high-poverty schools (Ingersoll, 2003b).

---

distribution and assignment of teachers to jobs and schools, and retention strategies for stemming high degrees of turnover among teachers (Ingersoll, 2003a). Each of these strategies reflects a different view of the key problems with staffing, with significant implications for policy and practice.

From a recruitment perspective, a shortage of qualified teachers leaves many schools—particularly schools in disadvantaged communities—without a qualified pool of applicants from which to draw when they have an opening. Responses to this problem often include policies that offer incentives (bonuses, higher salaries) and eliminate or simplify certification or other entry requirements in order to encourage people who have the potential to be effective teachers to choose teaching over other job opportunities.

From a distribution or assignment perspective, however, even with qualified candidates available, incentives to keep costs low and constraints on time and scheduling encourage principals and district administrators to hire unqualified teachers, to assign teachers to out-of-field jobs or other roles for which they are unprepared, or to distribute teachers and teaching responsibilities in inequitable ways. Responses to this problem focus on changing the conventional school structures—schedules, staffing patterns, budget allocations, and so on—that limit the flexibility leaders have in matching available personnel to the needs and demands of work in schools.

Those who take a retention perspective focus on the fact that even after teachers choose to join the teaching profession, many may not stay in teaching for very long and those who do may change teaching jobs relatively frequently. As a result, many schools, particularly low-performing schools and schools in disadvantaged communities, experience high turnover rates and constantly have to spend time and money searching for and training new (and often less-experienced) staff. Changing entry requirements does little to alleviate the problem. Instead, efforts to address turnover focus attention on improving the working conditions in schools, taking steps to make teaching more like other professions like law and medicine, and creating a "level playing field" so that all schools can have an equal chance of hiring the teachers they need.

Although policies often emphasize a recruitment perspective, many recent federal and state approaches to staffing problems pursue many different solutions at once. Thus the No Child Left Behind Act seeks to improve quantity and quality of the teacher labor pool and to reduce out-of-field teaching by ensuring that all teachers are "highly qualified" in core academic subjects they teach. At the same time, NCLB also requires states and districts to distribute "highly qualified" teachers equitably and encourages states and districts to provide incentives for bringing highly qualified teachers to low-performing schools and schools in disadvantaged communities. Many states and cities also strive to improve the labor force by supporting the development of alternative pathways into teaching. Like Teach for America, many of these programs provide a way for individuals who have strong educational backgrounds or relevant career expertise to enter the teaching force and start working in "high needs" schools without having to go through traditional teacher education programs. Simultaneously, pilot programs in many states and districts also provide mentoring and other forms of support for new teachers and strive to improve working conditions and reduce turnover considerably.

The Local Problem: Finding the Right Teachers

Regardless of what happens to the national labor pool, schools have to deal with a local labor pool that contains a range of more and less qualified candidates for teaching positions, and they have to figure out how to find and hire those most likely to meet their needs. In that effort, they have to compete with other local schools and with other schools with similar philosophies looking for the same kinds of teachers. In short, they can either invest their time and resources in finding the right staff or suffer the costs and consequences in turnover and other problems that result when hiring does not work out.

While focusing on finding the right candidates and providing them initial support can be costly, it can also significantly reduce turnover. For example,

---

Costs of Turnover

Costs related to turnover include recruiting and hiring new teachers, special incentives to recruit and retain teachers, personnel processing and transfer costs, training for new hires, and the cost to student learning in the "learning curve" of new teachers (Barnes, Crowe, & Schaefer, 2007).

- In 1999–2000 Chicago spent $5.1 million to recruit and hire new teachers.
- In 2001–02 New York spent $8 million just for an advertising campaign to hire 12,000 new teachers (Goodnough, 2001).
- In Texas the recruitment, hiring, and training costs to the state run into the hundreds of millions of dollars every year (Texas Center for Educational Research, 2000).
- In 2003–04 turnover costs ranged from $4,366 in a small district in New Mexico to $17,872 in Chicago (Barnes et al., 2007).
- In 2005 a national study reported average costs of a teacher leaving a school at $12,652 (Alliance for Excellent Education, 2005).

---

in a study of all the beginning teachers in the United States in 1999–2000, Thomas Smith and Richard Ingersoll (2004) reported:

- 40% of new teachers who did not participate in any support or mentoring programs were likely to leave their school at the end of the year.
- 28% of those who received some support (such as a mentor or common planning time with other teachers) were likely to leave at the end of the year.
- 18% of those who received the most significant support (including a seminar for beginning teachers and support from their principal) were likely to leave at the end of the year.

Given that some estimates suggest that the costs of initial support may be a third of the costs incurred when a teacher leaves a school and a new teacher has to be hired, savings for both individual schools and school systems as a whole could be substantial (Barnes, Crowe, & Schaefer, 2007).

Despite the common perception that schools have little control over the process of hiring and firing their personnel, a growing body of research suggests, that, on the whole, individual schools may be able to exert much more influence over the staffing process than they believe. For example, a study by Edward Lui and Susan Moore Johnson (2006) of 1st- and 2nd-year teachers in California, Massachusetts, Maine, and Florida, revealed that

- 45% of new teachers applied directly to their schools, with hiring decisions made at the school level
- 30% of the new teachers went through a screening by the district but the school made the final hiring decision
- 23% were hired based on a decision at the district-level

Yet even in schools that controlled the hiring process, principals and staff members engaged in relatively limited efforts to get to know the candidates and to find those that might be a good fit. Fewer than half (45%) of the new teachers participated in job interviews with other teachers at the school where they were hired, and in Florida one in five of the new teachers reported that they did not participate in any interview as part of the hiring process.

In part, these results may reflect another of Liu and Johnson's (2006) findings: Many schools and districts hire teachers quite late, with over a third of teachers in California and Florida hired after the school year has started. These results may stem from the timing of budget decisions at the state level as well as enrollment levels that may change even as the school year begins. With little time to waste, many schools make hiring decisions quickly, without much chance to get to know the candidates or vice versa. Nonetheless, those schools and districts that recognize the problems associated with late hiring and do whatever they can to make hiring decisions earlier in the year can gain a significant advantage in the competition for the most desirable teachers.

While most charter schools, like Horizons, still have to deal with the constraints of uncertain budgets and enrollment levels, they can determine their own hiring processes and make independent hiring decisions. Nonetheless, even when district administrators make budget, enrollment, and final hiring decisions, schools like Peninsula, City, Manzanilla, Dewey, and Emerson can control or influence many aspects of the hiring process. Regardless of how much hiring authority they have or when states and districts make their budget decisions, schools do not have to wait until the right candidates find them. Schools can recruit teachers who fit their requirements, arrange visits for applicants, conduct interviews, and develop their own selection procedures to help them learn about candidates. With a strong applicant pool and good information about the candidates, schools have more flexibility in the hiring process and more leverage when decisions are made. Taken together, these recruiting and hiring procedures also serve as key means of selling the school to some candidates and weeding out others who seem like a mismatch with the schools' missions and goals. With this up-front investment in getting the right candidates in the first place, schools can identify the most promising applicants and advocate for their hiring; schools can also increase the chances that both the candidate and the school will be happy with the decision, and they can decrease the amount and costs of turnover.

BEFORE SELECTION: THE POWER OF RECRUITMENT

Schools can develop their applicant pool by encouraging staff and community members to develop relationships with educators both inside and outside their districts (Jennings, 2008). Through these relationships, school members meet interesting candidates and get the word out about the school's work and any job openings they may have coming up. Schools that establish partnerships with like-minded teacher education programs and reform organizations and join networks with similar schools can also increase the chances that staff members will meet candidates with the kinds of interests and expertise the school values. In some cases, cultivating long-term relationships with external partners may create the school's own pipeline of suitable job candidates.

The development of these kinds of relationships and the recruiting efforts that go along with them take time and energy. The amount of time and energy required depends upon the turnover rate and the number of jobs the schools have to fill at a particular time; the number of teachers in the area whose skills and interests match their needs, and the schools' access to and reputation in the other schools and networks where they are most likely to find candidates. Schools like Peninsula that have little turnover, a strong reputation, and a traditional academic approach can rely on informal networks to find experienced teachers when they need them. In contrast, schools like Dewey, Emerson, and Manzanilla may have to spend much more time finding appropriate external partners and explicitly cultivating the development of more formal relationships for recruiting the right candidates.

Relying on Reputation, High Demand, and Informal Networks

It goes almost without saying that schools with good reputations, in popular locations and in good condition, are more likely to attract candidates than those with poor reputations and more problematic circumstances (DeArmond, Gross, & Goldhaber, 2008). Combined with low-levels of turnover, some schools may find that they have a wealth of qualified candidates even when others struggle to fill spots. Even with a larger pool of candidates, however, a school may still struggle to find and select those that fit their needs.

As a consequence, having a distinct identity and a set of key practices may be just as important for a school as having a reputation for success. Schools known for a particular approach can narrow and focus the applicant pool by helping applicants themselves recognize whether or not they fit and discouraging them from applying if they do not. Schools with limited turnover may also have significant time to develop an informal network of contacts who may be interested in joining the school. These informal networks provide a kind of waiting list of interested parties who serve as a buffer in case a spot suddenly opens up.

This kind of informal approach to recruitment and selection character-ized work at Peninsula. Although the school had a well-known approach to instruction, low levels of turnover, and a reputation as orderly and suc-cessful, the hiring process was not left simply to the fates. When Peninsula had an opening (and sometimes before), members of the faculty spread the word about the school through their colleagues and contacts within the district. For example, when Paula Williams, a second-grade teacher at Pen-insula, knew there would be an opening the following year, she encouraged Janet Stark, a 16-year veteran she knew from the district literacy committee, to apply.

As Stark explained it, through their joint work, Williams knew both that Stark's instructional approach fit Peninsula's and that Stark was growing tired of her current placement. As a result, when Williams told her, "I'd really love it if you'd come over to Peninsula. There's going to be an open-ing," Stark thought, "maybe it's time for a change." Peninsula's reputation and traditional methods of instruction appealed to Stark because, as she explained, she had a more "curriculum-focused" approach than many of her friends in the district. That traditional reputation may also have helped to scare away other candidates who might not be as good a fit. "Why do you want to go there?" Stark was asked by her colleagues. "They feel that it is just so traditional that you can't do anything," she explained. "[They think] you can't even breathe. I think they picture the desks being in rows and every kid sitting there just working in their math book or whatever." But because Stark knew Williams, she knew the school was not like that. "So I came over and I looked at the philosophy and read it and talked to the principal at the time, and he said, 'We'd really love to have you come over.' So I said 'Okay, fine.'" While Peninsula's principal still had to go through a formal transfer process, he got approval at the district level, and Stark was hired and moved to Peninsula.

A good reputation and informal networks aided hiring at City as well. Margaret Evans, a sixth-grade teacher, joined the staff at City when a friend of City's principal at the time recommended her. Evans, who had only one year of experience when she interviewed at City, would have stayed where she was even though it was a school that was not nearly as success-ful as City because she felt supported by the principal and her colleagues. "That was my first choice," she explained. But the school was in the midst of "reconstitution"—which consisted of closing and then opening the school again so that the school could be restaffed. Evans ultimately chose City over several other positions she was offered because, as she put it, the principal, Julianne Fredericksen, was "a good salesperson":

She just convinced you that this was a good place to work and she had a lot going for her. . . . It's a small school and there aren't a lot of behavior issues here and a lot of real difficult things, and so that is a selling point. In that sense, it can be much less stressful than other schools.

Building Local Pipelines

Even successful schools, however, may find that informal efforts fail to yield sufficient numbers of qualified candidates. In particular, schools with unusual or innovative approaches that call for specialized expertise may need to develop more explicit efforts to find the right candidates. Of course, high degrees of turnover—common among new schools like Horizon and other schools like Emerson and Manzanilla that depend on elaborate meeting and professional development structures to support their alternative approaches—increases the demand for these specialized applicants. Under these conditions, schools may find that formal or informal partnerships with like-minded organizations give them an even stronger basis for developing an appropriate and stable pool of applicants.

Although schools with unconventional approaches may sometimes look for experienced teachers, they may find that many veterans—even effective ones—who are accustomed to work in more conventional settings may not have the skills or interests that match the school's needs. Instead, schools with unconventional approaches may prefer to draw on teachers who are relatively new to the profession and who might be in a better position to benefit from the support and professional development these schools can offer. These schools do not have to settle for the average new teacher, however. To help them gain access to a strong pool of young teachers, schools can establish relationships with well-regarded teacher education programs, reform organizations, or teacher networks with whom they share goals and philosophies. These partnerships can create a kind of extended exploration or try-out period in which schools learn about the candidates and make informed choices about whether or not these applicants will fit. In turn, the candidates have opportunities to learn about the schools and some even have the chance to work directly with the school's veteran teachers in mentoring relationships. As a consequence, as Warren Lovejoy, a veteran teacher at Dewey explained, at least some new hires can begin their work already "pointed in the right direction."

At Dewey, like Peninsula, the success of the school as well as the high pay in their suburban district helped to attract a wide range of experienced applicants. But it was the long-standing connections to local teacher education programs that provided the school with a steady supply of young teachers whose interests and philosophies aligned particularly well with Dewey's approach. These programs and their student teachers sought out placements at Dewey because it stood out among schools in the area that take a progressive approach. Lovejoy, who first came to the school as a student teacher in the 1970s, explained that even at that time "Dewey was always in conversation" in his local teacher education program. "There was a movie that was made about some of the teachers [at Dewey] that we [the student teachers] all watched and all of us kind of drooled at." Being born and raised in the district, Lovejoy also knew of the school and had met the founding principal, who told him, "When you get to student teaching, come and see us."

Similarly, Marielle Henkel, a second-grade teacher at Dewey as well as a parent with children in the district, pursued a position at Dewey because she had heard about it from friends who had children there:

> I had always heard of the philosophy, admired the philosophy, and then I had friends who were there who were talking about different things that were happening in the classroom and I was very, very interested in that. So I was introduced to Georgeanne Kim [a fourth-grade teacher there] and had a discussion with her about whether she would be willing to take a student teacher, and she was interested . . . but she wanted me to come in and observe her first.

After visiting Kim's class several times, Henkel thought "this is my type of teaching, absolutely," and she ended up student teaching there for a semester. As a consequence, as a student teacher, Henkel had an opportunity to learn about the "Dewey way" and the specific curricula, practices, and demands of teaching at Dewey.

The experience at Dewey impressed Henkel so much that even after she took a job as a long-term sub in another building, she kept in contact with Charlene Moore, the principal at Dewey at the time, telling her how much she wanted to be at the school. She even invited Moore to visit her own school and see for herself if Henkel fit:

> For me to have my own classroom and to have her [Moore] observe and see what I was doing really, I think, helped our relationship develop, and I was able to really talk to her about what kind of a teacher I wanted to be and what kind of environment I wanted to be in.

Ultimately, once there was an opening at Dewey, both Moore and Henkel were convinced the job should be hers.

Like Dewey, Manzanilla benefited from connections to teacher education programs as well as links to other reform initiatives in the area. In some ways,

Manzanilla's status as a low-performing school may have made it a more attractive partner for organizations seeking to make a difference and provide help for schools in less affluent communities. In addition, Manzanilla's strong and engaged faculty, well-known commitment to bilingual education and equity, and an inquiry-based approach to professional development, all made the school an appealing partner. In fact, three different teacher education programs in the Bay Area placed a number of student teachers at Manzanilla over the years. At one point, a highly respected local program placed almost 20 student teachers a year at the school and also staffed an after-school English Language Development program there. Through these relationships, Manzilla's staff members got to know many job candidates before they applied and frequently hired their student teachers once they graduated from their programs. In addition to allowing these new hires to learn about the school before they applied for jobs, the fact that these new hires shared a common teacher education background with more experienced members of the staff helped to create an instant bond and kinship. "They all have relationships with each other," Elena Rivera the literacy coordinator said, "because they are friends from their programs," and as a result, they share a sense of collegiality and common learning habits.

Manzanilla also drew a number of staff members from one of their key support providers, Partners in School Innovation (PSI). One student teacher asked her teacher education program to place her at Manzanilla because she had heard so much about the school when she worked as a member of Partners. Barbara Silver, Manzanilla's reform coordinator, was also hired by the school after she fulfilled a number of related responsibilities when she was a Partners staff member who worked at the school. Silver's hiring not only tightened the connection between the school and Partners, it also meant that Silver had a source of support and mentorship that most new hires do not have. As she explained, "Partners has been helpful because that's where I came from, so I know how to use them. I can ask for help there, I can feel comfortable." In fact, her former team leader at Partners became the Partners coach at Manzanilla, and continued to serve as an unofficial support for Silver throughout her first two years on the job. Without that relationship and that support, Silver acknowledged that she probably would have left the school because of the demands of the job.

All in all, through these partnerships with both teacher education programs and external partners, many of Manzanilla's new staff members benefited from a kind of informal internship program—and an extended audition—that allowed the school to make well-informed hiring decisions. Further, the school managed to make those decisions in the context of a district bureaucracy and a human resources department widely viewed at the time as one of the worst in the area.

Establishing a National Reputation

Developing local relationships takes time. Furthermore, when a school is just starting out or takes a particularly unusual approach, even with some local connections, the local pool of candidates may not suffice. Under these conditions, schools need to look beyond the local community and establish their own means of recruiting on a national level. That work may involve the same kind of formal and informal networking and partnership building that benefits some schools at the local level; but school members may also have to find the time to attend job fairs and make recruiting visits to schools and meetings around the country. In either case, those efforts are likely to be enhanced once those schools experience some success in bringing in national recruits and develop a good national reputation.

Even with a relatively good reputation, Emerson always found it difficult to get suitable candidates from the local area. In fact, in its early years, with a limited number of teaching positions and a high demand for positions, bureaucratic restrictions required Emerson to hire candidates from within the district. As the hiring restrictions in the district eased, however, Emerson's pool of candidates expanded. Subsequently, their growing national reputation as a model progressive and project-based school in an urban district helped to attract candidates from around the country. As a result, new teachers arrived from places like Seattle and Chicago after learning about the school through the publications of national networks like *Horace* (produced by the Coalition of Essential Schools), through the Internet, or through their friends in the Bay Area.

As a charter school, Horizons did not have a pool of district candidates to turn to. In fact, limited access to job fairs and networking events held by the district hampered their local recruiting efforts. Drawing on his background and contacts from his work in independent schools, however, founding principal Paul Archer spent some of his time traveling to job fairs and visiting colleges and teacher education programs on the East Coast and in other parts of the country. When the school's reputation grew, the school's charter status and its distinctive focus on providing a college preparatory education for students with many different learning needs helped attract candidates both from around the Bay Area and around country.

The appeal of working in a charter school environment, particularly a stable one, drew the attention of Michael Jenkins, the curriculum director. When he and his wife relocated so she could begin a graduate program in the Bay Area, he knew he wanted to be at a charter school:

This [Horizons] is the one I wanted to come to because it was, at the time, the most stable of the four [charter high schools in the Bay

Area]. It had a good facility; its leadership was stable; the staff was stable. The humanities teachers there—they were losing no humanities teachers. Paul was the founding principal and had been there a long time. And that to me was very appealing. At all the other schools, there was huge turmoil.

Sally Reese, who joined the school as a humanities teacher, found out about Horizons when she was working on the development of a proposal for another charter school. When she was looking for a job for a year before her own school opened, a friend she knew through the alumni network of her local teacher education program told her that Horizons was "a great place to be." After her first year, rather than joining the staff of the charter school she helped plan, Reese stayed on at Horizons and within several years became dean of students and then principal when Archer became the executive director.

A general interest in "making things different in the public education field" attracted Reese to Horizons and a charter school setting in the first place. But the "commitment to kids with learning issues," rather than the school's charter status, attracted the attention of Allison Henry, the director of the Learning Center at Horizons. She discovered the school on the Internet when she began thinking about moving to California from the East Coast. A subsequent conversation with Archer and the hiring committee made it clear to her that the school would be a good match for her. The chance to participate in redesigning the Learning Center—an opportunity she could not find in many, if any, other schools—was also particularly appealing.

Despite all of the work invested in networking, establishing partnerships, and recruiting nationally and locally, however, even relatively successful schools face significant shortages of teachers in high-needs areas like Spanish and mathematics. But the challenges that even relatively successful schools experience also illustrates another of the catch-22s that make it difficult for schools that are not already doing well to make improvements and manage the change process: Unknown schools, schools facing difficulties, and schools known solely for poor test scores will have a hard time attracting the very staff they need to develop and carry out a distinctive approach. In contrast, those schools with distinctive approaches, shared understandings, and good reputations may not have to expend as much time and energy finding the staff they need to sustain their work. These problems are compounded when struggling schools are in districts with poor reputations, low achievement levels, and little money to attract stronger candidates in the first place (DeArmond, Gross, & Goldhaber, 2008; Wilson, Bell, Galosy, & Shouse, 2004).

USING THE SELECTION PROCESS TO FIND THE RIGHT FIT

Beyond recruitment, schools can either use the hiring process to mechanically fill positions that become available or as a strategic means of selecting organization members who fit the school's goals and approach. That strategic work begins with establishing a baseline or set of criteria that help to distinguish those who are likely to fit from those who are not. It includes using the selection process to launch the socialization process and to increase the chances that new hires will start their work "pointed in the right direction." Further, it expands into the careful orchestration of staffing throughout the school in ways that take advantage of individual strengths and organizational needs. With a broader understanding of how new staff fit into the organization as a whole, school leaders can also make strategic decisions about whether to use the selection process as a means of sustaining or changing a school's approach.

Screening: Determining the Initial Criteria

Hiring decisions in any organization often involve a tension between candidates who bring specific expertise or experiences needed to carry out a particular job and those who seem to provide the best overall fit with the organization. In some cases, a candidate may possess both qualities; but often organizations have to make a choice. In managing these tensions, organization leaders have to ask themselves "Who's available?" as well as "What's needed?"

Sports teams face this choice every time they prepare for a draft: Should they draft for need—selecting a person who plays a position that they have to fill—or should they pick the best player overall? To some extent circumstances may dictate the choice. If a football team needs a quarterback, they may not be able to wait to find the best candidate; they may need to take someone who can fill that particular position. Similarly, if a school needs someone to teach calculus or a foreign language, only a limited number of people will fit the bill; but if a wider range of candidates possess the right background, then schools can focus on those who are most likely to share the school's mission and understand the school's approach.

In order to manage these kinds of trade-offs, schools have to have a sense of their bottom line. As Jim Collins puts it in *Good to Great* (2001), when in doubt, don't hire—keep looking. Even if a school has a desperate need, hiring someone who does not share any of the school's values and disagrees with the school's approach can be disastrous. That's why Paul Archer at Horizons opted for fit over specialized expertise whenever possible. He explained that in his initial conversations with candidates, congruence with the school's mis-

---

Fit and Versatility in Personnel Decisions

In football, the New England Patriots are well-known for putting together and maintaining a powerful team through thoughtful player selection. Their approach reflects an awareness of the general qualities that make those players a good fit for the organization and attention to the specific demands of the roles those individuals may be asked to play in the organization. On the one hand, according to Vice President of Player Personnel Scott Pioli, he and coach Bill Belicheck look for "smart people":

> People that are professional, people like him and myself that are committed to being the best at whatever their job is. . . . We want people that care about football and are disciplined. And when we talk about discipline, it has nothing to do with how long their hair is or how much jewelry they're wearing. It has everything to do with being disciplined about your job—showing up on time, working hard and being accountable. (Quoted in Flynn, 2008)

On the other hand, Belicheck adds that before they even begin discussing the players they talk about "What do we want them to do? What role do we envision and what spot do we see on the team that the player could perform?" They do not envision those roles in conventional ways, however. They don't just look for players who play a particular position; they look for "versatility" and for individuals who can serve multiple functions on the field and in the locker room. As Pioli puts it, "Versatility is very important. You look for certain traits and one of the most important traits for any player to be versatile is intelligence." The fact that a number of Patriots players play multiple positions—including ones they never played before they joined the Patriots—demonstrates the team's commitment to this idea. It also reflects that their personnel decisions do not simply focus on what players have done in the past. As Pioli explains, it's all about how "they learn football and how they process it." (Quotes from Flynn, 2008)

---

sion more than the experience was the key. "We don't do any conversion here," Archer reported; "if you're not converted, you don't get hired." In his words, his interviews with job candidates included "tests"–open-ended questions about grading and assessment–in areas in which the Horizons faculty saw itself as differing substantially from common educational practice:

> The question I always ask in an interview is, "What's your reaction to the situation of a student who asks for extra time on a test?" There's obviously a right answer if the person paid any attention to Horizons, but if the person says, "Well, you know, I can see that happening but I have a question about whether or not that's fair to the other kids and I'd want to think about it." Well, you know, pull the

plug [he lifted up his arm as if to pull a lever to a trapdoor] and there goes the candidate.

While Archer looked for teachers who have had experience working with students with learning differences, their level of commitment to the idea, not their level of skill or preparation, provided the first cutoff for candidates. As Archer described it, "I haven't filled the school with people with LD backgrounds."

In addition to asking themselves "Who's available?" and "What's needed?" school members also have to ask "Who can learn?" and assess the extent to which the organization can support the development of new members and tolerate those that do not fit as well as others. Schools with a strong community among staff members and a shared understanding already in place, for example, are in a better position to accommodate new hires and help them develop in productive ways. Organizations with a smaller staff and those struggling to develop a shared understanding, however, are particularly vulnerable to the problems that come with new hires who are not already prepared to fit in.

Merging Selection and Socialization

Beyond screening initial candidates to see if they have the right general characteristics, schools can develop more substantial selection and hiring procedures. Even if schools cannot make the final decisions on hiring, this process eliminates some candidates who might be just as happy (or happier) somewhere else. This process also sends crucial messages to candidates about what the school values and what the work entails.

As at Peninsula, a school's hiring process may only involve school staff and other school members in the hiring process in informal ways. However, schools can also use the hiring process as a focus for considerable collaborative activity. At Horizons, in addition to the interview with Archer and, often, one or more parents, the members of the relevant teaching teams with open positions all conduct separate interviews with the candidates. While the interviews with the other teachers create opportunities for many staff members to gain a perspective on whether the candidate passes the litmus test for Horizons, they also serve as a means of enabling the candidate to go beyond the mission statement and learn about the school's philosophy directly from the teachers. Sarah Vance, who was relocating to the Bay Area with her husband, flew out from New York for a one-day visit to the school. She spoke with five other teachers and quickly got the sense that their approach would fit with her own:

> Their philosophy of teaching was consistent with what I felt: A
> strong sense of wanting to make sure that they started where students

are at, wanting to be demanding and high achieving, but recognizing that students can walk into your class in all kinds of ways and need to be handled from there. [The staff's] ethnic diversity; their diversity of opinion at the same time; there wasn't necessarily a party line. The only party line was their sense of purpose in working with kids.

In the process, Vance also got a clear sense of what working in a charter school environment entailed, and the staff got a glimpse of what working with Vance might be like.

At Emerson, staff developed a similar formal selection process that involved a number of members of the organization, but they went even further to establish an explicit interview protocol that instructed the interviewers to make sure to talk about the important practices of the school: challenge-based projects, interdisciplinary curricula, diversity, multiage classrooms, parent involvement, and the teacher-run administration. They also provided candidates with materials about the school and made sure to include an extensive meeting schedule that specified all the meetings that teachers were expected to participate in every week. Simply by highlighting the workload, level of collaboration, and number of required meetings, staff at Emerson discouraged many candidates who did not share their goals and philosophy from applying. Particularly in the early years when the school had to hire from within their district, Emerson staff spent almost as much time meeting with eligible local candidates to talk them out of applying as they did trying to recruit the right candidates. "We'd say, there's all of this work," Diane Kirsch reported. "This is what we do. We know that teaching is a hard job anywhere, but the expectations here are really over the top." At the same time, by making these aspects of the school clear to candidates that look like a good match, the recruitment and selection process begins to build the understanding and commitment that new teachers will need to enter smoothly into their work in the school.

Although these kinds of selection activities focus attention on finding the right personnel, the collaborative activities of explaining to candidates what the school values and what the work involves also provides existing staff with another opportunity to develop their understanding of one another's expectations and their views of the school's needs. While hiring decisions are not always easy, they also serve as a way for school members to interact with and get to know colleagues they might not work with on a regular basis, and they serve as the crucial first step in developing relationships with new staff. When the selection process is handled well, it can also reinforce members' investment in the organization and help them develop a sense of collective responsibility for the success of their colleagues and the organization as a whole.

Defining Roles and Responsibilities

As Jim Collins (2001) explains it, getting the right people "on the bus" (or into the organization) is only part of the task; getting the right people into the "right seats" is also crucial. Traditional job positions for teachers and school staff focus on school level (elementary, middle, or high school) and subject area and seem to leave little room for flexibility. Furthermore, districts usually determine formal job responsibilities and when these positions can be filled. However, whether a teacher teaches third or fourth grade in elementary school or English or mathematics in high school may not make as much of a difference as what roles and responsibilities they take on outside the classroom. In that sense, getting school staff into the "right seats" means figuring out what those key roles are and who can play them. What kinds of committees or task forces (if any) should there be? How should the school present itself to parents and the community? What kind of support for new teachers should the school offer? Each one of these activities presents opportunities to put staff to work in ways that can have a significant impact on the culture and effectiveness of the organization.

Criteria for hiring and a bottom line that reflects more general qualities and emphasizes versatility may put the school in a much better position for finding candidates who can play multiple roles and learn on the job. In turn, those individuals provide a school with an ability to adapt to changing conditions that organizations with employees locked in to particular positions cannot replicate. At Dewey, Charlene Moore paid particular attention to the roles that different staff members could play outside their own classrooms. As Warren Lovejoy reported, Moore often gave informal jobs to several veterans—Rob Rhodes, Georgeanne Kim, and himself. Rhodes, in many ways, acted as the assistant principal, although the district never created that position in their elementary schools. According to Lovejoy, Kim became "more a curriculum mentor in math, and I became the mentor for new people that came in." Moore also asked Lovejoy to investigate several topics of interest to the school and then make presentations on them for the staff as well as parents and others in the district. "I think she sees me as the vocal chords" of the school, Lovejoy explained.

Manzanilla and Emerson, with their emphasis on shared decision making also established a wide range of official and unofficial roles including membership on a number of committees (focusing on issues like budgeting, retreat planning, and professional development). Although leaders at these schools often made these assignments, taking on these kinds of responsibilities and dealing with problems proactively also became a part of the culture. As a consequence, individual staff members often stepped up and took on jobs or led initiatives if they saw a need rather than waiting for an assignment or worrying about whether or not it fit their formal job description.

Schools can also use funds and support from external partners to create positions for coordinators that do not have classroom responsibilities. School leaders and the individuals in these positions themselves can define and redefine these roles regularly in order to take on whatever work needs to be done. Elena Rivera at Manzanilla, for example, explained her job as one third coaching teachers, one third running an intervention program, and one third "kind of undefined" including anything having to do with assessment and all kinds of other things like "sitting on leadership bodies and planning professional development." Similarly, many of Barbara Silver's responsibilities as reform coordinator at Manzanilla got carved out of things that other people did not have time to handle but that still needed to get done: "There were all these things that weren't really anybody's job that were maxing out other people's time," she explained. "So they said, 'Let's ask Barbara to do it.'" The fact that she did not have a schedule of classes also meant that she could help engage other people in the work of the school, when it worked for them:

> One important thing is just being able to go run around and catch up with people and show things to people and having that time and flexibility built into my day where I can say, "I'm not the only one that should be thinking or looking at this. Who can I get and how can I make it work for them on their time?"

By distributing formal and informal responsibilities, school leaders can also help build the individual skills and organizational capacity that can ease leadership transitions. At Dewey, Moore even encouraged her unofficial assistant principal, Rob Rhodes, to enroll in a principal certification program. At Manzanilla, Melora Vasquez managed to divide up leadership responsibilities for the middle and elementary school by hiring Consuela Soto, a veteran staff member from the elementary school for an administrative position at the middle school. In practice, however, Vasquez and Soto worked it out informally so that Soto could take on some of Vasquez's administrative responsibilities at the established elementary school (the level where Soto had more experience), and Vasquez could focus her energies and her administrative experience on the middle school and the challenges of establishing a new school.

All of this work in getting the right people to do the most important tasks, however, depends on a shared understanding of the school's approach and goals and thoughtful orchestration on the part of school leaders. From Lovejoy's perspective, Moore's invitations and requests for himself, Rhodes, and

Kim to take on different roles reflected considerable planning: "Charlene's got my life planned for me," he laughed. "She actually told us that, she told all three of us–Rob, Georgeanne, and me–that she has our lives planned for us."

At the same time, that orchestration is far from easy. Roles and responsibilities get blurred, with the potential for some work to fall through the cracks. As Barbara Silver reported, her job was always "cloudy." "You can't just look in the book and say, 'Oh, okay. I know that that's coming up and that I'm going to have to do it.'" The effort, energy and stress that go into the work that lies beyond formal job descriptions also adds up and contributes to the challenges of retaining the staff the school depends on.

Finding Staff to Change a School's Approach

Although the interview and selection process can be used to weed out candidates who might bring different expectations or approaches to a school, that same process can also be used to turn a school in a new direction. While excessive turnover creates significant costs for organizations, no turnover at all can bring problems as well. Stagnation, in particular, can result if staff continue with "business as usual." As a result organizations with limited turnover may have trouble developing the new ideas and expertise that can enable the organization to adapt to changing conditions. Furthermore, professional development and mission-building initiatives may meet considerable resistance from veterans and may do little to dislodge entrenched positions. Under these conditions, increasing turnover rather than trying to improve retention may actually be a better strategy.

This resistance from veterans contributed to Julianne Fredericksen's decision to focus more attention on bringing in "new blood" than on establishing a common understanding. When she arrived at City, Fredericksen found some of the school's teachers were unable or unwilling to adapt their traditional instructional approach to the growing diversity of the school's student population; their refusal, in turn, was contributing to tensions with some parents and to general racial tensions at the school. As a consequence, while Moore saw class-size reduction and turnover as part of the problem at Dewey, at City, Fredericksen saw it as an opportunity to bring in new teachers who had explicit training and experience in working with diverse students. "When we took on a couple of new teachers with class-size reduction, that's really when we first started to change," she explained. Coupled with a buyout that the district offered to veteran teachers, class-size reducation enabled Fredericksen to hire a number of new teachers in close succession. She used that opportunity to develop a faculty that included teachers who were not only good teachers but teachers who "could work with all children in all types of families." As James Anderson, one of a few veterans who stayed described the situation, Fredericksen made sure that she didn't replace the veterans with teachers with a "traditional style. . . . She wanted the kids–and I say kids–that have come out of schools with the new train of thought."

In particular, Fredericksen looked for teachers who were certified to work with English Language Development (ELD) students and who were trained or had experience meeting the needs of diverse students. She also encouraged veteran teachers to get certified to work with ELD students so that the school would not have to have separate classes for ELD students and General Education students. Fredericksen explained:

> I wanted every teacher to get their certification for a couple of reasons. One, it allowed me the most flexibility at placing students. And two, then I didn't have to deal with the parents who felt that their child was in the class that was [designated] ELD, they were in a class that was inferior. . . . This teacher here who had only General Ed children, her test scores for sure were going to look better than this teacher's who had General Ed and English Language Development children.

In order to determine whether prospective teachers met their criteria, Fredericksen and her assistant principal, Jacqueline Edwards, carefully screened all the candidates to look for those that fit the new directions for the school. Like Archer at Horizons, Fredericksen and Edwards had a litmus test of their own:

> My assistant principal was African American, and we asked questions like, "How will you teach African American students that don't tend to respond to lectures? . . . And how will you work with their families?" And if we didn't like the answers to those questions at an initial interview, the teacher did not move on.

Those candidates that passed this initial review were then interviewed by a hiring committee composed of parents and teachers. The committee ranked the candidates and explained their rationale. In all but one case, the decision was unanimous, and, in every case, Fredericksen took the committee's recommendation. By screening candidates and sharing the hiring process with representatives of the staff and parents in this way, Fredericksen was able to bring in new faculty with a somewhat different approach than the veterans while still enabling those veterans and the wider community to feel some ownership in the process.

In the end, Anderson explained, the change was "incredible." "Maybe there's like 5 of us that have been there around at least 15 years. The rest, like 25, must be all new. I mean, all new. So, a big turnover. . . . It has really changed." Of course, once a school like City changes, then the same issues arise again. School leaders have to figure out who fits and how to get them to select the school and stay long enough to contribute significantly. But they also have to remember that a time may come where retention needs to give way to turnover once more; they have to try to find the right balance between stability and change in staffing and recognize that different times and different conditions call for different strategies.

SUMMING UP

All in all, the investment of time and energy in recruiting and hiring enables schools to influence the development of their applicant pools and increases the chances that suitable candidates will follow through with their applications and accept an offer. At the same time, whether schools use recruiting and the hiring process to sustain an approach or to change it, influencing the selection process and managing turnover are far from exact sciences. For one thing, less successful schools and schools experiencing more problems may have a harder time attracting the most qualified candidates. Furthermore, regardless of the efforts they make, those same schools may have trouble holding on to some of their best teachers as teachers gain more experience and become more attractive job candidates.

Even if recruitment and hiring efforts help select staff who are "pointed in the right direction," they cannot ensure that new staff actually understand what working at these schools will entail or that the experience will be a successful one for either party. At schools that recruit applicants through informal networks and formal partnerships and that make explicit efforts to screen candidates, many new hires still arrive with little more than a superficial understanding of the school's philosophy and approach. "Recruiting teachers has been the bane of our existence," Moore sighed when talking about her work at Dewey. Lovejoy estimated that even after Moore arrived and reestablished the "Dewey way" the faculty was still composed about "half and half" with those hired with some knowledge of the school's approach and those hired with little or no advance knowledge or experience with the school. Even when the selection process seems to reveal a match, things do not always work out. In one instance, a teacher "came across terrific in the interview," Marielle Henkel explained. "She knew how to talk the talk, but when it came down to it, she didn't know how to do it. . . . So it just didn't work. It wasn't a good fit." Ultimately, that teacher was encouraged to leave the school, and she did.

At Emerson, even with its extensive investment in recruitment and selection, some new hires still arrived at the school through serendipitous routes, and as Yolanda Smith explained, most "still don't really get it until they actually get in here." In fact, Diane Kirsch, who eventually became a lead teacher, actually came to the school when she "swapped" her full-time job at a middle school with a friend who was a half-time resource specialist at the school: "It was a fluke. I did not know about the school. I was actually singing in a band and wanted to teach part-time, and I knew the resource specialist at the school who was there and wanted a full-time job and we said we would switch jobs." For her part, Claire Marx, a 4th-year teacher and later lead teacher at Emerson, didn't know anything about the school other than the fact it was a K–8 school when she applied in 1997.

> I faxed my resume and they called me [and interviewed me], and it worked. . . . [But] on my first day of school here, I didn't know a whole lot.... I worked here 2 years before I felt like I really under-stood how it all fit together and what our vision was.

Although Fredericksen's efforts to hire new teachers benefited from City's good reputation, not all of the teachers that Fredericksen brought in were able to fulfill her expectations. After one month on the job, one teacher, who had been enthusiastic about the approach to instruction that Fredericksen de-scribed to her, came to Fredericksen and said, "I can't do it. . . . I know I said I would do this but I just can't do the things that you had expected." Even at Peninsula, where turnover has been minimal, principal David Summers acknowledged that not everyone "bought into" the school's approach.

As a result, although many new teachers fit well into their new contexts, turnover and new hirings still contribute to the tensions, conflicts, and oc-casional "mission drift" within schools and other organizations. When these problems arise, school leaders and staff have to turn their time and atten-tion to professional development, building shared understandings among the staff, and, in some cases, removing or "counseling out" those who really do not seem to fit.

Chapter 5

Creating a Productive
Work Environment

Once staff members are hired, they need to gain a better understanding of the organization's goals and expectations. They need to learn their roles and how to work with their peers, and they need to continue to develop the skills and knowledge that will help them carry out their work in that context. In other words, they need to be socialized; they need to be organized; and they need to develop their professional expertise.

Traditionally, schools try to accomplish the goals of socialization and organization in a few orientation activities at the beginning of the year and then in weekly or monthly staff meetings that often focus on administrative issues. Similarly, professional development is often relegated to a few staff development days that are sprinkled throughout the year (and often controlled by the district). This traditional model treats professional development as an add-on—outside of a teacher's normal classroom responsibilities—in which teachers can pick up a few ideas or strategies or enhance their content knowledge in a particular area. Correspondingly, traditional professional development often follows a transmission model of learning in which teachers participate in one-shot workshops and listen to outside experts cover a different topic in each session.

In recent years, however, many reform efforts have worked explicitly to challenge this traditional model and to expand views of professional development and of what it takes to create a productive work environment in schools. Several major trends over the past 50 years have fueled this attention to professional and organizational development. In education in particular, changes in the student population and the general aging of the teacher workforce have contributed to concerns that the backgrounds and skills of teachers no longer match the needs of many students. Changes in the nature of many jobs and the development of new technologies also contributed to calls for higher standards in the K–12 system and reinforced concerns that current teachers and traditional school practices may not be sufficient to enable all students to meet those standards.

At the same time, concerns about the productivity and efficiency of American businesses in general during the last half of the twentieth century

91

Features of Effective Professional Development

Research and practice over the past 20 years in education has supported the development of a new consensus about professional development (Corcoran, 2007; Desimone, Porter, Garet, Yoon, & Birman 2002; Elmore, 2002). That consensus suggests a need to shift from involving individual teachers in a roster of short-term activities that cover a wide range of topics to engaging groups of teachers in a series of related activities that are more closely connected to teachers' day-to-day classroom responsibilities and are focused on the improvement of student learning in a specific content area.

Findings from a national study of 93% of public school districts in the United States carried out by Laura Desimone, Andrew Porter, and their colleagues (Desimone et al., 2002), for example, found 6 different features of professional development that were related to reported increases in teachers' knowledge and skills and teaching practice:

- Reform-oriented activities, such as a study group, mentorship, network, or research group rather than traditional workshops, courses, or conferences
- Activities that involved more hours and took place over a longer span of time, rather than shorter activities
- Activities that emphasized collective participation of teachers from the same school, rather than individuals from many schools
- Activities that involved active learning
- Activities that were coherent and connected to school goals, aligned with state standards, and linked to other professional development opportunities
- Activitities that focused on relevant content

Follow-up studies suggest that "change would occur if teachers received consistent, high-quality professional development" (Desimone et al., 2002, p. 105), but that most teachers do not receive professional development of sufficient quality. In the absence of increased resources, Desimone and her colleagues suggest that in-depth, focused professional development with a small number of teachers may be more effective than more superficial efforts to address the needs of all teachers.

created a flurry of interest in new management approaches, many of which focused attention on the social and cultural environments in which work is carried out. In addition, recent research and thinking on adult learning led to a transformation in views of what it takes for workers in many different fields to learn how to do their jobs well. In particular, growing recognition of the ways in which workers learn on the job and in social interaction with peers and other people has increased interest in job-embedded professional development—activities woven into the daily schedule that provide opportunities for workers to share their ideas and expertise with one another. These efforts recognize and build on the expertise that exists in the workforce by creating groups, mentorships, and other arrangements in which more experienced or expert colleagues can provide modeling, guidance, and feedback for others.

These work arrangements emphasize that the skills and knowledge needed to carry out complex tasks cannot be contained in the head of one individual. Instead, completion of these tasks depends on many different people, playing many different roles and bringing different kinds of expertise. For example, no single individual has the knowledge needed to construct and launch a satellite for space exploration; but engineers, scientists, and others can "put their heads together" to build on one another's skills and knowledge and reach a goal that none could accomplish on their own. This view of collective expertise highlights the fact that in schools, individual teachers rely on a host of other people and resources to do their jobs well. They may need advice and support from other teachers and administrators who have more experience with a particular content area, aspect of the curriculum, or assessment; they may benefit (or suffer from) administrators' abilities to find or design appropriate professional development experiences; and they may require the assistance of school counselors, special educators, or others who can help them meet the needs of each student.

This emphasis on the development of collective expertise also contributed to the emergence of learning communities as a key focus for organizational change. In this view, rather than trying to transform beliefs and practices individual by individual, establishing learning communities creates a culture that encourages everyone and the organization as a whole to reflect on their work and improve their performance. Researchers and consultants in education and a number of other fields describe learning communities with different terms (including communities of practice, professional communities, and professional learning communities) and in different ways. In general, *learning communities* refer to groups of people who work together to develop their skills and understanding in a particular area. Beyond that simple definition, being part of a community means that people feel connected to one another and to a larger group: Community grows out of common values, common purposes, and common experiences. Community thrives when those commonalities give rise to shared commitments that encourage individuals to identify with the group as a whole. Being part of a community gives individuals a meaningful role in a larger enterprise and can help individuals feel a sense of efficacy and impact on the world that goes far beyond their individual activity. In the process, membership in a community provides emotional and personal support that motivates people to do their work when they can and sustains them when it seems like they cannot.

Many efforts to foster learning communities in schools emphasize the development of a sense of shared purpose and a commitment to collective work, not just the delivery of information or ideas to teachers to put into practice (Louis & Kruse, 1995; Stoll & Louis, 2007). In addition, while they may involve some workshops and instruction from outside experts, approaches to learning communities often emphasize the creation of opportunities for teachers to share their own ideas and expertise with one another and to work alongside coaches, mentors, or others who provide modeling, guidance, and feedback.

At the same time, there is no simple equation between the strength of a community and the extent of a school's investment in professional development and its performance. Nor does having a learning community necessarily mean that everyone will find the work environment more desirable. Some strong communities may be resistant to change and may w ork to block improvement efforts; and strong communities that develop in different departments or units within an organization may come into conflict, constrain the sharing of knowledge, and undermine the collective performance of the organization. Furthermore, there may be some individuals–including some highly effective, experienced or innovative members of an organization–who would prefer to blaze their own trail or work on their own rather than participate in extensive group activities.

As a consequence, a law of diminishing returns comes into play when building community and investing in collective professional development activities. Establishing some level of community and shared practice provides numerous benefits. However, at some point, investing more time and energy in creating closer and more collaborative work may not increase those benefits substantially. As a consequence, schools have to find the right balance between collective and individual activities and formal and informal learning opportunities. Schools need to establish enough of a sense of community to organize work effectively and to share expertise productively, but they also have to provide enough flexibility in their approach to professional development to meet the diverse needs of subunits and individual staff members. The organization needs to find that balance without spending so much time on coordination, community building, and collective professional development that staff members feel constrained and overwhelmed and the organization itself lacks the time, energy, and resources it needs to invest in other activities.

WHAT BRINGS COMMUNITIES TOGETHER?

Within an organization, being part of a community means more than working together. It even means more than developing a shared understanding

---

Communities, Communities of Practice, and Professional Learning Communities

A *community* is "a unified body of individuals," "a group of people with a common characteristic or interest living together within a larger society," "a body of persons or nations having a common history or common social, economic, and political interests," or "a body of persons of common and especially professional interests scattered through a larger society" (*Merriam-Webster Online Dictionary*, 2007).

Jean Lave and Etienne Wenger (1991) used the term *communities of practice* to describe groups of people who interact regularly, either informally or formally, to share information, experiences, ideas, and expertise in an area of common concern (practice). A community of practice can describe a group of weavers in a preindustrial society; groups of engineers within a company who are working on similar problems; groups of writers and producers who meet over lunch to share ideas and talk about their work; or a regular online meeting of superintendents who share problems and give one another advice.

In education, Milbrey McLaughlin and Joan Talbert (2001) define a *professional learning community* as a group of workers who share beliefs and responsibilities. In their groundbreaking study of teaching in high schools in California and Michigan they described both "weak" communities of teachers in which work is private and highly variable, and "strong" communities who share common work patterns, expectations and beliefs that evolve and are sustained over time. They found that strong communities may form around different expectations and practices (some reinforcing traditional approaches to teaching; some reinforcing more progressive approaches) and suggested that those communities could have either a positive or negative impact on students and student learning. They also found that in the high schools they studied, different kinds of communities could exist side by side and often grew out of the teacher's department affiliations and disciplinary associations.

---

of the organization's goals and approach. Being part of a community means that members trust one another: They share the belief that the members of the organization can carry out their responsibilities and live up to common expectations. Mutual trust arises when individuals look beyond their own self-interest (or that of the subgroups to which they belong) and care about other members of the community and the community as a whole; have the competence they need to fulfill their roles and meet their obligations within the organization; understand and respect one another's work, roles, and perspectives; and have the integrity to behave in ways that are consistent with the values and purposes of the organization. When these conditions are met, responsibilities can be divided up effectively, with staff able to work together efficiently or work independently when the situation calls for it.

Social Capital and Trust

In *Bowling Alone* (2000) Robert Putnam argues that societies in general and democratic organizations in particular rely on social capital and trust between members. According to Putnam, "social capital refers to connections among individuals—social networks and the norms of reciprocity and trustworthiness that arise from them" (p. 2). These connections provide individuals and groups with access to information, expertise, and support that in turn can increase efficiency, create opportunities for innovation, and foster a sense of well-being.

Building on this idea, Tony Bryk and Barbara Schneider (2002) suggest that the social connections and trust that develop between members of a school community act as crucial resources that enable and motivate them to work together effectively. According to Bryk and Schneider, schools can build the trust that helps to bring communities together by

- Fostering mutual understanding and *respect* for all the different roles, responsibilities, and perspectives in an organization
- Developing the *competence* that enables individuals to rely on one another
- Fostering the personal regard, *care,* and concern individuals have for one another
- Supporting *integrity,* facilitating behavior and actions that are consistent with the stated values and goals of the school

---

The need to develop this kind of mutual trust and to sustain learning communities over time creates a new set of demands for school leaders. Instead of focusing on planning a few orientation and professional development activities, school leaders need to think about how they can support productive interactions among individuals and groups on a daily basis. Leaders can foster these interactions in formal meetings, structured group activities, and explicit collaborations. For example, formal meetings and activities designed to engage school members together in organizational decision making, in studying and learning together, and in observing and assessing one another's work all provide ways for schools to establish trust and build social connections among staff. Beyond formal meetings, however, the careful orchestration of time, space, and staffing can also give staff numerous opportunities to interact productively in more informal and spontaneous ways.

Sharing Responsibility

Providing roles in school governance and decision making for many people creates a number of opportunities for members of the school community

Key Elements in Shared Decision Making

Shared decision making can take many different forms, with different purposes and different members of the school community involved. Whatever the form, however, the research suggests that overall the results of shared decision-making arrangements in schools have been ambiguous with no clear, consistent positive or negative affects on students (Leithwood & Menzies, 1998, and Murphy & Beck, 1995).

In one attempt to get past the ambiguity and understand how shared decision making might work, Patricia Wohlstetter and her colleagues (Wohlstetter, Smyer, & Mohrman, 1994) looked at the extent to which Edward Lawler's (1986) framework for "high-involvement management" might apply to schools. Lawler's framework suggests that employees need to have

- Power to make decisions and influence organizational practice in key areas like budgeting, personnel, and work processes
- Knowledge that enables employees to contribute to organizational performance (including the technical knowledge to do their jobs well; the business knowledge for managing the organization; and the interpersonal skills to work as members of a team)
- Information about the performance of the organization (including information on how the performance of the organization compares to others)
- Rewards for high performance (including a compensation structure aligned to the skills, abilities, and behaviors required for high performance and performance-based pay allocated on a group or team basis)

Wohlstetter and her colleagues concentrated their study in schools that had been engaged with shared or site-based decision making for some time and compared those that were successful in making changes in curriculum and instruction and those that were far less successful in making changes. While the more and less successful schools did not differ substantially in compensation structure and the kinds of rewards they offered, the study confirmed the value of knowledge, information, and power: The more successful schools invested more heavily in team-building skills and staff development; they created more opportunities for sharing information across classrooms and grade levels; and they had more mechanisms for teachers to participate in governance. In the struggling schools, however, teachers remained isolated, and they had few, if any, mechanisms for interacting and sharing information around instruction in particular.

to develop the trust, care, and respect they need to work together. These potential benefits, however, can quickly erode if individuals end up feeling tired and frustrated from spending too much time in meetings debating procedures and meeting processes rather than discussing key issues of teaching and learning (Smylie, Lazarus, & Brownlee-Conyers, 1996).

Schools that embrace democratic principles, like Emerson and Manzanilla for example, reflect the idea that many members of the school community have the expertise and deserve the authority to make decisions. Correspondingly, these schools created a series of groups and meetings to engage many different stakeholders in the management process. As often as staff members cited those meetings and the opportunities for shared responsibility as key elements of their schools' approach, however, staff members also struggled with the time and energy these commitments took and regularly looked for ways to simplify the process. At Manzanilla, in particular, staff constantly wrestled with a shifting array of meetings that included

- A monthly school site council meeting in which parents, administrators, and teachers focused on major issues like the review of the site plan and budget
- A biweekly meeting of the management team (composed of representatives of all instructional teams, staff, and parents), who focused on day-to-day operations and planning
- A regular weekly meeting of each instructional team to plan instruction and provide information and feedback to their management team representatives
- A weekly meeting of a literacy leadership team, and a math leadership team (composed of their reform coordinator, some content specialists, and representative faculty), who take responsibility for overseeing curriculum development and professional development in these areas

Ultimately, the meeting structure grew so complicated that the school convened another weekly meeting—a meeting of the A-Team (an administrative team composed of the principal, the lead teachers, the reform coordinator, and other coaches)—to try to facilitate communication and coordinate the work of the other committees.

One alternative to what could be called full-involvement models like Manzanilla's is to engage staff on committees or task forces when there are particularly pressing issues or major organizational changes under consideration; or staff members can be enlisted in helping oversee and monitor a few key aspects of the organization's operation (like hiring, curriculum planning, and/or professional development). Horizons, for example, had a traditional administrative structure (which grew to include an executive director, a principal, and several deans), and administrators took primary responsibility for decision making. However, administrators also assigned all faculty to one of five different "study teams" designed to address key issues and problems (like the professional development needs of the school, the school's definition of student success, the school schedule, and the nature of the senior-year experience).

Just like democratically run schools, however, schools with more traditional management structures can also overwhelm their members with committee responsibilities and other formal and informal roles in guiding the school. Therefore, from the perspective of building community, the precise nature of the management structures a school adopts matters far less than the extent to which the work of making decisions fosters the common experiences and interactions that help to build commitment, trust, and collective expertise.

Shelly Henry, a humanities teacher at Horizons, gave a teacher's viewpoint:

> One of the things that's really important here is understanding you have this authority in the way you're working with the class. And because you teach those students, you need to be part of helping to make other kinds of decisions that are important in the school, like scheduling, like what should happen with the projects, like how professional development should occur in the school, like how to support students in a better way, like how to best integrate the learning center into the classrooms.

From Henry's perspective that means that "institutional decisions are also teacher decisions and not just administrative decisions."

Taking on these kinds of larger responsibilities can encourage individuals to look beyond their own responsibilities and consider the needs of the whole organization. In addition, participating in some decision making activities can build coherence in the thoughts and actions of individuals throughout the organization. In particular, activities like the study teams at Horizons can give staff an opportunity to participate in what many businesses refer to as "cross-functional teams" and to see and hear from individuals they don't interact with on a more regular basis.

Developing short-term task forces and delegating key tasks to representative groups can also serve as productive ways to build coherence and foster a sense of the bigger picture. Every year at Manzanilla, for example, a different democratically elected set of representatives of the schools' stakeholder groups developed the annual budget. In turn, that committee sent out a survey asking the staff for their input on the key needs and priorities, and presented a draft budget for the staff to discuss before coming to consensus. Involvement in this kind of major organizational decision helped school members understand the trade-offs that had to be made and increased the chances that more staff would feel a commitment to and a responsibility for those decisions. Melora Vasquez, the principal, described the collective thinking that went into one decision to spend enough money to hire a credentialed teacher to serve as school librarian:

> In the past we had had an instructional assistant in that position that cost us less than half of what a credentialed teacher cost. But because that person was not credentialed, it was not a prep for teachers and it wasn't learning for kids; it was just checking out books, just managing to make sure the books got put in the right place. So we decided that by adding to the money that we used to provide somebody to be in the library, we could benefit by having a credentialed teacher or a credentialed person in there. Teachers could have an additional 50-minute prep, and students would learn library skills. That was a decision that was made based on looking at what the conditions were that we needed to put in place in order to do the work that we had identified.

Involving staff in key decisions can also work particularly well when it helps to break down traditional divisions between governance and instruction. Efforts by small groups to study data or develop new curriculum in planning and professional development meetings can lead to reflections on goals and purposes at whole staff retreats. Grade-level meetings designed to plan curricula can lead to the reexamination of professional development needs.

Emerson sought to build these connections between governance and instruction by establishing weekly developmental team meetings that went far beyond the usual curriculum planning and coordination of instruction that may (or may not) take place when teachers from the same grade level share a planning period. These developmental team meetings served as a crucial linchpin that connected the decisions made by the full staff at Emerson with the work done in individual classrooms. "We try to make sure that those things that we're thinking about at the whole-staff level get actually put into practice and evaluated," explained Claire Marx, a fourth-grade teacher and subsequently lead teacher. For these meetings, Emerson staff specified five different issues they addressed on a rotating basis. First, these issues included curriculum planning and development where "we sit down and we say, 'Okay, we want to do group work in math,'" Marx explained. "'These are the standards we need to cover this year. How are we going to organize that? What's that going to look like?'" Second, Emerson staff used the meetings to share results of a schoolwide inquiry they had undertaken to look at what is and is not working with low-achieving students. Third, they looked at student work: "We do a student work protocol in the developmental meeting to get a feeling of . . . or a sense of what are you trying? What do you notice about . . . what this child is learning from the way you're teaching?" Fourth, staff used the time to conduct "safety net" meetings in which they discussed any students about whom they are particularly concerned. Fifth, they focused on standards and standardization: "Because we do projects and we switch kids four times throughout the year," said Marx, "we need to have some things that are standardized between our classrooms to make sure that there's some continuity of experience."

Of course, even if schools develop complex meeting structures like Emerson's, staff members can still choose not to pay attention. Furthermore, school members can second-guess and critique decisions whether they are made by an autocratic leader, an elected committee, or the entire staff. As a consequence, in the end it all comes back to trust. School members need to have the trust that whatever decision-making processes they have in place will work without too much wasted time and effort, and they need to trust that school leaders will not subvert the process. But that trust has to go both ways. Leaders need to provide enough guidance to keep committees and decision-making processes running smoothly, but they also have to have the trust and patience to let the process work.

Taking Control of Professional Development

Professional development activities serve as another crucial opportunity for staff members to learn about one another's work, contribute to one another's effectiveness, and develop a sense of trust and shared responsibility. When schools rely on the district or other support organizations to provide those professional development activities, they can get access to expertise that may not exist inside the school, and they can make valuable connections to people in other schools and districts. However, outside professional development also reflects the needs and concerns of many other groups and agendas, and it does not always allow or encourage staff members to work together or share their expertise.

While schools that bring professional development in-house may lose some connections to other schools, they can increase the chances of addressing what they perceive as their most pressing needs, and they also can design their own collaborative, focused, and sustained approaches. Manzanilla, for example, used their own professional development funds and assistance from partnerships with a number of support providers to make whole-staff retreats (usually held at the beginning of the year, but sometimes the middle or end as well) a consistent part of their schedule. These retreats gave members regular opportunities to reflect on the school's progress, to address critical organizational issues as they arose, and to pursue their work on literacy and mathematics in more depth than they could do during the regular week. The fact that many staff members also participated in planning for these activities and deciding what issues to discuss increased the connection between these activities and the day-to-day work of the organization and helped the staff to feel that they had a stake in and a responsibility for making good use of this time together.

Explicit efforts to bring members back together to share what they have learned can also turn individual professional development experiences into a sustained collective enterprise. Emerson, for example, often sent groups as large as half the staff to summer institutes and professional development activities related to the school's goals and plans for the upcoming year. In turn, staff participating in those activities shared what they learned and helped lead follow-up activities during retreats, orientation activities, and professional development activities throughout the following school year. Although staff at Dewey did not regularly participate in summer activities as a staff, Moore often suggested conferences and courses in which interested faculty might participate, helped arrange the necessary funding, and then created opportunities for those individuals to share what they had learned during the school's orientation activities and regular professional development days.

How much time staff members need to spend in collective professional development depends in part on where the organization is in its development. Relatively new organizations, struggling organizations, and organizations requiring tight coordination may need collective opportunities to bring many staff members together. Those operating relatively smoothly can encourage and take advantage of the work of individual members. At Horizons, initially, whole-staff retreats took place over the summer, but the structure and purposes of these summer activities evolved as the school, and the staff grew. Where the staff initially spent a significant amount of time together getting to know one another and developing their expertise on learning differences (at times, spending as many as 4 weeks working together), retreats gradually became more individualized. Subsequently, new staff went to one set of professional development offerings, and veterans went to others. While this limited the time staff could spend together, it also allowed members of the organization to learn about many different issues at once and enhance their collective expertise.

Similarly, Dewey strived to find a balance in their professional development activities between the collective needs of the whole school and the specific needs of individuals, particularly their new teachers. From Moore's perspective, few teacher preparation programs provided training in a developmental approach to education. Therefore, the school took it upon itself to provide an orientation for the new staff, or what she called "our teach-in; our own training." One year, for example, the first day of the retreat that began the school year focused on what Moore described as "who we are, the core values," and it included a demonstration lesson from one of the veteran Dewey teachers that showed how she was putting those values into practice in a social studies unit on Egypt. The second day the staff discussed the practical implications of the book *Emotional Intelligence* (Goleman, 1995), which many of the staff had read together the year before. "For many of our older teachers it reinforced what they already did. For the new ones, it gave them ideas," Moore explained.

Developing an Inquiry Orientation

Developing an inquiry orientation throughout the school provides another way to connect activities over time and can help to bind individuals together in common pursuits. This inquiry orientation also helps to launch formal and informal investigations that both serve as a means of professional development and help inform decision making. They also serve as another invitation for staff to work together and share their perspectives and expertise. In addition, the inquiry orientation places all staff members—new and veteran—in the position of learners who then go on to develop expertise that they can share with others.

"Maybe the biggest things that I see schoolwide going on around all these goals that we set," Kendra Hopkins, a Manzanilla teacher in the Sheltered English Program, explained, "are the conversations that teachers have to question themselves or question the school." As she put it, "it's not just a 'what can I do' question, it's a 'why' question. It's a deep thinking question that isn't always answered, but it's investigated." These questions provide a rationale for staff to pursue professional development activities and encourage them to constantly reflect on whether or not those activities are worthwhile. Informally, staff at schools like Dewey, Horizons, Manzanilla, and Emerson can demonstrate this inquiry orientation in their constant questioning of the utility and effectiveness of their work and constant efforts to look for new information and share ideas. However, schools can also formalize this inquiry orientation in collaborative inquiry projects that serve as the backbone of many of their professional development meetings.

Of course, simply participating in inquiry projects does not guarantee any collective benefits. Schools have to take into account both the desire of individuals to investigate their own personal and professional questions and the need for some organizational focus, and then the school has to establish ways for those inquiries to feed back into collective work. At Emerson, in addition to some individual and small-group inquiry projects, all staff participated in a schoolwide effort to explore the achievement gap between the school's African American and Hispanic students and their White and Asian peers. That work included collective examinations of the data from the district and school's assessments as well as pilot experiments in which individual teachers tried out different approaches for dealing with these issues and then reported back to their colleagues.

At Manzanilla, although many of the teachers' inquiry projects grew out of issues they encountered in their own classrooms, their investigations were also informed by discussions with colleagues in planning meetings and by concerns raised in management meetings or retreats. Further strengthening the collective aspects of these inquiries, the teachers then discussed their progress in a monthly meeting with peers with similar interests and reported out and discussed the implications of their inquiries in meetings with the whole staff that took place once or twice a year. In turn, teachers often ended up trying new instructional approaches or techniques as a result of their inquiries, and in a number of cases these investigations led directly to major discussions in the management team and changes that the whole school decided to adopt.

"I was so tired of the writing samples that they [the district] gave us," reported Lonnie Dean, a fourth- and fifth-grade bilingual teacher at Manzanilla:

> There were these little pictures and the kids had to find really interesting stories to tell about a little picture that really had no meaning to them. And then we had this really horrible rubric that we kept using year after year, and every year people would complain about it: "Oh, this rubric is horrible, it doesn't tell me about what my kids really can do."

Therefore, Dean decided to address the issue that had troubled many of the members of the staff for sometime—their writing assessments:

> What do I really want? I really want to fix kids' writing. And how am I going to do that? I really need a decent rubric and I need to really be explicit. I want the rubric to show me exactly how I'm going to get them to that next step.

In response, she decided to pilot the use of another instrument: ALAS, the Authentic Literacy Assessment System:

> I looked at how ALAS is done, and I came up with three prompts per grade level based on books that are more like personal narra-

tives, because I thought the kids might write more about something they're more familiar with, like their lives. And then I piloted it with a couple teachers and brought it in a presentation and people seemed really excited about it. And then at the retreat, just a couple weeks ago, we voted to do it schoolwide.

As a result, in addition to building community by engaging staff members in collaborative work together and building expertise by involving some staff in the use of a new instrument and rubrics, the inquiry project also helped to build common understanding among the whole staff.

Managing the Informal Learning Environment

In addition to the establishment of a wide variety of meeting structures and group activities, faculty can also take advantage of opportunities outside of meetings to see and hear what their colleagues are doing, to develop trusting relationships, and to learn from one another. As Lonnie Dean commented, she learned a lot about Manzanilla's beliefs and goals just from seeing, observing, and talking with other teachers. Similarly, at Dewey, learning from one another does not have to take place in a formal activity. "You might go in the staff room," reported Marielle Henkel, "and have conversations with people about activities you have done with kids or your philosophy and how you're working it out in your own classroom." These conversations provided a chance for staff members to "debrief events or people or situations, and constructively, collaboratively give some ideas on how we might go about solving them," explained Warren Lovejoy. In many cases, these conversations started over lunch and turned into regular lunchtime meeting groups; in turn, these conversations spawned new initiatives for the school. "There was a lunch group that existed for about 2 years," Lovejoy continued, "of teachers who were just getting together–Marielle, myself, a few other teachers. I don't know if there was really a charge. I think maybe there started out to be one. I think it was like, 'anybody want to get together and talk about math?'" Ultimately, the group tackled issues like how to handle place value across the curriculum and brought their ideas to the rest of the staff during staff meetings.

Of course, spontaneous meetings like these may be rare in many schools. For the most part, teachers are more likely to spend their time in their own classrooms than they are in interacting with one another (Lortie, 1977; Little, 1990). In order to combat the kind of isolation characteristic of teachers' work, school leaders can create job arrangements that encourage informal interactions and, in the process, support teachers' development and foster improvements in the collective activities of the school.

These arrangements reflect a tremendous amount of work and planning behind the scenes to put people in positions and in physical locations where they can help one another. In particular, staffing and scheduling decisions about who works with whom and when individuals and groups have unrestricted time shapes informal interactions. Spreading veterans throughout a school can provide different groups with the organizational knowledge and expertise needed for consistent performance; or pairing individuals with diverse expertise or clustering experienced and creative staff members may establish an atmosphere of experimentation and innovation. It's no accident, for example, that Henkel was able to learn a tremendous amount from Georgeanne Kim, another fourth-grade teacher at Dewey. Moore placed Henkel in a classroom next to Kim's when Henkel returned to the school as a full-time teacher precisely so that the two of them could have a chance to work together on a regular basis. "We have a door that connects our classrooms," Henkel explained, "and that door was open a lot the first year. And I really feel that Georgeanne went out of her way to make things really work for me."

Creating common periods when members of different groups can interact also helps break down group boundaries and facilitate the sharing of information and ideas throughout an organization. In fact, Horizons created a schedule that allowed some teachers as many as three common planning periods a week. Those periods enabled Shelly Henry to partner with another humanities teacher and plan the curriculum together. As she put it, the "small bonds" that developed in these meetings created "big bonds in terms of developing and understanding people's work and being able to work well with them." Similarly, the lunchtime conversations at Dewey took place because Moore built common lunch periods into the schedule and because Dewey had a relatively attractive lunch room where staff could meet or simply hang out on their own.

Creating opportunities for staff to observe one another's practice—what one could call creating "windows into practice"—provides another avenue for staff to learn what their colleagues are doing and to see who does—and does not—have what it takes to fulfill their organizational responsibilities. Seeing how their own work compares to that of others can motivate teachers to improve their practice and help them recognize their own expertise.

Like many of the interactions at Dewey, "the sharings," as fourth/fifth-grade teacher Georganne Kim referred to them, took place largely on an informal basis when faculty invited their colleagues and often other students to see the results of particular projects: "Like we finished our electricity unit," Kim explained, "and the kids put together all their inventions, and we invited our buddies, the four/five classes, to come and see what we had done." Although informal, Moore supported these kinds of sharings through her classroom visits: When she saw projects going particularly well, she encouraged teachers to invite their colleagues to visit and made sure to post "visiting hours" on a central board for all to see.

At Emerson, although the intense meeting schedule and a lack of a common lunch period made it difficult for many of the teachers to get together informally, the teachers got the chance to observe the results of one another's work all the time. First, because they shared students during the projects, they could see the progress that students made with different teachers. Second, during their meetings and retreats they spent time as a whole staff looking at student work throughout the school. Third, faculty at Emerson created a formal structure—a semiannual open house for the community—in which students presented the results of their projects. Through the open house (and the free flow of people from one room to another), the school made student learning visible for everyone. As Yolanda Smith, a veteran fourth-grade teacher, explained,

> You go to open house and you see all this fantastic stuff and you ask the child, "show me around your room and tell me what you've learned." And one class can tell you all kinds of things with really good details, and the child is clearly in charge of their learning and clearly knows what they know. If somebody else is hemming and hawing. . . and they show you some stuff with a big "A" or "Excellent" on the paper and you're saying "excellent according to who," then we know we have to line up our standards a little bit more.

Providing Support for New Staff

Fostering mentoring relationships between new and veteran faculty serves as another means of socializing new members and creating connections among staff that might not otherwise develop. Although many of the schools took advantage of formal mentoring and support programs for new teachers, such as California's Beginning Teacher Support Program (California Department of Education, 2008b), a lot of work with new teachers at Dewey and Emerson went on informally as well. At Dewey, in earlier years, veterans like Warren Lovejoy occasionally had formal paid responsibilities for working with new teachers, but more recently he and colleagues like Georgeanne Kim simply found times when they could "check in" with new teachers. In particular, for Lovejoy, the common lunch periods allowed him to touch base with new teachers who often wanted to know, "Does this happen at this school? Is this normal? Is this all right?" Similarly, the "open doors" at Dewey, made it easy for new and veteran teachers to mix.

In turn, in order to know who needs help and who may have ideas and expertise to share, Moore regularly checked in with the veteran teachers she paired up with newcomers. Georgeanne Kim explained that in the weekly meetings between Moore and the "old guard," they often discussed what was going on in the school, which units or projects were going really well, and who might need some assistance. In addition, Moore constantly slipped in and out of classrooms looking for people—new or veteran—who might need some help and seeking examples of the ideas that could be shared at staff meetings or retreats:

> I just drop in and the teachers are used to it. I just go in and I sit
> at the back of the class 5 or 10 minutes. Sometimes they know I'm
> there; sometimes they don't, and I leave. And I do that all the time.
> That's how I know what the best practices are.

Beyond the development of specific mentoring relationships, many of the other formal and informal occasions that bring teachers together can also enable veteran teachers to see what new teachers are doing and vice versa. At Emerson, Yolanda Smith pointed out that their professional development activities, such as those designed to improve and assess student writing are designed for everyone, but with an eye toward the needs of new teachers:

> The new teachers have never done it before, so they need a little
> bit more, and we try to pace it along. So we set up practices and we
> share what we're going to do to prepare our students and make sure
> they have all these different aspects in their writing and we share the
> writing rubrics that the district has as well as the ones that we have,
> and we help develop lessons to meet these things so the kids are pre-
> pared.

For Claire Marx, when she was in her 2nd year at Emerson, the effort to look at the theory and research behind effective class meetings and the opportunity to draw on the experiences of veteran teachers who had been doing class meetings for some time was particularly powerful:

> I didn't do class meetings before I came here. And my 2nd year
> here, we decided everybody in the building should be doing class
> meetings, because we believe that class meetings are a vehicle for
> creating classroom community and giving students voice in how
> the classroom runs. And the combination of literature that was put
> out there by the professional development team for us to read, and
> then conversation, structured conversation around the literature that

we talked about . . . and what it would look like, whether it would be successful, and hearing examples from other teachers, and then try[ing] it for a month and then coming back as a staff and talking about it, reflecting on it, and thinking about how we learned from it, what we learned from it. That's the kind of pattern or sequence of professional development that really . . . it solidified class meetings as part of my classroom practice.

WHAT UNDERMINES COMMUNITY AND COLLECTIVE WORK?

Whether a school invests time and effort in formal structures for sharing authority and building collective expertise or relies on informal networks and the power of peers, the connections, commitment, and sense of community people feel constantly evolve. A sense of community comes and goes as members arrive and leave, relationships among people grow and dissolve, and feelings of commitment wax and wane. However, these shifts are not entirely unpredictable or uncontrollable. Changes in a number of factors can work to bring people together or pull groups apart, including

- Changes in the "infrastructure" people rely on to conduct their work and carry out their personal lives—the tools, technologies, and resources available
- Changes in what people think—their ideas, beliefs, and tastes—often inspired by changes in the tools and technologies they have available
- Changes in the membership of groups

In addition to changes in these factors, the development of a sense of community reflects the size and complexity of the organization. Although advocates of small schools often focus on the benefits of low teacher-student ratios and close relationships between teachers and students, the small numbers of staff members also means that there are fewer divisions among the staff and fewer obstacles to getting the whole staff to meet and work together. Larger organizations and organizations in which different people or groups are responsible for very different kinds of work and responsibilities are more likely to have divisions or departments that can make it easier to get to know some peers and harder to meet others. At the same time, larger organizations may also be able to bring together individuals with a wider range of expertise and perspectives.

Regardless of the size of an organization and the divisions imposed by management, a sense of community may also grow spontaneously out of shared backgrounds, values, or common interests. While shared experiences can help the members of both "imposed" and spontaneous groups develop common bonds, these common bonds may begin to distinguish them from other groups within the organization and contribute to divisions that can limit the exchange of information, the development of collective expertise, and the maintenance of an overall sense of community. These divisions may be exacerbated if groups from different generations or different divisions develop different perspectives around critical issues of teaching, learning, assessment, and school organization. Those divisions may become particularly problematic if groups become embroiled in the issues of race, class, gender, and culture that simmer throughout schools and society in general.

Predictably Divisive Issues

Schools regularly experience differences of opinion over key educational issues. At Emerson, for example, projects remained a central feature of instruction since they were introduced in the 1990s, but debates regularly focused on how best to carry out the projects and how much time to focus on them. Increasing demands on test scores and the school's decision to concentrate on reducing the achievement gap even led some teachers to question anew whether or not projects were the best form of instruction for their students. Peninsula's commitment to having only one teacher in each classroom (with no aides or parents allowed after kindergarten and no team teaching) also caused regular concerns. At one point, what one parent termed a "big brouhaha" erupted when two teachers wanted to share a class in a part-time arrangement, but were told they could not. Janet Stark, who arrived to teach at Peninsula the year after that debate, felt the effects as well. "I wanted to team teach with the other fourth-grade teacher," she reported, "and one of the fifth-grade teachers who had been here for a long time found out about it. She said, 'Well, you can't do that at Peninsula. That's just not acceptable.'"

In many cases, these kinds of differences of opinion can be exacerbated by enduring conflicts among the perspectives of different groups. "We have an ongoing debate about homework," acknowledged Sarah Reese, a humanities teacher at Horizons (who later became dean and eventually principal). "We say [in the handbook] 25 minutes per kid, but one of the things we say at the school [is] none of our kids are the same, so how does that apply? Does that mean they do what they do in 25 minutes, or should some kids have to spend more [time]?" From the math teachers' perspective, Reese explained "they have to do this, they have to get it . . . if it takes longer, that's what it takes for them." But for many humanities teachers, like Reese, "if the kid gets to [25] minutes and they haven't finished the assignment, and they come and explain to us, that's okay."

Even if the initial discussions are relatively focused, they can frequently spill over into other issues that can be even more contentious. At Horizons, the discussion of homework evolved from a focus on the amount of time students were spending to the nature of the work students were being asked to do. Reese reported, "Then there are people saying, you know, 'kids complain that some of the homework is just pointless, it's just to get homework and what do we think about that?'" In part, a school like Horizons can have these discussions because they have strong relationships to begin with and because they realize that their mission of both responding to individual learning needs and enabling all students to get a college preparatory education itself reflects a fundamental tension that they have to face on a regular basis. "The undercurrent of it," Reese explained, "is how do you hold kids to the same standards if you're trying to treat them all individually?"

Divisions Between Old and New

Although schools like Dewey and Emerson can use the development of distinct missions and approaches as a foundation for building community, those missions and "normal" approaches inevitably shift as times change and members come and go. In turn, these shifts (which do not affect schools that have no common sense of a collective mission or approach) also serve as some of the biggest threats to their sense of community and their collective efforts. These shifts may contribute to tensions between veteran faculty who often adhere to practices and approaches associated with the school's history and newer faculty who often bring new ideas and less familiarity with the "old ways."

At least in part, the tensions between different generations may reflect the fact that they have been educated in different eras that reflect different values, beliefs, and knowledge. The constant "swinging of the pendulum" between traditional academic approaches and more "progressive" approaches means that schools with different instructional philosophies are likely to experience these tensions at different times. Thus veteran and newer faculty at Dewey drifted apart and "did their own thing" as wider interest in their child-centered approach waned in nearby schools and teacher education programs. At Peninsula and City, however, the tensions grew as newcomers to the school brought backgrounds that emphasized more collaborative teaching and differentiated instruction. Megan Lawrence, a teacher who joined the staff of City a year after Julianne Fredericksen became principal, reported, "When I came in [the veteran teachers] would complain 'Oh, look at those grades. Those sixth-grade teachers, all those kids are getting As and Bs. That's going to bring down the quality of the school.'" In this case, the issue was not simply whether the newcomers were "too easy." The veterans expressed concerned that the more hands-on approaches the newcomers used to address the needs of an increasingly diverse student population watered down the school's standards.

Tensions do not always arise between new and old, however; divisions and subgroups within organizations may also reflect different values and approaches, and limited opportunities for cross-group interaction may make it difficult for them to learn about one another's work and points of view (McLaughlin & Talbert, 2001). In turn, these divisions can be exacerbated if the groups are responsible for different levels of students or different content that may involve different techniques or pedagogical approaches. The fact that veterans were clustered in the upper grades (and in different parts of their buildings), for example, contributed to the tensions at Dewey and City; and at Horizon and Emerson conflicts sometimes emerged among teachers associated with different disciplines like mathematics and English or the sciences and the humanities.

Unaddressed Issues of Race, Gender, and Cultural Difference

While it is difficult to predict exactly which tensions may grow into conflicts, particularly problematic are occasions when groups of students break down along lines of race or gender, with students from one group or another more likely to be high- or low-performing, attending advanced or remedial classes, or in gifted classes or special education. The same tensions can also emerge from instances when teachers of a particular race or gender are assigned to work with some students and not others (such as high- or low-performing students). These tensions can be especially divisive because these groupings are not always immediately visible and may require careful analysis of students' performances, patterns of course taking, and distribution of opportunities and resources.

Manzanilla faced a particularly difficult challenge because it was organized into the bilingual program that served a substantial portion of the students (all of them Hispanic), while the much smaller Sheltered English Program served all of the school's African American students as well as a small number of Asian and Hispanic students who were taught entirely in English. The staff members working with these two groups spent most of their time with colleagues from the same program, and they needed different kinds of professional development. Furthermore, they dealt with different pedagogical issues, different issues of race and diversity, and different groups of parents, all of which led them to take different perspectives and points of view. The relatively small size of the sheltered program and the different racial composition of the two groups of students also contributed to concerns–recognized by both groups of teachers–that the needs of the sheltered program and its largely African American student body were often overshadowed by the needs and demands of the bilingual program and bilingual students.

Compounding the challenges, in 2002 Manzanilla decided to apply to open a small middle school. The primary impetus came from a concern of members of the bilingual program that their students were not always well-served in middle schools. They felt that by creating their own middle school program, they might be able to capitalize on the relationships they had already established with their students. While the district approved their proposal and promised the middle school its own building, no building was immediately forthcoming. As a consequence, Manzanilla had to squeeze the middle school into its own building. As the middle school grew, the elementary school had to shrink. In turn, the school had to face difficult decisions about how to trim the staff of the elementary school and whether to decrease the size of the sheltered program, the bilingual program, or both. Throughout this debate, the school had to face the questions about how students of different races were treated and whether or not all of their needs were being addressed adequately.

Although these issues get swept under the rug in many organizations, staff at Manzanilla frequently discussed them as a regular part of their conversations, decision making, and professional development. Efforts were made to ensure that groups and committees included a mix of teachers from both the bilingual and sheltered programs and that the topics addressed in schoolwide activities reflected the concerns of both groups. Nonetheless, even these efforts created some tensions as the small size of the staff for the sheltered program meant that their members had to spend more time participating in schoolwide committees while their colleagues in the bilingual program could share those responsibilities among a much larger group.

HOW CAN SCHOOLS GET BY WITHOUT AN EMPHASIS ON LEARNING COMMUNITIES?

Although some schools can create an effective mix of collaborative activities and informal interactions, for others, group activities end up producing what Andy Hargreaves (2000) called "contrived collegiality": a sense that leaders have simply invented reasons to make staff collaborate rather than a sense that collaboration is an integral part of the organization's work. Particularly in schools like City that are doing well in terms of student performance, individuals may see no reason for more collaborative activities. As Monica Wilkinson, a sixth-grade teacher at City, put it, from her perspective, staff development is something to be endured rather than a crucial support for her practice. When asked about staff development she had participated in, she mentioned "a whole bunch of emergency stuff" related to school safety and security and then added, "Oh, yeah, we [also] had to go through all of the test data because you have to get your test scores up. You know, blah, blah, blah,

blah, and again it's kind of like the same thing. It's coming from above." For Wilkinson, "it's fine to spend a day together," but the primary value of these activities lies in getting a break or a respite from the usual activities: "Then, it's kind of like, oh, well, I don't have to teach but I'm going to hang out with the staff all day. That can work."

Relying on the Power of Peers

Schools like Peninsula and City can survive and even prosper—at least for a while—without much investment in collective professional development and without an explicit attention to building community. Rather than devoting considerable time to group meetings, they may allow individual members substantial leeway in carrying out their own activities and can rely on the informal interactions that are a normal part of the school day to share information, ideas, and expertise. At Peninsula, for example, "there's a real camaraderie at the school and a willingness to help each other and work together, but it's unofficial," Janet Stark explained. In fact, Peninsula managed to maintain its approach without establishing many group meetings or structures to support collective activity. Instead, they relied largely on a regular monthly staff meeting, on participation in the professional development offerings in the district and in the surrounding area, and on the informal support that teachers got from one another. As Paula Williams described it,

> There are no cliques, no "ins" and "outs." I've been in staff rooms where these people always sit together and those people always sit together and this group would never sit with that group, or you'd have the young teachers and the old teachers, or whatever, and I don't see that happening here. . . . I think people are pretty good about talking and sharing stuff. Somebody will say, "I need so and so," and whether it's magnifying glasses or whatever, somebody will always come up with something. People are willing to help each other.

Correspondingly, the school had few formal mechanisms to support new teachers or introduce them to Peninsula's approach. Instead, during the summer, when teachers were setting up their classrooms for the coming year, Paula Williams and other veterans often checked in with new teachers on a more informal basis. "We do go around and say 'Oh, do you need some help?'" Williams explained. "And we just sit around and talk." Those conversations revolved around things like "What makes Peninsula Peninsula," materials the new teachers need, how to set up their rooms, or other issues. The fact that most new teachers who come to Peninsula are actually experienced teachers whose approaches seem to fit the school's makes it easier for them do without an emphasis on more formal professional development activities. As Williams explained,

> We haven't gotten a lot of brand new teachers. Like our new first-grade teacher this year, we were talking about "How are we going to do guided reading?" We're not talking about "What is guided reading?" We're talking about how you implement it in this particular situation. So there's a lot of just talking to people, "How do you do this?" or "How do you do that?" And then I will take them through all our literacy stuff, the binders which we have with all our assessments, and talk about all that. And I try and do that on a fairly informal basis before they're totally stressed out [when the school year starts].

In fact, even when Janet Stark was new to Peninsula, she was a veteran within the district, and already worked with Paula Williams in leading some of the district's summer activities for teachers who were new to the district.

During the year, Peninsula did hold a regular staff meeting to discuss important issues, but it did not depend on meetings of teachers from the same grade or other arrangements in order to promote collaboration or collective work. The interactions among teachers remained informal with conversations among colleagues taking place on a largely ad hoc basis. As Janet Stark put it,

> I'll go next door to Tina [another fourth-grade teacher] and say, "Oh, I'm going to be doing this. Do you want to do it? This is a project I'm going to do." Or she'll share things with me, and we'll talk about where we're at in our subject areas to see how we're keeping [up]. Are we both in the same place or has one of us gotten ahead? I think the teachers do that on their own because it's an important part of the way you keep your program going. But at the same time, we haven't had formal meetings.

Within this kind of context, teachers can make their own decisions about where to focus their energies and how much time to spend working with others.

In addition to having a strong veteran faculty, schools like Peninsula and City may be able to survive without paying as much explicit attention to formal and informal interactions as schools like Dewey and Manzanilla because they have a more traditional academic approach. As a consequence, they can take advantage of the many traditional professional development offerings in their district and traditional courses at their local universities that reflect and reinforce their values and needs. In short, the demands of socialization and professional development are different in traditional schools and in less conventional schools. Traditional schools like Peninsula and City may be able to manage without a more extended investment in collective community building and professional development as long as any tensions within the staff or with the larger community do not turn into full-fledged conflicts, parents continue to be happy with their students' experiences, and the school remains successful in the eyes of the district and others.

Sowing the Seeds for Collective Activity

Although some schools may survive without investing much time or attention in developing a learning community or in organizing collaborative activities, maintaining an individualistic orientation has significant downsides. Even with high levels of performance overall, some teachers in these schools can "coast," and inequities in performance and achievement gaps can persist. Furthermore, these schools often lack a key mechanism for making changes and for adapting to changing circumstances.

This is the situation Julianne Fredericksen faced at City. Despite the concerns of some parents and administrators at the district level, the school had excelled with those same teachers for many years and without much emphasis on schoolwide professional development. Fredericksen even reported that when she arrived at the school, "the word on the street was that the City teachers didn't do professional development because they knew everything." Even teachers who agreed with Fredericksen's efforts to make classroom practices more responsive to student needs saw little value in their staff meetings and collective professional development activities. From Megan Lawrence's perspective, although Frederiksen wanted to engage the staff in collaborative professional development, the meetings mostly ended up focusing on administrative issues:

> Julianne would have a list of things, directives or business to attend to that was districtwide, like you need to boost up your test scores or you need to do this or whatever. It was the stuff that she would get from downtown that she would have to kind of pass on . . . she would tell us things about workshops or positions that needed to be filled or responsibilities or duties that had to be filled. Sometimes she would address issues if there had been a discipline issue that was relevant to the staff in general. Then a lot of time was spent discussing how money was going to be spent if there was a kind of school pot money. That was it. People don't like staff meetings.

Even without much success in creating formal opportunities to bring the staff together and develop collective expertise, however, the careful recruiting and hiring Fredericksen did, along with the placement of new teachers around the school, enabled her to foster the development of an entirely different adult learning environment that seeded the school with new kinds of expertise and encouraged all the teachers to stretch their skills. In addition to hiring new teachers who were certified to teach English Language Development students, Fredericksen tried to take advantage of the influence that the teachers could have on one another by making sure that every grade level had at least one especially strong teacher who could "be the cheerleader and the role model" and bring the others along. While placing veterans into these positions could be useful, Frederiksen mainly drew upon the energy, enthusiasm, and training of the new teachers she hired. She also made sure that these new teachers had roles in schoolwide committees and activities. In one instance, she hired a particularly dynamic new teacher who quickly got the nickname "Miss Bubbly." Although she only stayed for 2 years, Miss Bubbly introduced a number of new ideas to the school—including a Spirit Day that continued to bring all the members of the school together once a month even after she left. Miss Bubbly helped other members of the staff "step up to the plate," as Fredericksen put it. "When you get one of those [teachers] that are so dynamite it's like turning the oven higher and that one is so hot that the others have to turn their ovens up a little too, so it sort of became contagious."

In order to spread ideas and expertise among teachers, Fredericksen also encouraged all the City teachers to visit one another's classrooms or the classrooms of mentors or model teachers in other schools. Rather than mandating these activities or organizing them as part of the school's formal professional development activities, however, Fredericksen left it up to the teachers to decide when and if they wanted to participate. She made sure to highlight that these activities were going on and figured out how to get funding and support for anyone who wanted to pursue them. She also made a special effort to carve out what veteran James Anderson referred to as a "protected" environment for the new teachers, one that really made them feel welcome despite the grumbling of some veteran faculty. "She had meetings for the new teachers," Anderson marveled, "got them special materials, anything that they put on a list, she seemed to get for them."

By bringing in these new teachers, consciously placing them in positions where they could have an impact on others, and supporting individual professional development, Fredericksen helped bring new ideas and a new peer culture that made some veteran teachers uncomfortable and led them to leave the school. But it encouraged others to extend their own development. Anderson felt the pressure to get certified to teach students who were designated as needing English Language Development; but Fredericksen "never pushed me," he explained. "I had a [grade level] partner that had his credential so he would get the ELD kids. I always felt bad about that because I thought I should carry more weight. So I got it. That was good, a load off my shoulders. I felt like one of the gang again." As a result, although the school did not change or expand its formal professional development activities, Frederiksen saw a change in attitudes toward professional development: By the end of her tenure at the school, she explained, "the word out on the street was 'Oh God, look at all these City teachers, they're signing up for this [professional development activity] and they're signing up for that.'"

SUMMING UP

Learning communities are no panacea. They bring benefits as well as problems, and they are difficult to develop and sustain. Ultimately, leaders have to figure out how to maintain an appropriate balance between collaborative and independent work. In developing that balance, school leaders need to take into account the extent to which staff members already have a common basis in shared values, shared purposes, and shared experiences. If schools can find new teachers who bring a commitment to the school's approach and relevant qualifications and experience, then a school may not have to devote as much time to formal activities designed to develop a strong learning community and bring newcomers "up to speed." If substantial numbers of new teachers are not that well prepared to carry out a school's approach, however, then the school has to find ways to help those newcomers learn about the school and develop appropriate skills and commitment. Similarly, if the school's approach coincides with common expectations, there may be many outside programs, resources, and experts the school can draw upon to support their staff; but if schools pursue a less common approach or strategy, there may be relatively few places or people they can turn to for help and they may have to develop their own learning community and their own approach to professional development.

Significant investments in formal collaborative efforts like shared decision making and collective professional development activities bring with them significant risks. The scope and complexity of decision-making processes and professional development activities can also bring inefficiencies and frustrations that have the potential to undermine the very trust in colleagues and in the organization as a whole that those processes and structures are supposed to build.

Given these challenges, the members of schools that pursue shared decision making and pursue their own approaches to professional development have to spend considerable time and energy working on their own process. They need to spend time and resources getting training in meeting facilitation, establishing meeting norms and protocols, and getting guidance about the available professional development resources and support. In turn, even as they seek to take control of their work environment, schools may need to seek the assistance of coaches, support providers, district administrators, and others who can provide some of that expertise. Ironically, seeking that assistance subjects them again to the outside demands and expectations that they have to figure out how to manage.

Chapter 6

Managing the
External Environment

Developing a common mission, finding the right staff, and establishing a productive work environment are hard enough, but these internal practices are not strictly under the control of schools themselves. School members can try to develop a commonly understood mission, but cannot assume that everyone will agree with that mission. They can attempt to hire teachers who share their philosophies, but cannot guarantee that those teachers will apply. They can try to build community and foster the development of collective expertise, but they cannot ensure that they will get the resources and support they need to meet their goals.

In order to carry out crucial organizational functions and to overcome the inevitable problems that come with work in a turbulent environment, schools depend on their relationships with a host of individuals, organizations, and institutions that operate outside school walls. These include relationships with school district administrators and school boards that may have direct oversight of schools; funders, support providers, and other external providers with whom schools have contractual relationships; parent and community members to whom schools may have some legal obligations; and more informal relationships with a host of community organizations, teacher education programs, educational professionals, public figures, and other individuals.

While schools often benefit from the resources, services, and support these groups and individuals can provide, many of these external players have the authority to direct and constrain some of the operations and decisions of schools, while schools have little bureaucratic control over these outside individuals and organizations. As a consequence, many critics place the blame for failed improvements on the system—particularly the district and state bureaucracies—in which schools operate, but those critics do not always agree on the key problems with this system or the possible solutions.

On the one hand, critics that take a "market-based" or decentralized approach to reform argue that the traditional authority structure creates numerous bureaucratic problems that undermine a school's ability to innovate and make improvements. In turn, these critics advocate solutions like disman-

---

Recent Developments in School Choice and Vouchers

In 1990 Milwaukee established the Milwaukee Parental Choice Program, the first of a number of cities and states to offer vouchers allowing some families to send children to parochial or private schools rather than their local public school. Enrollment began with 341 participating students in 1990–91, but by 2007–08, over 18,000 students participated in that program. (Carnoy, Adamson, Chudgar, Luschei, & Witte, 2007; Wisconsin Department of Public Instruction, 2008; Witte & Thorn, 1996)

In 2007, 13 states and the District of Columbia provided some form of private school choice, with approximately 150,000 children using publicly funded scholarships to attend private school (Lips, 2008):

- Arizona, Florida, Georgia, Maine, Ohio, Vermont, Utah, Wisconsin, and the District of Columbia have policies that provide taxpayer-funded scholarships to help students attend private elementary or secondary schools of choice.
- Arizona, Florida, Illinois, Iowa, Minnesota, Pennsylvania, and Rhode Island offer incentives for contributions to scholarship programs or allow tax credits or deductions for education expenses, including private school tuition.

---

tling burdensome administrative structures or developing voucher programs and charter schools that vest more authority in the schools themselves.

From their perspective, schools that operate outside of the traditional bureaucracy can respond more effectively to the needs and concerns of parents and the local community. Furthermore, market-based approaches assume that giving parents and students the opportunity to choose between schools (instead of having to go to a school designated by a school district) will create market pressures that lead the least popular and least effective schools to make improvements.

On the other hand, many "systemic" reformers fear that such decentralized systems can never ensure a level playing field in which all students have an equal chance of attending an effective school. They argue that while the most informed and capable parents and students may find their way to effective schools, many students in disadvantaged communities will end up in schools that remain mired in problems, without sufficient support or pressure to make improvements. Rather than seeing the constraints of the bureaucracy as the key problem, systemic reformers argue that the current system does not work as well or as efficiently as it could. In turn, they have pursued a variety of strategies to create more coherent policies and administrative structures that can raise expectations for all students and foster changes

The District Role in School Improvement

Views of the district role in school improvement efforts have evolved over time. In the 1980s, a surge of interest in "effective schools" and other school-based reform programs often cast districts as either irrelevant or as obstacles to improvement efforts. The dissatisfaction with trying to make improvements one school at a time, however, and the growing attention to developing more systemic approaches to school reform contributed to a resurgence of interest in the district as a key player in producing improvements on a large scale. Subsequently, research elaborated the roles that districts can play in mobilizing key resources and generating physical, human, and social capital needed to undertake improvements. However, that research also cautioned that effective resource allocation and policy implementation at the district level depends on how well district personnel understand those policies and reform initiatives and on the stability of district personnel, particularly district leadership (Anderson, 2003; Hightower, Knapp, Marsh, & McLaughlin, 2002; Marsh, 2000; Spillane & Thompson, 1997). The resurgence of interest in districts was also reflected in several ambitious wide-scale improvement efforts in Community School District #2 in New York City (Elmore & Birney, 1997), Chicago (Bryk, Sebring, Kerbow, Rollow, & Easton, 1998), and San Diego (Darling-Hammond, Hightower, Husbands, LaFors, Young, & Christopher, 2005; Hess, 2005; Hightower, 2002).

throughout the educational system. These systemic reformers have worked to establish curriculum standards, assessment systems, and incentives and rewards at the district, state, and federal levels that are more consistent and aligned. They have also concentrated on strengthening, rather than diminishing, the control of districts over schools by establishing clearer common goals and supporting initiatives intended to be implemented across many different schools.

Ironically, over the past 30 years, both the efforts to decentralize and to strengthen the traditional school system have gained some ground. As a consequence, at the same time that schools face increased pressure from parents and students who have more options for choosing schools, schools also face additional demands from the new curriculum standards, assessments, and policies put in place at the district, state, and federal levels.

Despite their different perspectives on the traditional authority structure of schools, these views of both decentralization and systemic reform cast schools as reactive, dependent on others (parents and students or policy makers and administrators) who need to pressure schools to initiate changes and hold them accountable for carrying those changes out. In the process, both views reinforce a sense of helplessness among principals and school staff and encourage school members to depict themselves as victims of bad policies and poor decisions made by others.

Distributed Leadership

Traditional conceptions treat leadership as an individual quality—an ability or propensity that one person can develop and exercise—and as a discrete role that an individual can play within an organization. In contrast, James Spillane and John Diamond (Spillane, 2006; Spillane & Diamond, 2007) and Alma Harris (2008) argue that leadership functions and responsibilities can be spread or distributed across a number of people, tools, and routines. From this perspective, formal authority and responsibility for developing a productive staff may lie with a school leader. However, teachers, coaches, or others who serve as mentors or who organize the work of grade-level teams can take on some of those responsibilities. Similarly, protocols and formal or informal reflection processes that facilitate peer observations can help to distribute the work of instructional leadership over a wider group of individuals. This distribution of the functions of leadership

- Allows the organization to benefit from individuals who have more relevant expertise or have access to more up-to-date information than an individual leader
- Lessens the burden of responsibilities that fall on a single person
- Contributes to greater stability and helps organizations survive and thrive through leadership transitions and other disruptions

At the same time, assigning formal leadership responsibilities to different individuals or creating structures for participatory decision making does not necessarily mean that leadership is distributed. The extent to which leadership is distributed reflects how leadership functions are actually carried out, regardless of what organizational charts or formal job descriptions specify.

In contrast to these assumptions, schools can play a proactive role in influencing the expectations of parents and community members, finding the resources they need, and shaping the demands that centralized bureaucracies and other external partners may place upon them. Schools do not have to wait for their local district, community groups, teacher education programs, or state policy makers to deliver to them the resources and people they need to do their work; and they cannot stand idly by while others develop goals and expectations that may not fit their missions or capabilities. Schools do not have to acquiesce when those who have authority over them demand that they implement initiatives that undermine the work they are trying to do or their mission as they see it. Schools can work to advance their own goals and missions.

Being proactive, however, does not mean that schools have to break away from district control or take an antagonistic stance toward policy makers, administrators, community members, or others who seek to influence or control what happens inside schools. Carefully cultivating relationships with key individuals and organizations on the outside can help schools to build social capital by connecting them to the ideas, expertise, and power that enables them to anticipate and influence the demands and expectations they may face in the future. Schools can also take advantage of these external relationships and the information they can gain from them to try to avoid or reshape demands and expectations that may be problematic. Ultimately, schools may be able to use their connections to develop allies they can call on to help them in times of crisis.

BUILDING RELATIONSHIPS AND DEVELOPING NETWORKS OF INFLUENCE

Recent work on educational leadership emphasizes that the principal needs to be an instructional leader as well as an administrator who can manage day-to-day operations. Juggling both responsibilities contributes to the overwhelming demands of the job because they require very different kinds of expertise, including both a knowledge of teaching and learning and a knowledge of finance, personnel, and administration. Adding to those demands, however, and often neglected amidst the focus on instruction and administration, the principal also has to act as an external leader, as the liaison to those outside the school and as the spokesperson, negotiator, and champion of the school's interests. Rosabeth Moss Kanter (2004) explains: "The ultimate work of leaders lies in the connection between their groups and the wider network that provides support, loyalty, revenues, or capital. Leaders must prove to those in the wider circle that their investments are warranted" (p. 341).

School leaders, like external leaders in other organizations, need to cultivate connections to knowledgeable and powerful outsiders that can help manage demands and expectations in the external environment and procure needed resources. At the same time, relying on one individual to take on all the responsibilities of developing these connections leads to several key problems:

- If individual leaders focus too much on the external environment, they may well find themselves growing distant from the work going on inside the school.
- Trying to fulfill the responsibilities of managing both the internal and external environment may contribute to the overwhelming demands that make the work of the school principal so difficult.
- When leaders do leave the school, like doctors or lawyers who leave their practice or firm for a rival, they take many of their contacts

and relationships with them, and the new leader has to begin again in assembling the network of contacts and relationships the school needs to be successful.

In order to combat these problems, the work of managing the external environment—like the work of managing the internal environment—can be distributed. Distributing that work entails enabling many members of the school community to develop a common understanding of the school's mission and approach. Without that understanding and some commitment to the work of the organization, individuals cannot effectively advance the interests of the school; instead, they may undermine it by sending mixed messages about the school and its needs or by deliberately working to block the efforts of others. With a common understanding of the school's mission and work, when members of the school attend meetings and conferences, take courses, and just walk around in the community, they can help to explain the school's mission and goals, recruit qualified staff, find resources, and advance the school's interests.

Developing the relationships needed to manage the environment means that schools have to not only get "insiders" out of the school and into the surrounding community but also give "outsiders" some opportunities to get inside the school. Like the opportunities for social interaction that build relationships among staff members, developing connections between staff members and parents, community members, district administrators, and others enables them to discover common interests and develop the wider understanding and trust they need to work constructively toward common ends.

Developing Shared Understanding Between Teachers and Parents

Although some schools may be able to get by without explicit efforts to build wider understanding and trust within the larger school community, limited opportunities for insiders and outsiders to learn about one another can create a distance between school staff and others that fuels ignorance, fear, and misunderstanding. In fact, struggling schools face the paradox that the lack of external relationships feeds the distrust that discourages them from inviting outsiders in and developing productive relationships in the first place. In particular, school members may be afraid to expose themselves to scrutiny and may fear losing power and control if they involve "others" directly in school operations. As they become more and more isolated, they may find it harder to build social capital and develop the power they need to do their work well. Differences in the racial and cultural backgrounds and economic and educational status of those "inside" and "outside"—particularly between teachers and parents—can reinforce these divisions and discourage many from taking the risk of developing the external relationships they need to manage the environment and make improvements (Fine, 1993; Warren, 2005).

Some of the common activities that bring parents and teachers together can actually exacerbate these divisions. For example, the short, formal nature of parent-teacher meetings, with a roster of individuals that shifts nearly every year, can create counterproductive power dynamics and pressures between tax-paying parents and grade-wielding teachers. Similarly, traditional PTA and school management meetings can pit parents and teachers with different perspectives and needs against one another, particularly when divisive issues arise.

Even at schools that demonstrate good performance results, the distance between insiders and outsiders and related misunderstandings can spill over into serious tensions and conflicts. At City and Peninsula, for example, the schools had high test scores for some time, and parents always provided considerable support in the form of fund-raising and a willingness to participate in school activities. At the same time, neither went beyond the norm of typical parent-involvement activities, and both schools had to deal with significant rifts and conflicts between parents and school staff. At City, the concerns of parents contributed to Fredericksen's selection as principal and helped fuel her efforts to "modernize" the school's instructional approach; at Peninsula, the concerns of parents contributed to the turnover in principals as well as to continuing tensions over how much influence parents should have over school decisions.

At some point, schools that do not pay explicit attention to developing connections between the inside and the outside have to take the plunge, break out of their isolation, and give themselves a chance to learn about those around them—or pay the price. In order to do that, schools need to create opportunities for outsiders to learn about what's going on inside. In contrast to traditional parent-teacher conferences and meetings, holding regularly scheduled open houses, forums, and informational meetings create informal environments in which school staff, parents, community members, and others can converse and learn about one another's backgrounds, interests, and concerns and facilitate the development of strong relationships. At Dewey, for example, the principal regularly hosted "parent coffees" to encourage parents who were dropping off their children to stop for a moment and talk to her and other staff members. The school also hosted evening sessions when teachers from the school shared with parents information on issues and new approaches that they themselves were learning about. At Emerson, the semiannual open houses provided both a regular, low-pressure environment for staff and many members of the community to get to know one another and a chance for parents, district administrators, and the general public to see what students (and teachers) were doing. Members of the wider school

Community Organizing as a Means of Developing Common Interests

Many typical approaches to community involvement begin by trying to get parents into schools and often run into problems when not enough parents come through the doors. An alternative approach focuses on connecting the school to life and work with community around it. These efforts recognize that parents, teachers, and other members of the educational system have diverse needs and perspectives, but strive to help find the common interests that can serve as the basis for joint work on school improvement.

The Alliance Schools, a network of schools in the southwestern United States, takes such an approach in their efforts to build a powerful constituency for improving education and other aspects of the local conditions in low-income neighborhoods (Hatch,1998b; Shirley, 2002; Warren, 2005). Building on the community-organizing tradition of Saul Alinsky and the work of the Southwest Industrial Areas Foundation, the Alliance Schools begin with efforts to build relationships throughout the community by

- Surveying the members of the community and school to find common interests
- Using that information to fuel conversations and identify critical issues that many members of the community and school care about
- Pursuing an issue that can be addressed in a reasonable period of time

These efforts may focus inside or outside the school—on improving school facilities, repairing a playground, establishing a health clinic, addressing traffic problems, or increasing safety. The joint work to address these issues builds relationships and establishes social capital that serve as a basis for further school improvement initiatives and community development work. Over time, the work together helps build a political constituency that can advocate for schools in times of crisis as well as apply pressure when schools or districts seem resistant or unresponsive to community concerns.

community could see the work of individual children in the context of others and get a sense of the work of the school as a whole. Without these kinds of possibilities to see inside a school, those who are not a part of the school's day-to-day operations have little opportunity to put any information they do get into perspective.

Establishing Connections with Other Educators

School members may have a number of formal meetings with district officials and other outside consultants and professional educators, but some explicit efforts to help those outsiders develop their understanding of a school may be useful as well. When Moore arrived at Dewey, as one parent put it, it was "obvious" that the district "really didn't get what the philosophy was about." Moore's conversations with board members and the new superintendent made it clear to her that none of them "had a clue" what the school did. In response to this situation, after the school reexamined its philosophy, Moore worked with the parents and teachers on the Community Relations Committee she had established to host a series of dinners with district administrators and board members. At these dinners, school members provided the same kind of orientation to the Dewey philosophy that they provided for new parents: describing the history, mission, goals, and practices of the school. They also invited the superintendent and board members to visit the school and talk with the teachers "anytime," which many of them did.

In addition to trying to get outsiders into the school, getting the insiders out creates important opportunities for the development of relationships and wider understanding of a school's work. At Peninsula, in fact, teachers like Paula Williams and Janet Stark helped to cement a strong relationship with district administrators through the regular interactions they had when they served as lead teachers for the district's professional development for literacy instruction.

Opportunities for productive external relationships go far beyond the district, however. Given their nontraditional instructional approaches, both Emerson and Manzanilla came to rely on relationships with external support providers like Bay Area School Reform Collaborative (BASRC) and Bay Area Coalition of Equitable Schools (BayCES). While school leaders played key roles in launching and maintaining these organizational relationships, many members of each school not only went to meetings and conferences organized by these groups, they also took on responsibilities to make presentations, provide advice, and lead activities that helped to build stronger connections throughout both organizations, enabling Manzanilla, in particular, to break out of what principal Melora Vasquez referred to as "its isolation."

Isolation can be a particular problem for charter schools. Although many charter schools are designed explicitly to evade the pressures and demands of districts, stepping outside traditional district structures means that charter schools can also get cut off from many of the people who have information, resources, and expertise the schools could use (Wohlstetter, Molloy, Smith, & Hentschke, 2004). Compounding the problem, the intense work of starting and managing a school can consume the entire staff and leaves little time for them to get outside school walls and connect with anyone. But, like Emerson and Manzanilla and other schools that develop their own approaches, charter schools do not have to cut themselves off from the outside world completely. They can develop relationships with external support providers, and they can also choose to negotiate their own relationships with their local districts.

Horizons developed a number of relationships with their district including contracting with the district for special education services and participating in some professional development activities sponsored by the Department of Curriculum, Instruction, and Professional Development (CIPD). Principal Paul Archer saw maintaining these relationships as a key means of getting crucial resources—he described some of the Horizons' teachers as "crying out" for professional development—and as a way to work "politically thoughtfully to make sure that what we're doing with the curriculum makes sense to the district even if we're doing it outside the box." The work of individual staff members also helped the school to maintain a strong relationship with the CIPD. Archer credited the school's academic dean with making the "face-to-face" connection with the district staff, but the "humanities people led the charge and they took the time to go over and meet and work with and talk about materials and go to meetings." For charter schools, these relationships with districts may be particularly important when it comes to issues like special education, bilingual education, facilities, and data management, which most charter schools do not have the capability to handle on their own.

Gaining Access to Information, Resources, and Power

The wider understanding that comes from cultivating connections between those inside and outside schools also creates avenues for the school to get crucial information, expertise, and resources and to build social capital. Just as good businesses can gain valuable information about the changing needs and desires of their customers from their salespeople in the field, school members who attend courses, conferences, and local meetings, and simply walk around the community act as "bridges" who can get and share information that helps connect those inside and those outside the school. Similarly, outsiders who come into a school—whether they are district administrators, coaches, educational consultants, visitors from other schools, parents or community members—can connect insiders to a wide range of other contacts, activities, and initiatives both locally and nationally. These connections give the school the capacity to "scan the environment": to see and hear about issues, concerns, and new developments and to stay abreast of how the environment around them may be changing. Getting insiders out into the surrounding community also enables the school to "seed the environment": to put individuals knowledgeable about the school into positions of power and influence. In turn, the information, contacts, power, and influence the schools can gain through a growing network of external relationships enable them to develop allies who are more likely to act in ways that are consistent with the school's needs and interests and who can help the school continue to expand their network.

The Role of Boundary Spanners
in Managing the Environment

Schools depend on a host of individuals—"boundary spanners"—who work in and between different groups and organizational settings (Wenger, 1998). Although school personnel often view boundary spanners like district administrators, coaches, professional development consultants, and other outsiders with suspicion, Meredith Honig (2007) describes how these individuals can play a crucial role in supporting improvement efforts by serving as

- "Bridges" who relay information, resources, and expertise from one group or setting to another
- "Buffers" who try to reduce the extent to which one group or organization is inspected, monitored and pressured by another

Honig argues that district administrators, in particular, can advance the goals and interests of schools by advocating for and assisting in transforming some district policies and practices and by helping schools understand how to work within existing central office policies. Individual administrators can play these roles even within district bureaucracies considered to be resistant and unsupportive and even though formal job descriptions often emphasize their work as monitors, compliance officers, and service providers, not as boundary spanners.

At Peninsula, Paula William's connection to Janet Stark helped to expand the school's network further when Stark joined the staff. Stark not only brought her experience in the classroom to Peninsula, she also brought along her connections and influence within the district's literacy program. As a consequence, both Stark and Williams could contribute to the discussions about literacy instruction in the district and advance ideas and opinions consistent with the Peninsula approach; in addition, they could build collegial and productive relationships with the district staff responsible for ensuring compliance with district policies. Given Peninsula's commitment to traditional instructional approaches, having teachers positioned in leadership roles within the district was particularly crucial during periods when the district experimented with newer approaches, like whole language.

At Manzanilla, Melora Vasquez came to the attention of BASRC staff members through her work as an activist in the Hispanic community, not her work as principal at Manzanilla. When BASRC invited her to join their board, however, she was in a position both to support the development of a formal relationship between Manzanilla and BASRC and to influence BASRC's work in the future.

Similarly, Emerson's project-based approach grew out of the involvement of veteran teacher and later head teacher Rosalyn Bird in Project 2061, a national initiative of the American Association for the Advancement of Science. Bird went to national meetings for Project 2061 for 3 years before Project 2061 launched an initiative with schools in Emerson's district. When they did, Bird was among a small group that was invited to develop the local district model. As a result, Project 2061 was, in a sense, "preimplemented" at Emerson: ideas, beliefs, and practices that were consistent with the Project 2061 model were already in place before the school formally decided to join the project. As Diane Kirsch explained it, "There's a lot in the [2061] model that is really based on Emerson. [Rosalyn] brought a lot to the model but then she also brought many things from the model back to the school."

At Horizons, the development of an organizational relationship with their district as well as with individual district employees enabled them to get some services and to have some control and influence over those services that they might not otherwise have had. In fact, Horizons's relationship with their local school district included a contract that specified the district as the local education agency (LEA). That contract enabled the school to receive special education services from the district in return for a negotiated fee. Those funds paid for the services of five district employees who acted as resource specialists for Horizons's special education students. In addition, as their LEA, the district assumed responsibility for additional costs such as transportation and equipment. "I see it as the world's best insurance policy," Archer explained, because he can avoid the problem faced by colleagues in neighboring charter schools who are in a "constant battle" to get their districts to transfer funds dedicated to serving the needs of special education students who have enrolled in charter schools.

Illustrating the power of developing connections with individuals who can become key allies, Horizons's organizational relationship grew initially out of contacts with one key district administrator, Maureen Tompkins. Tompkins applied for a job at the school when the school first interviewed for the position of director of Horizons's Learning Center. Although the school did not select her for that position, the initial contact helped to convince both the members of the school and Tompkins that they had something to offer each other. Ultimately, as part of the district's arrangement with the school, Tompkins agreed to serve as one of the resource specialists in the school's very first year and remained one of their prime resource specialists even as she continued as a senior employee in the district. As Archer explained, "She has so much seniority that she gets to tell the district where she's going to work and where she's not going to work, and she wants to work here."

Expanding Networks of Information and Influence

Part of the power and social capital that comes with productive external relationships comes from the fact that relationships, in a kind of snowball effect, provide opportunities for more relationships, more information, more access, and more allies (Jennings, 2008). Establishing relationships with district administrators, for example, can lead to a cycle of benefits for both parties. At City, Julianne Frederiksen supported the district's work with new principals, including offering presentations and mentoring on teacher evaluation and the formation of classes each year. Through her connections at the district, Fredericken learned about and joined a leadership project supported by a local foundation. Through her involvement in that foundation initiative, she got support to develop a mentoring project for struggling students at her school that proved to be extremely successful. In turn, Frederiksen led workshops to encourage other principals in the district to develop similar programs. Ultimately, Fredericksen was selected as School Master of the Year for the district, a nice recognition for Fredericksen, but an opportunity for the district to highlight good work going on there as well, and more good publicity for the foundation that supported Fredericksen's work.

Growing connections between school and district staff also creates opportunities for school members to take on other roles and responsibilities within the district, potentially increasing the number of well-informed allies a school has working on the outside. In fact, Fredericksen worked in the district office before she became a principal, and when she left City, she went on to take charge of key aspects of personnel and human resources in the district. Just as Stark brought her connections and influence to Peninsula, Fredericksen took her district knowledge and contacts to City and her knowledge of City and her contacts and relationships with City's parents and teachers back to the district.

Similarly, as schools like Manzanilla and Emerson develop relationships that help them establish their own focus and goals, they develop a distinct identity that is more likely to attract the attention of organizations outside their districts. That attention creates opportunities to develop more relationships with more individuals and groups that can help them make further improvements. In turn, the increased visibility that comes from the development of a distinct identity and a large network of relationships brings visitors and recognition to the school that can help validate the work they are doing.

For example, the information about Emerson that spread through the reform community helped the school manage hiring and turnover by influencing the pool of teachers who applied to the school. As a consequence, as jobs in the district became more plentiful, the school was able to hire teachers from outside the area who already knew something about the school and already believed in project-based instruction, thus lessening (though not eliminating) the need for initial professional development and socialization of the newcomers. The staff also gained numerous opportunities to meet with people outside the school and the Bay Area who could help them learn about the latest research, practices, policy ideas, and funding opportunities long before the members of many other schools.

Isolated schools with limited contacts and few allies face a more problematic situation. Their isolation means that they lack access to the resources and information that could help them find and use the resources, help, and support they need. In a sense, they have to depend on whatever happens to come through the door, regardless of whether or not the help that arrives fits with their goals and needs. But once they do start building a productive network of outside contacts, previously isolated schools can begin developing the capacity to find and use outside expertise more effectively. At Manzanilla, the information and knowledge about BASRC that Melora Vasquez gained from her participation on the BASRC board led her to propose to the staff that they consider joining; in turn, Vasquez's knowledge helped them navigate BASRC's application process. Then their initial work with BASRC brought a host of people into the school as well as numerous opportunities for Manzanilla staff to get out and meet others and visit other schools. Those contacts in turn contributed to the development of relationships with other organizations, like BayCES.

Along with the contacts, funding, and educational opportunities these relationships brought, the school also gained the assistance of several experienced coaches. Several of those coaches were so inspired by the kind of approach that Manzanilla was taking in a bilingual school in a struggling district, that they acted like part-time staff members, regularly sitting in on leadership meetings, helping to plan retreats, and bringing in other experts to try to help troubleshoot some of the difficult issues and crises the school faced. Through those relationships, the members of Manzanilla developed a better understanding of what they needed from their external partners.

In the end, the school was transformed from an isolated organization in need of help, to a reform-minded community, proactively seeking cocollaborators whose approaches fit the school's mission and values. Correspondingly, members of the school community became more resistant to external support that tried to dictate solutions without consulting the Manzanilla staff or taking into account their needs or previous work (the kind of top-down approach characteristic of their district).

SHAPING EXTERNAL DEMANDS

When it comes to managing the environment, building bridges to district administrators and external partners serves as one half of the equation. In order to advance their own interests, schools also need to be able to protect themselves from unwanted demands and to temper inappropriate expectations. Given the fact that those who work inside and those who live and work outside schools—like district administrators, members of support organizations, funders, parents, and others—have different roles and responsibilities in the educational system, some tension between them should be expected:

- School districts are primarily responsible for meeting the needs of all students across schools.
- Schools are primarily responsible for their own students.
- Educational support providers usually support work in a number of different schools in a particular region or around the country.
- Parents and guardians serve as the chief advocates for their children, ensuring that each child gets needed support.

Those outside the school also face different kinds of incentives and rewards, experience different demands, and have different ways of doing their work. Funders have to take into account the expectations of their own boards and the wishes of their founders. School board members and other elected officials have to pay attention to politics, the popular press, and voters, and they have to rely on developing policies, passing resolutions, and making budget allocations in order to influence what goes on in schools.

Within this context of diverse perspectives and responsibilities, schools have to figure out how to take advantage of the benefits of external relationships without getting overwhelmed or undermined by the conflicting demands and pressures that come with them (see Figure 6.1). School members have to ask themselves how close they can get to these external partners without compromising their independence and flexibility; and they have to determine how far away they can stay from their partners without losing access to crucial resources and expertise. In answering those questions, school members have to carefully calibrate how important the demands are to those making them: Are the demands central to the publicly stated goals and initiatives of policy makers, district officials or support providers or to the expressed interests of many parents? Are there acceptable alternatives that would accomplish the same goals? In turn, schools have to take into account how problematic the demands are: Do these demands interfere with the school's basic identity, key goals, or central approach? Finally, school members have to consider the work that would go into resisting the demands

Figure 6.1. Key Considerations in Responding to External Demands

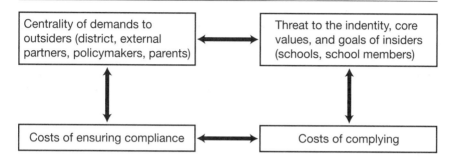

or coming up with more suitable alternatives:

- Do the "outsiders" have the resources and will to ensure compliance, or can the schools get by with little or no response?
- Can schools provide a superficial or symbolic response that makes it look like they are complying without actually making any changes?
- Can schools negotiate a more suitable alternative?
- Would they be better off saving all the time and energy it would take to resist and simply acquiesce?

In some cases, schools may find that they can safely ignore or escape demands and monitoring from outsiders. Many schools, however, particularly those that are recognized as having a distinct approach or are designated as "low-performing" depend on developing information, expertise, and social capital in order to negotiate with powerful partners and to shape activities and expectations outside the school.

Finding the Right Position

"Market position" reflects how particular products, companies, or people compare to others (Ries & Trout, 1981). Companies poised to meet the needs of a new audience or meet a new demand or who have a product that can offer needed services and other benefits are "well-positioned." Businesses can develop a competitive advantage over others by trying to anticipate how their products and services compare to those of others and positioning their products and services so that they offer benefits that others do not. Furthermore, whatever the products and services, advertisers, marketers, and media specialists can use "branding" and public relations campaigns to try to establish their market position and influence how the general public perceives the relationship between their products and clients and those of competitors. Political candidates use similar strategies when they highlight what they think the wider public will see as favorable comparisons between their positions and their personal attributes and those of the other candidates. When these groups and individuals explicitly work on establishing, maintaining, or changing their market position, they are attempting to manage the environment.

Although some efforts to establish favorable comparisons amount to little more than crass attempts to manipulate the public, schools have to face the fact that those on the outside have a perception of what schools do, and schools can either try to play a role in shaping those perceptions or run the risk that those perceptions—accurate or not—will lead to problematic expectations and demands. Efforts to develop an identity and a broader understanding of a school's goals and instructional approach function as one means of establishing a position in comparison to others. Schools that choose to emphasize how different they are from other schools (including those in their district) may develop a distinct identity, but that identity may put them in opposition to others and lead members of other schools, their district, and other educational organizations to view them as resistant and problematic; but schools that cultivate a distinct identity while still emphasizing their connection to other schools and highlighting some similarities to traditional conceptions of education may be viewed more favorably. Therefore, by trying to manage how outsiders perceive the school—and whether outsiders see them as unique or normal, resistant or consistent with dominant expectations— schools can position themselves in ways that have significant implications for how closely they are monitored and how much pressure outsiders put on their operations.

Positioning plays a particularly important role in a school's efforts to manage the environment because members of districts and other educational organizations have limits on the time, resources, and attention they have available to monitor activities and ensure that their school partners act in ways consistent with their demands and expectations. These outsiders have to make choices about which initiatives and expectations should serve as the focus of their attention and often have to concentrate their time and energy on a limited number of the schools with whom they work. Under these conditions, schools can position themselves in ways that lead to less pressure and less monitoring from their districts and give them more flexibility in adapting demands to their goals and needs, and they can try to position themselves in ways that will get them the most advantageous resources and support as well.

Doing what's expected without making waves—or cultivating "benign neglect"—serves as one means of positioning the school so that outsiders do not monitor it too closely. What passes for "doing what's expected," however, is a matter of interpretation that often gets worked out informally as the individual representatives of a district or support organization or parents themselves try to observe and understand what a school is doing. In some cases, demonstrating some acceptable level of performance may be sufficient; what schools do to achieve those results may not matter at all. In other cases, schools may be able to publish school improvement plans, hold a few meetings, or make other superficial changes in order to be in compliance without fundamentally changing what they are doing (thus achieving "symbolic compliance").

Successful schools with approaches consistent with their districts are in a particularly good position to cultivate benign neglect without having to expend much organizational time and energy in developing a collective response. At Peninsula and City, while their districts have at times required more attention to the implementation of new curriculum programs, the development of new curriculum standards, or the examination of standardized test results, for the most part, the principals shared district directives with school staff, the schools participated in district professional development, and the teachers and schools went about their business. In a sense these were win-win relationships because the schools could do their work without close monitoring, and district administrators could save time and focus their attention on what they perceived as more pressing needs.

Already existing consistencies between the goals and approaches of districts and schools and wider demands and expectations also puts schools in a relatively good position to respond to new initiatives and comply with district and state policies. Thus state and district demands to make sure that English Language Development (ELD) students and English Language Learners (ELL) participated in standardized testing caused far fewer problems at City than they did at Manzanilla.

In fact, City's focus on academic preparation led them to test their ELD students even before testing was mandated. City's parents, in particular, told Fredericksen that they wanted their students tested. "I'm saying, 'Why do you want to put your child through that? He hardly speaks English.' But, 'No, we want our child tested.' So I learned very quickly just to be quiet. They want their child tested, let them have their children tested." As a result, City did not have to invest time and energy in complying, nor did it need to develop or draw on relationships with outsiders either to help them implement the policy or try to explain why they would not. City had little additional work to do, and no learning curve in carrying out a policy change.

Manzanilla, however, had never tested many of its ELD students before, and the new testing demands conflicted with some of the basic goals and values reflected in Manzanilla's approach to instructing students in their native language as well as in English. As a consequence, staff at Manzanilla had to spend considerable time and energy in figuring out how to make adjustments and in lobbying to maintain their approach.

Developing the Knowledge Needed to Negotiate

Although some schools may position their work as consistent with the demands of outsiders, whether schools choose to cultivate benign neglect or to resist external pressures, they engage in negotiation at some level. They can choose to engage in that negotiation explicitly or implicitly, collectively or individually. In order to carry out these negotiations effectively, schools have to have the relationships that provide avenues for discussion and exchange, and they have to have a good understanding of the "system," as well as the strengths and weaknesses of their outside partners. Paul Archer at Horizons quickly learned that in order to manage Horizons's relationship with the district, he had to be both a lawyer and a politician who knew the laws better than the members of the district did. As he gained this knowledge, Archer's approach evolved considerably until he didn't "roll over and play dead any more."

Archer needed this knowledge because Horizons's efforts to maintain connections with their district meant that they entered into a gray area where they might be expected to comply with district policies and expectations that conflicted with Horizons's approach and that could enmesh them in the red tape that charter schools are supposed to be able to avoid. At the same time that the school was receiving support from the Department of Curriculum, Instruction, and Professional Development, for example, district administrators from that department also began to participate in reviewing the school's curriculum. Horizons welcomed this relationship in order to show the district that they were providing an appropriate education and valuable service to the community (and the district) without having to comply with all the regulations and policies that the district established.

However, Archer noted a number of instances in which the district's requests for information and reviews of the school's practices seemed to him to be outside the realm of the district's legal authority or responsibility. At one point, Horizons was asked to complete a school accountability report card, which all schools in the district complete annually. Archer felt that they were not obligated to do so since charter schools are required to submit separate annual reports to the district, but he completed the report nevertheless. In doing so, however, the school opened itself up to further pressures as part of their report was questioned by district administrators. "One of the things I said in the report," Archer said, "was that most of the materials that we use are on the district's approved materials list. It was like alarms went off [in the district] with the use of the word *most*. It was circled; I got it back [with the question] what does this mean?" Archer wrote back that "it means just what it says," and the discussion ended. In this case, Archer had gained enough experience and enough confidence to know that he did not have to acquiesce, and he chose to draw the line rather than risk further complications.

Knowledge of the system can also help schools, particularly those in dysfunctional districts, from getting into situations that can lead to problematic negotiations or situations where negotiations are unlikely to pay off. Manzanilla, for example, regularly encountered issues around paperwork, personnel, and timely receipt of funds that no amount of negotiation could address. In one instance, a teacher left the school in the middle of the year, but the district's hiring process involved several requirements that could interfere with the school's ability to find someone whose interests and experience matched the school's goals and approach. Barbara Silver, the reform coordinator, explained:

> If we hire somebody [through the district], the priority goes to people that are consolidated from another school. But if we hire somebody that was consolidated from another school that has district seniority over somebody here, in June they could decide, "I want to stay at Manzanilla" and bump one of our teachers that are *our* teachers.

Complicating matters further, going to the district to hire a new teacher could lead the district to recognize that the school was 22 students under capacity—the equivalent of a full classroom. However, Silver pointed out that those empty seats were spread across grades and programs:

> So we either reconfigure the entire school and put some bilingual [students] into sheltered and sheltered into bilingual, change the grade levels the teachers were teaching, and put everything in chaos or find the money in the existing budget to pay for a position until June.

Given the multitude of complications and difficult conversations with the district that could result if they tried to negotiate for a new teacher, Melora Vasquez pored over the school's budget to find pockets of unrestricted funds she could use to pay a long-term substitute to serve as a temporary replacement. In this case, Vasquez's knowledge and experience with the system enabled her to know there was a problem, and her knowledge of the school's budget (and the "portable budget" spreadsheet she carried around in her pocket) enabled her to come up with a workable solution.

Part of understanding the system comes from a sensitivity to the underlying issues, pressures, and incentives that different organizations face. In particular, schools need a sense of which demands and pressures are likely to go away and which are likely to remain or grow. At Manzanilla, that often meant responding to professional development demands with what might be called "creative compliance": sending a representative or two from the school to mandated professional development and asking them to report back on whether or not others should attend. This response both showed some effort to comply while giving the school a chance to scan the environment—collect information and learn how the initiative is being received in other schools—and to make some guesses about what the district might do in the future. When the district began implementing Open Court—a structured reading program it hoped would help to boost reading scores districtwide—district administrators increased the pressure on the school to send the staff to the trainings. Rather than try to ignore the increasing demands or cave in to the pressure, the school chose to study Open Court and the district's adoption of it: interested representatives of the Sheltered English Program attended the district's Open Court professional development sessions, but they did it as part of a collaborative inquiry project and reported back to their colleagues, who could then take what they were learning and make their own decisions about how to implement Open Court in their classrooms. In this case, the demand to implement Open Court grew and the district went on to mandate it for all schools, but Manzanilla was in a much better position to deal with the mandate than they would have been if they had simply ignored the initial pressures (which they often did with other district demands around professional development).

By knowing how the system applies to them, schools may be able to get the upper hand in negotiations with administrators and other partners who have to manage relationships with numerous different individuals and organizations. At the same time, approaching relationships with external partners as opportunities for both sides to learn about the other can help schools minimize the amount of negotiation they have to do down the line. With open avenues for communication and some common understanding, both sides can anticipate potential conflicts, imagine alternative solutions, and deal with problems before they arise. These relationships make it possible for schools to position themselves as distinct and unique while still trying to minimize the problems and conflicts that can come from those differences.

It takes time, however, to establish that kind of mutual understanding. At Dewey, a high-performing school in a well-off and well-functioning district, even Moore and her colleagues' initial efforts to help the superintendent and other members of the district understand the "Dewey way" were not sufficient to avoid conflicts when the district mandated the use of a standardized report card. When Moore heard about the plans, she called the superintendent to explain that Dewey does not use report cards: "We tell the parents, we don't compare children with each other," Moore related to the superintendent, "and that's what a report card does—it's a comparison of you with somebody else." In response, the superintendent said, "Well, because we are looking at standards, it is not a comparison of the child." After what Moore called a "long philosophical discussion," the superintendent told her to request a waiver, and he would consider the issue. As Moore put it, "I was not going to do a report card, I'd made up my mind"; and she was not content to simply apply and see what might happen. Instead, she organized a daylong study session in which several parents, teachers, a board member, and a representative of the district reviewed Dewey's approach to assessment. Moore described it:

> We spent a whole day looking at it, with teachers reporting, how do you do it, where do you do it. I brought samples of the end of the year letter to them, because we write an end-of-the-year letter to every parent, and what I did, I sort of looked through some amazingly good letters . . . and some letters I would downright change. . . . Then I did letters for one child, who had been at Dewey for 6 years, so they could see the letters about this child throughout, and what they came up with, and then I had a second letter from the same teacher about a child who was going to be retained, so I really wanted them to get a global view.

After reviewing all their work, she went on to joke with the administrators that doing a report card might be easier: "You know, in May, if I came to the teachers and said, 'Here's a report [card for you to fill out],' they would all say yes."

In the wake of this demonstration, the superintendent granted the waiver, and the board member reported back to the school board that Dewey had a reason not to do the report cards. What's more, the exchange enabled the school to have an impact on the district as the district adopted some elements of Dewey's own approach to assessment into the report card the district rolled out in the other schools.

For Moore and Dewey, the benefit of engaging in this negotiation and the educational exchange that went with it had implications that went far beyond the report card itself. In fact, when the new superintendent arrived in the district, Moore had a particularly difficult time getting the district to agree to let Dewey use one of the districtwide professional development days at the beginning of the year to carry out the school's own orientation. As a consequence, the school staff agreed to meet on their own time, on a Saturday, in order to help newcomers get situated and to get everybody on the same page. The following year, however, after the school's efforts to help the superintendent learn about the "Dewey way" and the negotiations over the report card, things changed. Moore laughed when she explained that the superintendent announced in a principals' meeting that for one of the professional development days opening the year "'the focus will be on writing, but Dewey doesn't have to do it. As long as Charlene can do it another day.' I didn't ask, he just said it. And I was sitting there saying, 'Is he talking about me?'" From Moore's perspective, it made all the work the school had been doing to cultivate relationships and build wider understanding worthwhile:

"So I think the bottom line is that he sees the efforts we've been doing and what's happening, and he knows. We're not trying to be ornery; we're not trying to be contrary; we're doing good work."

By positioning themselves in contrast to others while still seeking to establish close relationships with their districts and other external partners, schools like Dewey that pursue their own approaches take a risk: They gamble that the up-front investment in engaging with outsiders (even with the added burdens it might bring) will facilitate negotiations down the line. In a sense, those schools choose the path of "some" resistance, hoping that path gives them more control over external demands and pressures than they would have if they tried to work in isolation from, or in opposition to, what's going on outside the school. In contrast, schools that cultivate benign neglect or that ignore district mandates pursue the path of what appears to be the least resistance; they gamble that they can get by without attracting attention and pressure that will lead to conflicts and much more problematic negotiations down the line.

Taking Advantage of Time

The timing and evolution of relationships with outsiders serves as another key influence on the ability of schools to manage external demands. The inevitable changes in personnel—changes in superintendents, other key district administrators, coaches, support providers, and school leaders themselves—can sever crucial relationships or provide opportunities to revitalize old relationships and establish new ones. Schools have to calibrate carefully whether new leaders in their districts or other external partners are coming in with an expectation or mandate for quick changes, thus potentially increasing the possibilities for conflict and raising the stakes on resisting, or with an interest in taking the time to assess the situation or establish relationships, thus potentially increasing the possibilities for initial flexibility and accommodation. When school leaders themselves change, schools often have to figure out how to replace one of their most crucial sources of information and knowledge about the system and one of their key points of contact with their external partners. In either case, schools may find themselves operating in a much murkier environment at least for a while: They have to make decisions about how to manage the external environment with much less information than they normally have about what's going on and what might happen in the future.

This regular turnover in leadership positions means that schools often have to reinvent their relationships, reposition themselves, and prepare for further negotiations. However, schools that distribute responsibilities for managing the environment, ones that have a dense network in which many members are well-connected to outsiders, are in a much better position to maintain relationships and to keep information and resources coming. If the new arrivals come from afar or are unfamiliar with their new organizations, schools with a dense network may actually find themselves in a more advantageous position as they are likely to have even more knowledge and information about what's going on locally than any new leader.

Even with a dense network, however, turnover can sever numerous relationships at once and dramatically alter a school's relationships with outsiders and their ability to manage external demands. When a new superintendent arrived in the district Horizons worked with, she instituted a number of reforms including "blowing up," as Archer put it, the Department of Curriculum, Instruction, and Professional Development, which led to the departure of many of the staff members with whom Horizons's staff had relationships. At the same time that the new superintendent arrived, a new school board was also elected that showed much more hostility toward charter schools than in the past. In addition to leading the charge to eliminate a charter school associated with the for-profit Edison Company, the new superintendent and board also voted to bar charter school principals from attending districtwide principals' meetings. A district administrator in charge of overseeing charter schools explained that the board and superintendent were concerned that these meetings involved information about district schools that they wanted to keep confidential. These changes both limited Horizons's ability to get access to resources and support and restricted their access to the knowledge and information that could help them to maintain a productive relationship with the district.

Beyond the issues of turnover, the costs and benefits of relationships shift as new initiatives and organizations evolve. In early pilot or experimental phases, new initiatives and organizations may be much more amenable to influence and may be much more responsive as they try to figure out "what works"; but because they have not yet established what works, the benefits of these relationships may be less certain. Once these initiatives and organizations mature, they may have more resources and expertise to offer, but they may be much more restrictive, and they may be less inclined to adapt to the goals and needs of individual schools. At Emerson, several staff members spearheaded the school's involvement with BASRC at a time in the mid-1990s when BASRC was developing their approach, which involved engaging schools in an inquiry process. As Kirsch put it, "they were figuring out what their tools were, so we got to figure it out with them." Furthermore, Emerson staff got to meet with and benefit from the expertise of the key leaders at BASRC (with extensive experience at the state level and in national reform work), who at that time were part of a small staff directly involved in developing BASRC's initiatives. These interactions with BASRC staff and consultants helped to establish teacher inquiry as a key part of Emerson's professional development activities, and Emerson was able to establish connections to other local and national leaders who could serve as powerful allies. In turn, BASRC was able to learn from their affiliation with Emerson and could take those lessons into account in the evolution of their own initiatives.

While there was considerable flexibility at these early stages, BASRC was under significant pressure to expand their work to large numbers of schools in the region, which quickly made such personalized and flexible relationships with individual schools much more difficult. Eventually, BASRC established a formal process that specified a number of requirements that schools had to meet to gain support, including producing a portfolio to apply for funds, engaging in specific forms of inquiry, and sharing results in a structured network meeting. In addition, the senior leaders, who had the power and authority to allow for exceptions and flexibility in BASRC's requirements, had much less time to spend developing relationships with or learning about the needs of specific schools like Emerson. Under these conditions, Emerson staff gradually became less and less engaged in BASRC activities, and they had to look elsewhere for support and assistance.

In a sense, schools like Emerson face the same issues that venture capitalists do when they consider whether to invest their time and energy participating in new initiatives or in partnerships with fledgling organizations. If they guess right, they can benefit from the growth of the initiative or organization, but they may want to turn to new endeavors once work becomes more established and the possibilities for further growth and innovation diminish. Similarly, just as successful venture capitalists benefit from growing expertise in making good choices, developing skills in building partnerships, and establishing a network of contacts in the "start-up" world, schools that develop the right relationships at the right times can benefit from a rapidly expanding network: They not only increase their chances of finding and selecting appropriate partners, they also increase their desirability. Their successful partnerships can make them sought after targets for other external organizations looking to work in schools.

Drawing on the Power of Allies

No matter what schools do, at some point they are likely to face crises that they cannot avoid and cannot negotiate away. No matter how schools position themselves, how well they understand the system around them, or how much attention they pay to the timing and evolution of their relationships, they cannot control the external environment. As a consequence, they have to be prepared to call on the clout and pressure that large groups of well-connected allies can bring. That means cultivating relationships with influential individuals and groups who may be able to provide schools with a kind of "cover"–the threat that those who take drastic action against a school will have to face significant repercussions.

In the wake of their battles over threats of closure, staff at Emerson, for example, explicitly sought to establish relationships with support providers like BASRC who could help protect them from the more traditional approaches reflected in the policies and actions of their district. "We needed outside recognition," Kirsch explained.

> I felt like we were never really going to get support from the district and that we really needed to make alliances with people outside the district who were going to support the school so that we would not be in a position of ever having to fight being closed down again.

Similarly, once the new superintendent and school board took a harder line against charter schools, Archer began to spend more and more of his time collaborating with other charter schools, including helping to establish a local charter school principals' network. Subsequently, the principals' network approached the district to talk about changes in policies regarding a number of issues, including oversight and financial charges and disbursements. Archer also took the lead on a number of occasions in suggesting that the charter schools develop common responses to some of the requests the charter schools got from the district. Even though many of these were seemingly innocuous requests–like asking the charter schools to send out satisfaction surveys to staff and parents–from Archer's perspective, routinely agreeing to them could bring the charter schools further under the influence of the district. At the same time, refusing ran the risk of annoying some of the same district administrators whose support Horizons sought in other areas. As Archer explained it, requests like these reminded him of the Chinese expression "death of a thousand cuts," and the ability to respond collectively allowed Horizons to both retain its independence and minimize stresses and strains in its own relationship with the district.

Ironically, despite the expectation that competition among charter schools would help improve schools, Archer found that establishing collaborative relationships with his peer organizations provided crucial benefits to the schools and critical support in battling the district:

> [The charter schools] were able to agree after a year and a half or so of our existence that we weren't really in competition with each other, that we really did need to work together even if there was some competition between us. So we started sharing projects.

These relationships facilitated the sharing of information and expertise, but they also provided the cover and the social capital that comes from what Archer called a "strength in numbers approach."

Strong relationships with parents and community members serve as another crucial foundation for bringing allies together and forming collective responses to problematic external demands. The threats of closure and changes in facilities that come with poor performance, declining populations, or shifting enrollments often lead to battles between districts and schools that schools are unlikely to win without the wide support and collective efforts of parents and community advocates. Both Emerson and Horizons had to rely on a constant supply of outside support so they could put pressure on their local districts to get and maintain decent facilities. Manzanilla regularly depended on parents to sign petitions and request the waivers needed to maintain their bilingual program and to free themselves from policies that adversely affected the school.

Even Peninsula drew on the support and influence of parents to oppose policies that seemed inconsistent with the structured approach that they chose for their children. For example, when Peninsula's district adopted a new math program in the mid-1990s, both parents and staff expressed extensive concerns. As Janet Stark described it, the new program was "conceptual" and did not focus as much attention on the skills and practice of traditional math. In response, parents took it upon themselves to mount a major campaign opposing the district policy and what they considered to be approaches to mathematics instruction that were too progressive.

Ultimately, even though the district went ahead with the math program, to a large extent Peninsula's parents got what they wanted, and Peninsula's teachers got the cover they needed to continue to pursue their own approach: The superintendent and district staff were well aware of parents' concerns and never exerted much pressure on the school to comply. The knowledge of the parents' support for the school's instructional approach and the parents' ability to mobilize reinforced benign neglect from the district, and many of the Peninsula teachers continued to use the same math materials they had used all along. According to Stark, district administrators gave teachers

> the freedom and flexibility to use what they prefer. And so you could get a recommendation that you really should be doing this [the new math program]. But if the students are doing well, and they're succeeding, no one's going to say, "Well no. You have to do this." It's never that emphatic.

Even on occasions when the superintendent who implemented the program visited the school, he simply asked if the school was using the program. "He didn't make a big issue of it," Stark continued, "but the question came up."

WEIGHING THE COSTS OF RELATIONSHIPS

Along with the challenges of managing the environment, schools have to decide how much time and energy they can afford to spend in building relationships, developing external support, and buffering themselves from unwanted demands. In some cases, the up-front investment in establishing relationships simply doesn't work out. At Emerson, they worked extensively with a corporation that had made a commitment to provide resources to schools in the district. The corporation wanted Emerson, because of its orientation and reputation, to serve as a pilot school for the use of its resources and offered to put computers in every classroom. "We didn't want 30 computers in every classroom," Terry Simon, the lead teacher at the time, explained. "We had been really clear about what our priority was, and it was people. We didn't want technology without human support for it." Ultimately, however, after the relationship between the company and the district soured, the school got 20 computers for a media center in the library. "We don't want 20 computers in there unless there's someone who can take care of them," Simon continued. "I've totally refused to go look at them. . . . I have yet to see them. But they're there."

Establishing relationships not only takes time in the first place, but it can lead to more complications and require more time down the road. If they choose to participate in initiatives, to get grants, or to develop new partnerships, schools have to deal with the burden of the reporting and administrative requirements that often come with them, and then they have to take on all the work required to sustain these relationships. At Manzanilla, for example, "the staff is always writing grants"; and as Melora Vasquez lamented, a lot of that grant writing focuses simply on grants that have to be renewed every year. As a consequence, Manzanilla chose to use some of the money they gained from their relationships with organizations like BASRC and BayCES to pay for a staff member to work as an in-house grant writer. In the same vicious cycle faced by many not-for-profits that depend on grants to survive, however, that grant writer had to spend a portion of her time getting more grants to continue to pay for her own position.

Even when these relationships go well, they often lead to more work and take more time that is only sometimes accounted for or anticipated. As their relationships with support providers developed, Emerson staff members took on more and more responsibility within the networks of support providers. Emerson served as a "lead school" that other schools could visit; the staff members participated in critical friends' groups and went on visits to provide support for others in the network; and staff members often served as models, presenters, or facilitators for the convenings and meetings of their various partners. As the school became better and better known both inside and outside these networks, its partners and others referred journalists, educators, funders, and others to visit and look at the school. In addition, staff members took the time to participate in numerous research projects, including several dissertations, numerous evaluations, a video series, and the research that went into this book, all involving countless interviews and observations.

SUMMING UP

Schools operate within a network of relationships. Schools can choose to consciously manage those relationships, or they can accept whatever opportunities and demands come with those relationships. In order to manage those relationships most effectively, schools need to be able to get insiders out and outsiders in, spreading a wider understanding of the school's goals and practices and putting members of the school community into positions where they can scan and seed the environment. Even as school members build bridges to people and organizations on the outside, schools also have to protect themselves from the unwanted demands and expectations that come along. That may involve cultivating benign neglect or engaging in extensive negotiations. In either case, schools need to draw on an understanding of the system and the needs and demands of their partners to sustain a network of allies who can provide their support in times of crisis.

Although managing the environment depends on identifying those who are outside the school and figuring out how to deal with them, in a sense it allows schools to draw their own boundaries. While a traditional organizational chart listing those who report to the principal or school leader formally defines who counts as being inside the organization, schools can focus their energies on building common bonds and common work solely among the school staff, or they can expand their attention to draw in parents, community members, district administrators, and other educators in order to develop a larger school community. In other words, instead of treating these groups as outsiders that they have to deal with, schools can treat them as insiders who have useful information and expertise, who can take on key roles and responsibilities, and who can help the school expand its network and increase its ability to manage the environment.

These boundaries are fluid, however, reflecting changing and evolving interests and shifting alliances. Sometimes parents may join together with school members to put pressure on the district, or parents may align with a district and a new principal (like Fredericksen) who strives to make changes.

At times they may act as outsiders who add to the external demands and pressures that schools have to manage. As a consequence, rather than treating schools as part of a system in which control and authority are clearly defined, it may make more sense to view the system as a collection of diverse constituencies, who have access to different kinds of information, expertise, and authority, and who can come together to pursue their interests in many different ways.

Within this context, the nature of a school's relationships with many different constituencies and not just the degree of regulation they face from their local district plays a crucial role in how much autonomy a school can have. Whether the schools are highly regulated (like Manzanilla) or generally exempt from district regulations (like Horizons) changes the nature of their relationships with outsiders, but it does not determine whether or not the schools will demonstrate the capacity to make improvements. Horizons expended considerable time and resources in developing a productive relationship with its surrounding district in order to get resources to address the wide range of student learning needs that was at the heart of its mission. Conversely, even Manzanilla, in a highly prescriptive district, earned some flexibility in its curriculum, assessments, and professional development activities. It did so because the principal, teachers, and parents all worked hard to get waivers from district policies they considered problematic, developed their own alternative practices, and aligned themselves with local reform providers and community leaders who shared their instructional philosophy and helped them develop the social capital they needed to sustain their alternative approach.

More than the degree of regulation that schools face, the fit between their goals, instructional approaches, and organizational practices and those of the districts, organizations, and people in their immediate environment determines how much effort and what kind of work schools need to do to manage the environment. Since the instructional approaches of the more traditional schools like City and Peninsula match those of their districts, they have survived and done well while relying largely on the resources and trainings available to them through the district and made do without much external support. However, with philosophies and instructional practices that distinguish them from many other schools, Horizons, Emerson, Dewey, and Manzanilla all developed their own approaches to professional development and reached out to numerous external sources—parents, community members, educational foundations, and other support providers—to help them meet their goals.

Although they vary in the extent to which they embrace district activities and engage in work with external partners, none of these six schools are closely tied to work going on in their districts; they operate on the margins of district activities. The cost is that these schools may be left out when districts enact policies and distribute resources designed to reflect the needs of the majority of schools. But the benefit of their marginal status is that the schools may not feel as much pressure to conform to the demands that come with those offers of support: They may have some organizational slack (Hirschman, 1970; McDonald, 1996) and the flexibility to shape those demands to their own requirements.

In part, these schools managed to attain their marginal status, their flexibility, and their support from external partners because they already had some capacity to make improvements. Emerson, for example, had a distinct identity, a relatively unique progressive orientation, good relationships among teachers, and staff and community members who understood that orientation and were already connected both educationally and politically to powerful groups and individuals in the area. As a consequence, the members of Emerson were not simply waiting for support to come along. Crucial functions (often the sole province of strong leaders) like seeking funding, bringing in relevant technical expertise and personnel, and building understanding of the school's mission and approach were already distributed across a number of people. This distribution of responsibilities, in turn helped the schools find the "right" partners. These relationships with the right partners further enhanced the school's ability to negotiate with the district and to preserve the flexibility it had attained.

Many struggling schools do not have these same advantages. They are more likely to be subjected to mandates and demands that require them to put in place particular programs or accept the assistance of "turnaround specialists" or other support providers. But those struggling schools are unlikely to be able to take advantage of that assistance and adapt it to the needs of their teachers and students until they develop the capacity to manage the external environment.

PART III

CREATING THE CONDITIONS FOR SUCCESS

In the preceding chapters, I have argued that schools cannot control what goes on outside their walls, but they can help create conditions that will contribute to their success. By carrying out the key practices described in this book, school members can work to establish some consistency between external demands and expectations and their own goals and values, and they can seek out and cultivate appropriate resources and support.

Schools can use these practices to calibrate or "tune" their performance (McDonald, 1996). The passage of time, changes in the supply of teachers, shifts in policies and public expectations can all result in schools becoming out of tune with their surroundings or can put pressures on schools that contribute to mission drift or break down common understandings or relationships among members of the school community. Under these circumstances, tightening the mission by rearticulating it and ensuring that the members of the school community understand it can make it clearer to job candidates and staff members whether or not their ideas fit with those of the school, provide a basis for making decisions about how and when to manage external demands, and enable schools to reestablish collective work. Or school members can change practices to be more in step with the times by focusing their efforts on hiring and developing new staff who may then help to establish a new mission. Similarly, investing more time and energy in building trust and in supporting the exchange of ideas among staff may minimize the need to focus specifically on rearticulating the mission.

How much time, energy, and resources schools have to spend on each of the key organizational practices depends on the fit between their approach and the goals and practices endorsed in policies, programs, and public discussions around them. As the examples in this book illustrate, schools like City and Peninsula, with more traditional approaches consistent with surrounding expectations and relatively good performance in the first place, may be able to get by without formal efforts to build understanding, manage hiring, or foster collaborative work, and without seeking additional resources and support. Yet members of schools like Dewey, Emerson, Horizons, and

Manzanilla–schools that take more unconventional approaches or schools that are struggling in the first place–cannot get by with such informal approaches. They need to create organizational structures and spend time in formal, collaborative efforts to build their capacity, make improvements, and sustain those efforts over time.

From this perspective, instead of a set amount of resources or a discrete set of abilities, school capacity is a function of the resources available and the demands that exist at any given time. Just as the analogy to managing the water supply described in Chapter 1 showed that conservation efforts have to take into account the changing conditions in the external environment, approaches to improvement need to consider what's going on outside school walls:

- How are students and parents likely to change?
- Where are good new teachers likely to come from?
- What new expertise or resources might become available?
- How are budgets likely to shift?
- What new policies are in the offing?

Dealing with these external conditions and making improvements on a wide scale entails work on both a local and national level. On a local level, some schools can use the key practices to try to create the "right" conditions, but improving the schools experiencing the most difficulties–those that may not have the capacity to carry out these key practices–may have to begin in the surrounding neighborhoods, towns, and cities, and draw on other sources of support.

That local work, however, remains constrained by the broader national context in which schools operate. As a consequence, efforts to build capacity in schools and their communities can also be enhanced by rethinking some of the fundamental assumptions that underlie many of the policies and reform initiatives pursued across the country. That national work needs to shift the focus from the quick implementation of a constantly changing roster of initiatives to the development and support of the basic organizational functions that enable schools to manage the demands and opportunities around them.

Chapter 7

Working to Build Local Capacity

Large-scale educational reform efforts have always struggled to deal with the fact that schools and districts face vastly different circumstances and vary widely in their capacity to make improvements and reach their goals. While some schools may be capable of carrying out comprehensive reform efforts that address many aspects of their operations at once, most schools cannot. Others may need to begin with more focused efforts that concentrate on one or two key strategies or one or two aspects of the organization before attempting more significant changes. Still other schools may be so overwhelmed that even limited efforts seem beyond their capabilities.

As a consequence, rather than one-size-fits-all policies and approaches, the work to improve schools needs to take into account each school's capacities and build on whatever strengths and assets each school has. Even in the most difficult circumstances, there are usually some bright spots—some people, some programs, some classrooms, some initiatives, some existing relationships—that demonstrate potential. These assets serve as the leading edge of capacity: places where work inside the school might be able to begin and where work already underway might be extended. For schools in the most difficult circumstances, those that have struggled repeatedly to make improvements, however, it makes more sense to look for the leading edge of capacity on the outside—in the places, programs, and people alongside the school who may eventually be able to support the work going on inside. That means taking advantage of the resources and opportunities that may exist for community and neighborhood development and viewing them as an integral basis of the work of school improvement.

WORKING INSIDE THE SCHOOL

When school members focus their attention on the inside, they need to envision work that is both focused and broad: work that provides a clear sense of priorities but also takes into account who will do the work and what support they will need to do it. When school members are engaged in work both focused and broad, they should be able to answer concisely three sets of questions (see Figure 7.1):

- What's the focus, and what's the work?
- Who will do it, and why will they do it?
- What support will those people need, and where will it come from?

Furthermore, school members need to understand the intimate connection between all three: developing a focus and defining the work can't be done without a sense of whether or not there are personnel who will embrace the vision and do the work; and determining who can do the work depends on understanding the kind of support that could be available. Thus, although many reform efforts focus on finding the right leaders, what those leaders do, not simply who they are, determines whether or not their efforts to improve schools will be successful:

- How can leaders take advantage of–or create–structures to build shared understanding around a common focus?
- How can they find or identify staff members whose skills and interests fit that focus?
- How can they organize the work environment so that staff members can get the resources and develop and share the expertise they need?

Initiatives that seek to build a broader and more explicit understanding of common goals at a school like Peninsula, for example, will founder if those efforts alienate key staff and there is no system for replacing them with those who are a better fit. At a school like Emerson, the challenges might run in the opposite direction. With numerous structures and mechanisms for sustaining shared understanding and developing collective expertise, the overwhelming burden of work and responsibilities outside the classroom also contributed to high turnover rates among the staff. That turnover then created pressures to maintain, if not increase, the number of meetings and collaborative activities. As one of the school's advisors from the Bay Area Coalition for Equitable Schools put it, if they're "dependent on single women without families who can stay until 8 o'clock 4 nights a week, that's not a sustainable way to run a school." Thus, at Emerson, building a more stable staff might mean streamlining and redistributing the workload and reducing the emphasis on collaboration. But school members have to remain aware that stability in staffing might come at the expense of the shared understanding and collective expertise that helped to fuel Emerson's improvements, and they need to be prepared to ratchet up those collaborative activities again sometime in the future.

In cases like these, school leaders can't be afraid to act, but they have to do so with a sense of what the repercussions will be and how they might deal with them down the road. Leaders have to have the confidence that they are

Figure 7.1. The Triangle of School Improvement

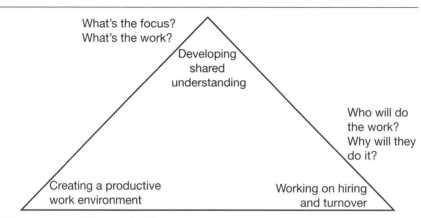

What's the focus?
What's the work?

Developing
shared
understanding

Who will do
the work?
Why will they
do it?

Creating a productive
work environment

Working on hiring
and turnover

What support will be needed?
Where will it come from?

doing what's right (Kanter, 2004). That confidence helps to sustain motivation and momentum even when improvement seems impossible and failure inevitable.

At the same time, there is a fine line between passionate commitment and blind persistence. Passionate commitment can accommodate different points of view, entertain alternatives, and take into account feedback and previously unanticipated setbacks and opportunities. At Dewey, Charlene Moore embraced many different ways for staff members to develop their classroom practices and share their expertise; but she never wavered in her belief that they should all exemplify the "Dewey way." Even when the superintendent mandated the adoption of the new report card, Moore was willing to compromise and improve Dewey's assessment system without giving up on what she saw as key aspects of Dewey's child-centered approach. In the process, Moore was committed to staying the course but was aware that she might not have all the answers and that room for improvement remained.

Some sense of the answers to all three sets of questions produces triangulated reform strategies that enable different schools to approach improvement in ways that respond to local circumstances. For example, Horizons's strengths included the fact that it had addressed "what" and "who." The school had established a clear and distinct mission and put in place a committed staff. But even with an extensive professional development structure, it continued to struggle with "how": how to develop the instructional practices to meet the needs of all learners. Under these circumstances, Horizons might benefit the most from gaining access to more effective professional development related to learning differences than from any change that could be made on the inside. On the other hand, until it can find that expertise, it may have to rely on its own efforts to bring staff together to reflect on, coordinate, and improve the work.

In contrast, even schools like Peninsula and City that appear to be successful but have few collaborative arrangements may benefit from the development of new mechanisms to foster the development of collective expertise and common work. But those efforts are unlikely to take off unless all involved perceive some common interest or compelling reason to work together. That may require getting more insiders out to learn about new developments and inviting outsiders in who can help to apply pressure and identify areas where further improvements may be possible. Rather than a new leader who brings a new vision or launches an ambitious new reform effort, this kind of school might benefit from a leader like Fredericksen, well-connected and knowledgeable about the educational community outside the school, who can slowly help open them up to productive external forces.

Along with addressing who, what, and how, school leaders need to think about "when": They have to have a sense of when work can begin productively, and they have to have in mind goals and visions that can actually be achieved in a reasonable period of time. If they pursue ambitious visions that initially seem far out of reach, they need to articulate the goals and steps to be accomplished along the way. As the experiences of schools like Emerson, Dewey, Horizons, Manzanilla, City, and Peninsula demonstrate, however, even for schools that have some capacity to make improvements, envisioning reasonable goals and achieving them is extremely hard work.

Pursuing ambitious reform efforts in schools that have little or no capacity to make improvements is an even more dangerous proposition. If leaders can't define what the work is, who will do it, and how it will be accomplished in ways that respect and reflect a school's circumstances and the external conditions, launching an ambitious reform effort can lead to a cycle of failure that can be much more destructive than not doing anything at all (see Figure 7.2; March, 1991). Building shared understanding of a powerful vision or ambitious goals can raise hopes and help to move work forward, but only if the people involved also have the expertise and motivation to pursue that vision and meet those goals. Getting people in place who have some of the needed expertise and motivation may help to get things started, but failure to provide the support that can lead to some initial success can erode their belief in the vision and goals and limit their ability to learn from and improve their performance. Then the raised expectations and inability to meet them can contribute to turnover and make it harder for the school to attract the capable help and support it needs. When that happens, what should be a powerful foundation for improvement ends up reinforc-

Figure 7.2. The Cycle of Failure

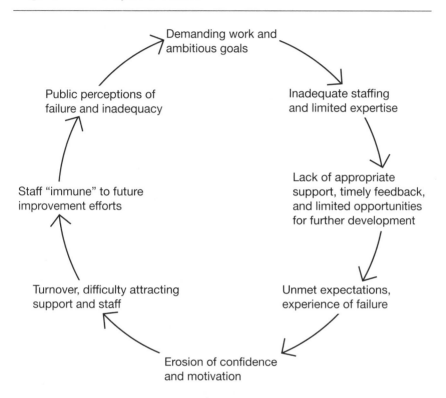

ing negative perceptions and contributes to the problems the improvement efforts were supposed to solve. This cycle of failure naturally leads individuals within an organization to become jaded and immune to the entreaties of future leaders no matter how compelling the visions or goals they offer (Little, 1996).

Given these dangers, avoiding the cycle of failure is as important as building the capacity for improvement. But that is no excuse for doing nothing; it means that in some cases work has to begin in the surrounding communities, towns, and cities instead.

WORKING ALONGSIDE THE SCHOOL

When repeated efforts to improve a school fail, then it makes more sense to turn the attention to finding and building capacity on the outside. Moving

---

**Allocations for Facilities and Children's and Youth Programs
Nationally and in One State (California)**

At the federal level:

- Over $33 billion was allocated for school construction projects in
  public and private K–12 schools in 2006 (National Clearinghouse for
  Educational Facilities, 2008)
- $11 billion was allocated for child-care subsidies from federal sources in
  2004 (Kreader, 2005).
- Over $1 billion was appropriated ($2.5 billion authorized) through the
  No Child Left Behind Act for funding of after-school programs through
  the 21st Century Community Learning Centers initiative (After-School
  Alliance, 2005).

In California:

- Over $35 billion was approved by voters to help build and maintain school
  facilities in California from 1998 to 2006 (EdSource, 2008a).
- $3.1 billion was proposed for child-care and development programs (birth
  to age 12) in California in 2008–09 (California Legislative Analysts Office,
  2008).
- $550 million was authorized for annual expenditures on after-school
  programs in California through Proposition 49, the After-School Education
  and Safety Program Act (Afterschool Alliance, 2005).

---

outside the school means changing the focus from school improvement to
community development. School members can still play a role, but community and youth groups, politicians, local philanthropies, congregations,
and others also need to step to the forefront to develop initiatives that can
serve as a source of support and a springboard for later work on the inside.
In doing so, the leaders of these community initiatives need to look beyond
the "what," "who," "how," and "when" of school-based improvement efforts
and ask "where" neighborhood development efforts are most likely to be
successful.

Following the example of community organizers, these efforts can begin
by identifying people from all walks of life who have leadership potential
and then bringing them together to identify common interests that they can
address in a reasonable period of time. These efforts help to locate the "latent
capacity" in the area and to establish the expertise, resources, and commitment that can serve as the foundation for the development of social capital.
Finding and building on the capacity in the surrounding community also provides the best chance to achieve the kinds of "quick wins" and "small victo-

ries" that give hope and help build motivation for and commitment to the improvement efforts that need to take place inside schools (Kanter, 2004).

Where to Begin?

Community organizing initiatives that focus on enhancing the physical environment, establishing local programs for children and youth, and developing the local workforce, in particular, may help to create the kind of foundation even schools in the most difficult circumstances need to begin building capacity.

Facilities and the Physical Environment. Improving the physical environment either inside or outside the school provides a reasonable goal that can help launch work in any community. In fact, many of the visionary and successful leaders of large corporations and major organizations that Kanter (2004) chronicles begin their efforts to turn around and improve their organizations with this same attention to the local environment: They paint the hallways, fix the physical plant, or update the offices, creating a better atmosphere and signaling that better times lie ahead.

Of course, most school and community leaders don't have the same budget flexibility that many CEOs do, but even without any money, community members can usually pull together a few people and some materials and make a difference by cleaning up a vacant lot, painting a wall, repairing broken windows, planting a garden, or fixing a playground. In addition, scheduled repair and building projects in the school also provide opportunities—and funds—that can be used strategically to jump-start work in schools. These efforts bring people together in ways that can help develop common interests and trust. They provide concrete demonstrations that improvements can be made, and they create places and spaces that foster positive and productive activities.

Programs. Beyond improving the local physical environment, efforts by community members to establish local day-care, preschool, after-school, and youth programs also produce numerous collateral benefits for schools. First, these programs can provide support for children's development that prepares them for success in school. Good day-care and preschool programs can support early language and literacy development and can help identify learning issues even before children reach kindergarten. They can ease the transition from home to school and create opportunities for social development and positive interactions with peers. Good after-school and recreational programs can expose children to the arts, sports, music, nature, and other activities that they may not have opportunities to pursue in schools. They can also create safe and supportive environments where students can spend their time. Similarly, effective youth programs can introduce students to college-level and real-world activities and experiences that help prepare them for life and work beyond school. Second, these programs provide support for parents, guardians, and other family members. With more day-care and after-school activities, family members have more time to spend developing their own careers, managing their own lives and families, and participating in other activities (including school-based events and other kinds of community work).

People. Work on improving the physical environment and the number and quality of programs for children in a neighborhood also creates opportunities to build the local workforce. With foresight and careful planning, some of these local initiatives could be designed to provide employment or training for people in the community. Meaningful job opportunities in programs for children and youth can help attract workers and volunteers to the area. In turn, this expansion of the local educational workforce can strengthen the local labor pool for schools and create a larger cadre of people who know the students and who can play key roles in school improvement efforts as staff members or volunteers.

Next Steps

In the same kind of snowball effect that can help schools to expand their networks and build social capital, the more good programs there are in a community, the more opportunities there are for community members to develop relevant skills and expertise. Similarly, developing new programs creates a demand for more and better facilities and can help attract the funds needed to improve the physical environment. In turn, better facilities can help improve programs and create the conditions that make it easier to keep and attract people who have relevant skills and expertise.

In a sense, this approach is like the effort to strengthen one part of the body like the knee. Any effort to work on the knee has to include the surrounding muscles—quadriceps, hamstring, calf, and hip—that can help develop leg strength. Particularly for those whose knees are weak, exercises aimed directly at the knee can cause further damage and can only begin slowly after working on the muscles around the knee. From this perspective, the school is just one of a set of related places, programs, and institutions outside the home where children spend their time. Strengthening all of them can help develop resources, personnel, relationships, and social capital that schools can draw on down the line to help them build the capacity for improvement.

Although the need and demand for investments in improving local facilities and developing children's and youth programs far outstrips the supply, significant funds are already being spent in these areas. Community leaders

Limits on the Capacity for Improving Schools

In 2005–06, out of roughly 100,000 public schools, over 11,000 or 12% of all schools were identified as "in need of improvement" according to the criteria of NCLB (Stullich, Eisner, & McCrary, 2007). At the time, roughly 600 schools had experienced repeated failures to reach their performance targets and were designated as "in need of restructuring." By 2010, projections based on these numbers suggest that almost 5,000 schools, serving more than 2,500,000 students, will be "in need of restructuring" (Calkins, Guenther, Belfiore, & Lash, 2007).

The evaluation of the implementation of NCLB commissioned by the U.S. Department of Education (Stullich et al., 2007) showed that support for schools "in need of improvement" was a moderate or serious challenge in most states. The specific challenges reported by states included the inadequacy of

State educational agency staff size (45 states)
State funds (40 states)
Federal funds allocated for state implementation (39 states)
State educational agency staff expertise (30 states)

In terms of district support, the report found that although schools identified for improvement often experienced a higher level of support than nonidentified schools, many districts failed to provide some of the assistance that identified schools were promised. In 2004–05, for example, 30% of districts with identified schools said they provided no assistance with identifying effective curricula, instructional strategies, or school reform models, and 13% of identified districts provided no assistance in analyzing assessment results, despite NCLB requirements to do so.

Furthermore, high-poverty districts with identified schools reported significant problems in providing support:

49% lacked needed expertise
46% lacked the necessary staff
56% lacked sufficient time
80% lacked sufficient money

The report concluded that, on the one hand, its findings show the widespread implementation of many of the accountability systems of NCLB, but on the other hand, also point "to limitations in the extent to which these may reach all low-performing schools" (p. 85).

need to use these funds strategically as a launching pad and complement for school-based improvement efforts.

Given that federal and state funds are unlikely to meet all needs, other sources for investing in communities need to be found. The emergence of a whole series of new ventures and new organizations dedicated to social entrepreneurship may help to make up some of the shortfall. Like entrepreneurs in business, social entrepreneurs seek to fund and develop new organizations, activities, and resources, but they focus on a social return—beneficial impact on the community—rather than a financial one. Social entrepreneurs have launched organizations like Teach for America and New Leaders for New Schools, for example, that focus specifically on helping develop the personnel and human capital needed to improve schools (see Hess, 2006, for one discussion of social entrepreneurship and education). Social entrepreneurs have also helped to create organizations like City Year and Citizen Schools whose work focuses specifically on creating and supporting the kinds of children's and youth programs that can improve the conditions in neighborhoods and towns around the country.

Those social entrepreneurs that focus on developing youth and children's programs outside the regular school system have the added advantage that they do not face the same bureaucratic and organizational constraints or public expectations that have frustrated educators for years. Under these circumstances, social entrepreneurs may find unusual opportunities to support the development of a series of organizations and small programs with some dedicated to early childhood programs and others concentrating on after-school and youth programs. Social entrepreneurs might also pursue opportunities to focus on the development of the people and resources needed to run these programs effectively. In conjunction with Lesley University in Massachusetts, for example, Citizen Schools has already established a National Teaching Fellowship Program that enables program leaders to get a master's degree in out-of-school learning. With qualified staff for child care, after-school, and other youth programs in short supply, the involvement of these kinds of organizations in the communities around struggling schools may serve as another crucial means of building the local educational workforce.

Implications for School Improvement

When communities improve the local environment, establish new programs, expand meaningful work, and attract social entrepreneurs, they may create what researchers in business refer to as "clusters": geographic concentrations of interconnected organizations, suppliers, and service providers in a particular field (Porter, 2000). Ideally, these clusters can help stimulate productivity, foster innovation, and spawn new organizations.

While there are no guarantees that local conditions will improve, these kinds of investments in the physical environment and in children's and youth programs are much more likely to lead to beneficial "collateral impact"—indirect local benefits—than many school-focused reform efforts. The contrasts between prominent school turn-around efforts and efforts to build support for school improvement efforts in the local community illustrate the trade-offs. In California, for example, the Immediate Intervention Underperforming Schools Program (IIUSP), launched initially in 1998, and the No Child Left Behind (NCLB) Act prescribe a specific set of steps to take when schools consistently fail to improve their performance. Both processes begin by notifying parents and members of the community that the school is low-performing, enlisting outside experts who are supposed to provide technical assistance, establishing an "action plan" that will lead to the accomplishment of short-term goals, and providing some funds (on the order of $50,000–$100,000) to pay for that technical assistance and carry out the plan. Although the IIUSP and NCLB approaches differ in their details, if growth targets are not met and improvements are not made within the next few years, another series of consequences kicks in, including allowing students to attend any public school in which space is available; requiring the provision of supplemental services such as tutoring; allowing parents to apply to create a charter school on the school site; enabling the state to reassign management of the school to another organization; and reorganizing or closing the school.

Both these approaches rely heavily on finding appropriate outside technical assistance and developing an action plan, but provide little support in doing so. The expectation is that struggling schools can find and get good technical assistance, and those who provide the technical assistance have the power to bring school community members together around a plan in ways those schools have never been able to accomplish before. In a sense, in order to build capacity in a particular school, these efforts seek to *borrow* capacity by importing people, resources, and expertise from somewhere else (see Elmore 2006 for a related discussion).

Rather than beginning by labeling schools as "failures," community development approaches can begin by looking at the challenges and opportunities in the physical environment and other aspects of the community outside the school. For example, community leaders might target available construction and repair funds from the district, city, state, or federal government to identify and make some immediate improvements in either the school facilities themselves or other places in the surrounding neighborhood. (Ideally, at least some of these initial investments could be made for far less than the $50,000–100,000 allocated to pay for outside technical assistance in the IIUSP and NCLB approaches.) This work on the local physical environment could be carried out by or in conjunction with neighborhood organizations that can use it to engage a wider group of people and build a broader constituency for improvements. Ideally, that growing constituency could then draw on local businesses, foundations, and social entrepreneurs to supply some of the capital, resources, and people needed to establish or expand local day-care, preschool, or after-school programs.

Once these projects aimed at the physical environment and local youth and children's programs begin to show some progress, work on the local school may be able to begin. Most likely, struggling schools will still need considerable technical assistance from outside groups, and they might benefit from new leaders, new instructional approaches, and some changes in staff. Or members of the community may be interested in establishing a new small school or a charter school. However, in any case, the community should be in a better position to play a part in those efforts and the school may be in a stronger position to use any outside assistance more effectively. Furthermore, these local improvements can create a more promising context for attracting (and retaining) the highest quality school leaders, educational support providers, and school staff available. These community development efforts can ignite the hope that something can be done, and help to provide the means to do it, without adding the kinds of demands and expectations that lead to the cycles of failure for schools that try to make it on their own.

Of course the need for new facilities, preschool programs, and youth programs far exceeds the funding available and extends far beyond the reach of the current generation of social entrepreneurs. The needs in many schools and in many neighborhoods are so significant that any universal and national efforts seem far beyond comprehension (although the amounts spent on the war in Iraq and the bailout of the financial sector seem incomprehensible as well). But viewed at the local level, the available funds and existing organizations provide crucial opportunities to improve the environment outside of schools and to break the cycle of failure in which far too many schools are trapped.

Chapter 8

Working Nationally to Create a More Supportive Educational Environment

While efforts to build the capacity of schools can begin locally, policy makers, funders, and others involved in education on a national level can play a constructive role in the process. In order to do so, however, they too need to keep in mind the paradox that it takes capacity to build capacity and recognize that well-intentioned efforts that fail to address what it actually takes to improve schools can be counterproductive. That means coming to terms with a series of long-standing myths that can promote a simplistic view of school reform and confronting the conventional expectations that make it hard to develop more supportive conditions for sustained and long-lasting improvements in schooling.

FOUR MYTHS OF SCHOOL REFORM

MYTH 1: *The educational system in the United States has the capacity to significantly improve instruction for all students; people just need to figure out how to unleash it.*

A Nation at Risk (National Commission on Excellence in Education, 1983), the report whose identification of a "rising tide of mediocrity" helped launch reform efforts in the 1980s, reflected this myth when it stated that "the essential raw materials needed to reform our educational system are waiting to be mobilized through effective leadership" (p. 15). This same assumption was reflected in some of the initial efforts to implement systemic reform in the 1990s that implied that aligning policies, incentives, and supports and streamlining the bureaucracy could unleash some previously hidden capacity that would enable all students to learn at high levels (Fuhrman, 1990b). Some of the recent efforts to develop small schools also proceed in ways that suggest that smaller schools and smaller classes and better relationships

165

between teachers and students will, on their own, equip previously unsuccessful teachers with the knowledge and skills necessary to enable all their students to reach high levels of achievement (Kahn, Sporte, de la Torre, & Easton, 2008). Policies like some of those contained in the No Child Left Behind legislation that focus on regulations, compliance, and testing with little or no investment in the development of the knowledge and skills needed to achieve meaningful learning goals also imply that teachers and schools know what to do to make improvements, they just need to be encouraged—or forced—to do it.

The turbulent conditions that schools face; the serious constraints on the resources, time, and people available; and the significant demands and expectations schools have to meet, create challenges that cannot simply be ignored. Even the best schools have to work hard to make improvements, and most need some kinds of outside support to achieve it. After a long career working for the most part in well-known private schools, Paul Archer called the faculty at Horizons the best he had ever worked with; but they were telling him, "I know what I want to accomplish. I know what the mission is. I know what I'm being asked to do in terms of having the kids succeed. I don't know how to do it." Even when the school turned to an expert Archer described as the "best thinker on learning differences," it turned into "a disaster" because the expert couldn't provide the kind of practical support the faculty needed. When one teacher asked the expert to think through how to approach a situation in a particular class, according to Archer "[the expert] didn't even know; he said, 'That's really interesting. . . .' And that isn't what the faculty wanted to hear." Subsequently, the school brought in specialists from one of the foremost colleges focused on learning differences to lead a day and a half of professional development, but again, it was a mixed success because the college was still struggling to address many of the issues Horizons' teachers were facing. In short, Horizons had the capacity to get the best professional development available; but even with the best professional development available, Horizons still did not have the capacity to meet the learning needs of all their students.

Schools like Emerson and Manzanilla, with larger concentrations of students from disadvantaged communities, faced similar capacity problems. The commitment, dedication, and long hours of the members of those schools would impress any visitor. These schools were focused on issues of equity and the achievement gap before NCLB came along, and they were well connected to some of the leading local and national organizations working on these issues as well. As a consequence, they had access to some of the latest information and to some of the best local and national expertise, but even those connections could not provide any easy answers. These schools and their collaborators faced problems of invention, not just implementation:

There were no already-established curricula or well-documented approaches that could guarantee the success of their students or ensure the closing of the achievement gap.

Illustrating these difficulties, even with all the calls for schools to use "research-based" practices and all the laments that schools do not take advantage of the latest research, in fact, educational research rarely provides clear and unambiguous guides for practice. The *What Works Clearinghouse* (Institute of Education Sciences, 2008), for example, established in 2002 by the U.S. Department of Education's Institute of Education Sciences, seeks to provide the most up-to-date reviews of research and guides for practice in key areas. By 2008, the *Clearinghouse* offered reports on approaches to eight different issues including beginning reading, character education, and dropout prevention. While these reports identify some practices in different areas that seem to have good evidence of effectiveness, the reports make it clear that for most practices there is usually more limited or mixed evidence of success, if there is any evidence at all. With only eight areas addressed so far, every day teachers have to teach complex subjects like writing, literature, mathematics, social studies, history, the arts, and basic and advanced sciences where there is relatively little specific and definitive research on what works with students at different levels, from different backgrounds, and with different learning needs.

Even if numerous questions about "what works" remain, however, it would be a mistake to conclude that there is no useful knowledge or information to guide practice. Too often reformers split into two camps with some arguing for the need to build capacity and provide more support for schools and teachers, and others arguing that schools need to be much more efficient and that teachers just need to be given the right incentives to work harder and do what needs to be done. To some extent, both are right. Even if schools and teachers do not have all the support they need, that does not mean that every school is working at "full capacity"—working as efficiently and effectively as they could be with the available resources. Focusing on one or the other won't work. Improving schools takes both greater efficiency and greater capacity.

MYTH 2: *If a school makes some improvements and hits some performance targets in one year, the school has the capacity to continue to make meaningful improvements in instruction over time.*

Reaching meaningful goals and outcomes deserves celebration. But there are many different ways to reach short-term goals and outcomes, and some of them can actually undermine the ability of an organization to sustain performance and to reach long-term performance goals. Professional sports teams demonstrate the tensions between short- and long-term outcomes as they try to balance the needs of creating a strong system for developing younger players and for getting the best players on the field at a given time. For example, a team may load up on high-priced, established stars in order to reach the playoffs and win the championship; but that same team may pay a price when those veterans retire or move on to other teams if the younger players have not had enough support and enough playing time to develop and carry the team to the championship in the future. The simple fact that a team reached the championship in one year does not mean they have the capacity to sustain such a high level of performance and reach the playoffs year in and year out.

Similarly, performance targets that give schools incentives to make quick improvements can lead to several superficial responses that inhibit long-term performance. First, schools may take too narrow a focus and may concentrate solely on making improvements on test items. For example, schools that drill students on test items repeatedly or that place their best teachers in grades and subjects where students are tested might produce a rise in test scores. However, those responses may not give students the opportunities and experiences they need to succeed in later grades and in college. Furthermore, these quick-fix strategies are unlikely to improve the quality or effectiveness of the faculty as a whole.

Second, rather than leading schools to put forth maximum effort, performance incentives that are either too low or too high may discourage many staff members from trying at all (Mintrop, 2003). If school members do not know what to do to significantly improve their students' performance or do not feel their students can perform at high levels, then even substantial rewards are unlikely to motivate them to do anything other than finds ways to "game the system." Similarly, performance targets that are too low also provide few incentives for schools that already meet those targets to do anything differently.

Third, improving enough to meet some performance targets does not necessarily mean that a school will continue to improve and develop the capacity to hit higher targets in the future. While making some improvements in average performance on standardized tests is a significant accomplishment, it does not mean that a school is necessarily on the way to meeting the needs of all learners, closing achievement gaps, or enabling students to develop deep understanding of key concepts. When *A Nation at Risk* was published in 1983, it emphasized that the key education goals should focus on enabling all students to reach "world-class standards" in major subject areas like English, mathematics, the sciences, and history. At least in part, the difficulty in reaching these ambitious goals has tempered expectations and contributed to the development of the narrower goals in the No Child Left Behind legislation.

Now, instead of "world-class standards" in multiple subjects, schools have to set their sights on enabling students to make "average yearly progress" primarily on tests of reading and math skills. But even if NCLB's goals are achieved, there is little evidence to suggest that those schools that do achieve average yearly progress in reading and mathematics will somehow also be on the way to achieving world-class standards in any subject.

Given these problems, funders, policy makers, and others need to recognize that specifying narrow outcomes and monitoring and holding schools responsible for them often creates short-term demands that many schools do not have the capacity to meet. Such short-term pressures may make it particularly difficult for low-performing schools to make the long-term investments in the basic organizational practices of managing staff, maintaining a productive work environment, and developing common understanding that contribute to a school's capacity to make improvements and sustain them.

MYTH 3: *The way to improve the system as a whole is to "scale up" the successes of individual programs and schools around the country*

While articles and books document many examples of individual schools that have succeeded and excelled under difficult circumstances, the primary problem is that too many other schools have not. In response, many reformers propose "scaling up" the successes they have achieved in individual schools by identifying key features, practices, and resources and replicating them in other schools around the country. This strategy is reflected in the work of many of the comprehensive reform programs and small school networks that attempt to put in place a particular model of schooling in a number of different communities. In many cases, these efforts reflect common practices in business in which companies try to expand on the success of stores or products in one neighborhood by introducing those stores and products into new contexts.

In education, however, despite the remarkable achievements that some networks have made, successes that spill over into thousands of schools remain elusive, and an extensive research literature chronicles the problems and challenges that many school reform organizations have faced when they try to scale up (see, for example, Bodilly, 1998; Datnow, Hubbard, & Mehen, 2002). In part, these problems reflect the inability of many scale-up efforts in education to address and re-create on a much wider basis the external conditions and resources that enable some schools to be successful. In business, the type of store and the character of products matter, but stores and products that are successful in one neighborhood or community—like Wal-Mart stores in the United States for example—may encounter significant problems when they try to expand in a very different context—like Wal-Mart stores in China (Gogoi, 2005; Huffman, 2003). In other words, the challenge for business goes beyond producing or scaling up more stores and products; the challenge includes finding and creating the markets and the conditions in which those stores and products can be successful.

Similarly, the experiences of schools like Dewey, Emerson, City, Peninsula, Horizons, and Manzanilla suggest that in part their ability to make improvements comes from the fact that they have distinguished themselves from others, escaped from burdensome requirements and inflexible monitoring, and captured scarce resources including such things as effective teachers, strong leaders, high-quality professional development, capable external assistance, adequate facilities, political influence, and foundation support. In most cases, these are not conditions and resources that can be scaled up. Many other schools cannot substantially improve their performance until those conditions and resources are more widely available and more equitably distributed. As a consequence, any attempt to scale up successful programs has to be accompanied by a concerted effort to create more favorable economic, organizational, social, and political conditions that will give *all* schools a better chance to manage the external environment and make improvements.

MYTH 4: *School choice and competition for students will create conditions that lead to innovation and improved performance in many schools.*

Arguments over school choice often boil down to whether or not school choice will increase competitive pressures among schools and contribute to improved outcomes. These debates, however, often fail to take into consideration the many aspects of choice and competition that affect an organization's performance. As explained in the final report of the National Working Commission on Choice in K–12 Education (2003), whether or not choice contributes to improved outcomes depends on a host of issues including parents' access to information, their ability to make "good" choices, the availability of suitable alternatives, and the personal as well as economic costs of moving students to another school. For one thing, students and parents may choose to attend a school for many different reasons—location, population of students, sports and other extracurricular opportunities, course offerings, size, schedule—reasons that are not necessarily linked to improved academic outcomes.

In addition, even when parents and students can choose schools, those schools remain dependent on the resources, personnel, and support providers in the local area. In areas where local resources and supports are inadequate, schools' responses to the competition for students will likely focus on superficial changes in themes, mission statements, program offerings, and

The Limits of Choice

- In 2004–05, 5.2 million students were eligible to transfer to higher performing schools because they attended Title 1 schools that failed to make adequate yearly progress under NCLB, but only 48,000 students participated, approximately 1% of the eligible participants (Stullich, Eisner, McCrary, & Roney, 2006).
- In 2003–04, 270,757 students in Chicago were eligible for transfer, 19,246 applied, approximately 7% of those eligible, and the district only placed 1,097 students, less than 1% (Hassel & Steiner, 2004).
- In 2004–05, 6,200 schools were required to offer their students the option to go elsewhere, but 39% of those schools did not.
- Twenty percent of the schools required to provide choice also reported that there were no higher performing schools available for their students to attend (Bathon & Spradlin, 2007; Stullich et al., 2006)
- Fifty-eight percent of the schools required to offer choice but not doing so were high schools, but 75% of all high schools are in districts with no other high schools (Bathon & Spradlin, 2007; Stullich et al., 2006).

other aspects of the organization without addressing the core of instruction. In other words, in addition to limits on their ability to choose, students and parents often lack meaningful choices (Hill, 2005).

This conundrum illustrates an often overlooked aspect of competition in the choice debates: competition over resources. Regardless of whether or not students and parents have a choice of schools, limited resources, difficult external conditions, and public perceptions of what counts as "real" school (Metz, 1990) constrain schools' abilities to provide innovative alternatives. Moreover, as illustrated by the experiences of the schools in this book, schools that capture scarce resources may be able to maintain a competitive advantage over others. For example, schools that establish partnerships with the best local teacher education programs may find it easier to get effective teachers. In turn, the effectiveness of those teachers, in turn, can make those schools even more attractive to other effective teachers, and less successful schools will have a harder time getting access to the same quality of personnel. In this scenario, choice reinforces the status quo rather than stimulating innovation, and it exacerbates the disparities that make it difficult for low-performing schools to make improvements.

While a growing demand for more effective teachers and better resources, facilities, and other forms of support might help increase the supply, exactly how that might happen remains to be seen. At this point, the possible effects of choice on the conditions in which schools operate require much more investigation. As Paul Hill, Chairman of the National Working Commission on

Choice in K–12 Education, describes it:

> No serious business would adopt a whole new corporate strategy without understanding its customers, supply chain, technical challenges, start-up costs, and competitive environment. But, in the absence of serious nuts-and-bolts [research and development], that is what communities that adopt choice, a profoundly different strategy for providing public education, are forced to do. (Hill, 2005, p. 149)

FROM SHORT-TERM DEMANDS TO LONG-TERM SUPPORT

Coming to terms with these myths of school reform can help policy makers, funders, and other members of the educational establishment shift the focus from implementing policies and scaling up programs to helping schools develop and maintain the basic organizational functions that enable them to manage the demands and opportunities around them. In this view, establishing and sustaining stable funding streams over time is far more important than infusing the system with funds when times are good and demanding cuts in budgets when times are bad. Similarly, tying new funding to new initiatives (and new demands) won't work unless schools and districts have in place some of the people, mechanisms, and external relationships that will allow them to build shared understanding, find qualified staff, and get appropriate professional development when they need to.

Establishing different policy and assessment contexts may also help take into account the fact that different conditions support increases in efficiency and the development of innovations. Clearer goals, tighter monitoring, and increased incentives can improve efficiency, particularly in circumstances where the knowledge and resources to meet those goals are available but not used or implemented well. However, when knowledge and resources are not available, in order to develop innovative approaches, schools may need more support and more latitude rather than tighter controls and more demands for more results in less time. Innovative efforts can still benefit from good assessments providing useful feedback on key indicators, but they also need a significant time period that allows for experimentation and improvement without immediate penalties.

While one could argue that some arrangements for charter schools and other alternative schools provide these conditions, the demands of getting new schools up and running in short periods of time and responding to conventional expectations can constrain their development as well. In fact, the very efforts to spread and scale up any successes can lead to the kinds of top-down pressures and tighter monitoring that constrain innovation and bring any alternatives closer to the status quo. The effort to replicate the success of an innovative school creates one more organization that produces more demands and expectations that other schools have to manage.

Given the constraints of conventional expectations, creating conditions that foster significant innovation also depends on developing a better understanding of effective instruction and addressing public perceptions of what "real schools" (Metz, 1990) and "good teaching" look like. Public understanding serves as a crucial driver of many of the demands that schools face. If schools like Dewey and Emerson or even charter schools like Horizons try to make changes that parents and other local educators do not understand, then they have to devote more time, attention, and resources to managing the external environment. Conversely, even if schools do not always perform at the highest levels or enable all of their students to reach high levels of achievement, many schools, particularly schools in more advantaged communities, can satisfy public demands by continuing to operate in ways that conform to public expectations.

If the wider public does not demand a teaching force that truly delivers high-quality instruction to all students or one that produces high levels of learning for all students, describing most teaching as "high quality" and labeling low levels of performance as "proficient" or "adequate" will continue to suffice. To address these conventional expectations, policy makers and funders have to go far beyond the usual efforts to publicize data on school performance or sway public opinion on education. They need to support the development of opportunities for parents and the wider public to see what goes on in classrooms and to develop an understanding of what it takes to enable all students to reach meaningful educational goals (Hatch, 2006).

In contrast to top-down, technical efforts that focus on aligning disparate parts of the educational system, these developments could enable schools to play a more effective role in coordinating the supports, demands, and expectations in the external environment and crafting more coherent instructional approaches (Honig & Hatch, 2004). At the same time, it is easy to see why many policy makers and funders might find it difficult to focus on investing in basic organizational functions, fostering innovation, and developing public understanding. Investing in these areas makes it harder for policy makers and funders to point to specific programs or interventions that they developed or to show direct causal links between their investments, specific initiatives, and measurable changes in student achievement over the short term. Of course, policy makers and funders operate under some of the same constraints and face the same economic, political, and public pressures that contribute to current demands for accountability and demonstrations of quick, measurable improvements. As a consequence, especially in this age of accountability, policy makers and funders need the vision and the courage to make basic investments in building capacity even though the results may be hard to see for some time.

FINAL QUESTIONS

Improving schools entails hard work on the inside of schools, in the communities schools serve, and among the policy makers, funders, and educators who help to shape the conditions in which schools operate. The approach described in this book provides some ideas and hypotheses that can help guide that work in the future. At the same time, this approach to school capacity raises a number of fundamental questions that require further consideration.

How Should Resources and Demands Be Defined?

Reflecting the complexity of the external environment, there is a fine line between resources and demands. For example, the supply of teachers serves as a crucial resource for schools, but if those teachers lack appropriate qualifications or bring expectations that do not fit those of their school or community, then their hiring may create a demand for the schools to find or create certain kinds of professional development. This problem suggests that resources and demands cannot be defined a priori but only in the interactions between the school and the surrounding environment. As in the implementation of California's class-size-reduction policy, some schools encounter increased opportunities to get needed resources at the same time that others may find themselves faced with new demands they do not have the capacity to meet.

Who Builds Capacity, and Who Impedes It?

Reflecting the fact that no definitive boundary exists between insiders and outsiders, it is also often hard to tell who represents a school and who represents other interests. Although she was the principal and technically an insider at City, upon her arrival Julianne Fredericksen was perceived by many veteran staff as an outsider and a representative of the district. Correspondingly, it is hard to know whether to characterize some of the changes she initiated as being made by the school or as being imposed upon it.

Similarly, in schools like Dewey and Emerson, parents were often seen as colleagues and allies who helped to manage the demands of the district. However, at Peninsula, at least in some cases, parents were seen as making some of the demands that needed to be managed (and, in fact, the school sometimes solicited the help of the district in dealing with those demands).

Given this complexity, studies of school capacity should not treat schools as monolithic organizations with a single set of interests that are either consistent or inconsistent with those on the outside. Careful descriptions should illuminate the variety of actors and interests that are involved in school improvement efforts and the relationships among them.

How (and When) Does Context Affect Capacity?

The experiences of the schools described in this book suggest that schools within the same district context can experience demands in distinct ways and may have to expend their energy and resources in very different ways as a result. In particular, being a "school of choice" may play a crucial role in a school's ability to manage change. Conceivably, since most of the schools in this book were not the focus of district policies and attention, they may have had more of the flexibility they needed to manage change than other schools in their districts. Further studies could usefully explore the role that flexibility and other aspects of the district and community context can have on a school's capacity to manage resources and demands.

Where Does Capacity Come From?

What sources can schools, particularly schools that routinely struggle to make improvements, draw on? As a member of the ATLAS Communities Project, I often heard Ted Sizer (founder of the Coalition of Essential Schools) quote James Comer (founder of the School Development Program and another leader of the ATLAS Project) as saying that the three most important things in improving schools were "relationships, relationships, relationships." That idea represents well the key role that interactions among people and the development of social capital have to play in building capacity.

At the same time, the experiences of the schools described in this book, as well as the reform experiences of countless others chronicled in the research literature, suggests that it is possible to build relationships and improve some aspects of school operations without improving student learning. As a consequence of those experiences, people like Richard Elmore (2002) might recite a different top three: instruction, instruction, instruction. From this perspective, any effort to build relationships has to go hand in hand with efforts to focus on the core of instruction, namely, students' and teachers' experiences in the classroom. Further efforts need to explore how to build capacity and improve schools while, on the one hand, respecting the strengths, values, and beliefs of the community members and the educators who are a part of those schools and, on the other hand, developing and bringing in instructional expertise that implicitly or explicitly suggests that those insiders do not know what to do or aren't trying hard enough to do it.

What might enable schools to take the next steps?

Even the best schools still have work to do: Some students continue to struggle; some needs go unmet; and significant and intolerable inequities persist. Schools that develop the organizational practices described in this book can try to manage the environment in ways that will help them to work on these issues and continue to make improvements. However, just like businesses and other organizations, schools can also use these practices to manage the environment in ways that enable them to maintain the status quo, lower expectations, and gloss over problems in operations and outcomes. That's why, as Michael Fullan emphasizes in his writings, improving schools also depends on "moral purpose": a commitment that goes beyond simply increasing organizational efficiency or survival and reflects some conception of the role schools play in the local community and wider society. In *Good Work: When Excellence and Ethics Meet*, psychologists Howard Gardner, Mike Csikszentmihalyi, and William Damon (2002; see also Gardner, 2007) explore the roots and manifestations of "good work"—work in many different fields that is excellent in quality, socially responsible, and meaningful to its participants. Their project includes a look at how some teachers manage to carry out excellent work in challenging circumstances; that same kind of lens needs to be brought to the work of educators more broadly—school leaders, district administrators, reformers, policy makers, funders, and researchers. Collectively, those involved in education need to develop a better understanding of what it takes to carry out improvement efforts that transcend partisan politics, ideological battles, and economic pressures and advance the common good.

In the end, the educational system can be viewed as a mechanical system in which policies and practices can be aligned to produce a narrow set of outcomes. This view may be particularly appropriate in contexts where the beliefs and expectations of school communities, the initiatives they undertake, and those reflected in state standards and accountability systems are all consistent. It can also be useful to view the educational system as a democratic political system in which diverse interests are constantly expressed. From this standpoint, establishing processes that schools can use to examine and negotiate diverse interests seems particularly important.

However, it is also useful to view schools as part of an ecosystem in which many different entities are trying to coexist (see, for example, Goodlad, 1994; Rowan, 2002). Viewed in this way, the initiatives of schools, improvement programs, districts, and states cannot be considered as the "start" of change efforts. Changes are constantly underway. In this context, new initiatives, whether launched by schools, districts, states, improvement programs, funders, the federal government, parents, or others have to be carefully examined in the same way that scientists have to consider how new species and new developments will affect the ecosystems into which they are introduced. Basic questions about these initiatives must be asked:

- Is there sufficient capacity to absorb and carry out the new initiatives?
- Do they extend and deepen efforts already at work?
- Are there high demands and hidden costs that can contribute to harmful and not just beneficial effects?

Educational ecosystems can accommodate vastly different designs for learning and schooling, but they cannot be pursued independently. Learning to deal with forces beyond organizational control and becoming more aware of the interaction among the many initiatives and programs currently at work in schools may be more than a step in the right direction. It may be part of a movement that embraces the complexity of schooling and the diversity of approaches to it.

References

Abelman, C., & Elmore, R. (1999). *When accountability knocks, will anyone answer?* (CPRE Research Report No. RR-42). Philadelphia: University of Pennsylvania, Consortium for Policy Research in Education.

Afterschool Alliance. (2005). *Afterschool for all: California's Launch of Proposition 49.* Washington, DC: America's Youth Policy Forum. Retrieved July 20, 2008, from http://www.afterschoolalliance.org/ambs/notebook/Background/California%27s_Proposition_49.pdf.

Alliance for Excellent Education. (2005). *Teacher attrition: A costly loss to the nation and to the states.* Retrieved July 28, 2008, from http://www.all4ed.org/files/archive/publications/TeacherAttrition.pdf

The American Heritage Dictionary (4th Edition). (2006). Boston, MA: Houghton-Mifflin.

Ancess, J., & Allen, D. (2006). Implementing small theme high schools in New York City: Great intentions and great tensions. *Harvard Educational Review, 76*(3), 401–406.

Anderson, S. (2003). *The school district role in educational change: A review of the literature.* (ICEC Working Paper #2). Toronto: International Centre for Educational Change.

Ballou, D., Goldring, E., & Liu, K. (2006). *Magnet schools and student achievement.* New York: National Center for the Study of Privatization in Education.

Barnes, G., Crowe, E., & Schaefer, B. (2007). *The costs of teacher turnover in five districts: A pilot study.* Washington DC: National Commission on Teaching and America's Future.

Bathon, J., & Spradlin, T. (2007). Outcomes of the school choice and supplemental educational services provisions of NCLB. *Education Policy Brief, 5*(8), 1–15.

Bidwell, C. (1965). The school as a formal organization. In J. March (Ed.), *Handbook of research on organizations,* (pp. 972–1019). New York: Rand McNally.

Bodilly, S. (1998). *Lessons from New American Schools' scale-up phase: Prospects for bringing designs to multiple schools.* Santa Monica, CA: Rand Corporation.

Brewer, J. & Smith, J. (2007). *Evaluating the "crazy quilt": Educational governance in California.* Stanford, CA: Institute for Research, Policy, and Practice.

Bryk, A., Sebring, P. B., Kerbow, D., Rollow, S., & Easton, J. (1998). *Charting Chicago school reform: Democratic localism as a lever for change.* Boulder, CO: Westview Books.

Bryk, A., & Schneider, B.(2002). *Trust in schools: A core resource for improvement.* New York: Russell Sage Foundation.

Bureau of Labor Statistics. (2008). *Projections data.* Retrieved August 20, 2008, from http://www.bls.gov/oco/ocos069.htm#projections_data

California Department of Education. (2008a). *Budget crisis report card.* Retrieved August 23, 2008 from http://www.cde.ca.gov/nr/re/ht/bcrc.asp

California Department of Education. (2008b). *California beginning teacher support and assessment.* Retrieved on August 27, 2008 from http://www.btsa.ca.gov/

California Educational Demographics Unit. (2006). State-wide enrollment by ethnicity, 2005–2006. Retrieved December 2, 2008, from http://dq.cde.ca.gov/dataquest/EnrollEthState.asp?Level=State&TheYear=2005-06&cChoice=EnrollEth1&p=2.

California Educational Demographics Unit. (2008). Time-series–Public school enrollment. Retrieved September 2, 2008 from http://dq.cde.ca.gov/dataquest/DQ/EnrTimeRptSt.aspx?Level=State&cChoice=TSEnr1&cYear=2007-08&cLevel=State&cTopic=Enrollment&myTimeFrame=S

California Legislative Analysts Office. (2001). *A new blueprint for California school facility finance.* Sacramento, CA: Legislative Analyst's Office.

California Legislative Analysts Office. (2008). Analysis of the 2008-09 budget bill: Education. Retrieved December 2, 2008, from http://www.lao.ca.gov/analysis_2008/education/ed_anl08.pdf

Calkins, A., Guenther, W., Belfiore, G., & Lash, D. (2007). *The turnaround challenge: Why America's best opportunity to dramatically improve student achievement lies in our worst-performing schools.* Boston: Mass Insight Education and Research Institute.

Carnoy, M., Adamson, F., Chudgar, A., Luschei, T., & Witte, J. (2007). *Vouchers and public school performance: A case study of the Milwaukee Parental Choice Program.* Washington, DC: Economic Policy Institute.

Carroll, S., Krop, C., Arkes, J., Morrison, P., & Flanagan, A. (2005). *California's K–12 public schools: How are they doing?* Santa Monica, CA: Rand Corporation.

Clark, B. (1970). *The distinctive college: Antioch, Reed and Swarthmore.* Chicago: Aldine.

Cohen, D. (1995). What is the system in systemic reform? *Educational Researcher, 24*(9), 11–17, 31.

Cohen, D., & Ball, D. (1999). *Instruction, capacity, and improvement.* Philadelphia: University of Pennsylvania, Consortium for Policy Research in Education.

Cohen, D., & Hill, H. (2001). *Learning policy: When state education reform works.* New Haven: Yale University Press.

Collins, A., Brown, J. S., & Newman, S. (1989). Cognitive apprenticeship: Teaching the craft of reading, writing and mathematics. In L. B. Resnick (Ed.), *Knowing learning and instructions: Essays in honor of Robert Glaser.* Hillsdale, NJ: Erlbaum.

Collins, J. (2001). *Good to great: Why some companies make the leap and others don't.* New York: HarperBusiness.

Collins, J. (2005). *Good to great and the social sectors: Why business thinking is not the answer.* Boulder, CO: Author.

Corcoran, T. (2007). Teaching matters: How state and local policy makers can improve the quality of teachers and teaching *(CPRE Policy Briefs, No. RB-48).* Philadelphia: University of Pennsylvania, Consortium for Policy Research in Education.

Damon, W. (1990). *The moral child: Nurturing children's natural moral growth.* New York: Free Press.

Darling-Hammond, L., Hightower, A., Husbands, J., LaFors, J., Young, V. & Christopher, C. (2005). *Instructional leadership for systemic change: The story of San Diego's reform.* Lanham, MD: Scarecrow Education Press.

Datnow, A., Hubbard, L. & Mehan, H., (2002). *Extending educational reform: From one school to many.* London: Routledge/Falmer.

DeArmond, M., Gross, B., & Goldhaber, D. (2008). Is it better to be good or lucky? *CRPE working paper # 2008-3.* Retrieved November 20, 2008 from http://www.crpe.org/cs/crpe/view/csr_pubs/226

Desimone, L., Porter, A., Garet, M., Yoon, K., & Birman, B. (2002). Effects of professional development on teachers' instruction: Results from a three-year longitudinal Study. *Educational Evaluation and Policy Analysis, 24*(2), 81–112.

Ed-Data. (2004). *Understanding California's Student Testing and Reporting Program (STAR).* Retrieved July 15, 2006, from http://www.ed-data.k12.ca.us/Articles/Article.asp?title=Understanding%20the%20STAR

Ed-Data. (2008). State of California education profile: Fiscal year 2006-2007. Retrieved December 2, 2008, from http://www.ed-data.k12.ca.us/Navigation/fsTwoPanel.asp?bottom=%2Fprofile.asp%3Flevel%3D04%26reportNumber%3D16

EdSource. (2004). How California ranks: A look at the state's investment in K–12 education over the past decade. Retrieved December 2, 2008, 2006, from http://www.edsource.org/pub_ranks9-04.html

EdSource. (2008a). Accountability overview. Retrieved December 2, 2008 from http://www.edsource.org/iss_sta_accountability_overview.html

EdSource. (2008b) Assessment overview. Retrieved December 2, 2008, http://www.edsource.org/iss_sta_assessment.html

Elmore, R. (1990). *Restructuring schools: The next generation of educational reform.* San Francisco: Jossey-Bass.

Elmore, R. (2000). *Building a new structure for school leadership.* Washington, DC: Albert Shanker Institute.

Elmore, R. (2002). *Bridging the gap between standards and achievement: The imperative for professional development in education.* Washington, DC: Albert Shanker Institute.

Elmore, R. (2006). *The problem of capacity in the (re)design of educational accountability systems.* Paper presented at the annual conference of the Campaign for Educational Equity, Teachers College, Columbia University, New York.

Elmore, R., & Birney, D. (1997). *Investing in teacher learning.* Washington, DC: National Commission on Teaching and America's Future.

Fine, M. (1993). [Ap]parent involvement: Reflections on parents, power and urban public schools. *Teachers College Record, 94,* 682–710.

Flynn, D. (2008). Patriots beat: Proven draft strategy. *The Milford Daily News.* Retrieved October 11, 2008, from http://www.milforddailynews.com/sports/sports_columnists/x1767335627

Fuhrman, S. (Ed.) (1990a). *Designing coherent education policy.* San Francisco: Jossey-Bass.

Fuhrman, S. (1990b). *The new accountability.* (CPRE Policy Briefs, No. RB-27.) Philadelphia: University of Pennsylvania, Consortium for Policy Research in Education.

Fuhrman, S. (1993). The Politics of Coherence. In S. Fuhrman (Ed.) *Designing coherent education policy: Improving the system* (pp. 1–34). San Francisco: Jossey-Bass.

Fullan, M. (1993). *Change forces: Probing the depths of educational reform.* London: Falmer Press.

Fullan, M. (1999). *Change forces: The sequel.* London: Falmer Press.

Fullan, M. (2003). *Change forces with a vengeance.* New York: Routledge & Falmer

Press.

Fuller, B. (2003). Education policy under cultural pluralism. *Educational Researcher, 32*(9), 15–24.

Gardner, H. (1983). *Frames of mind: The theory of multiple intelligences.* New York: Basic Books.

Gardner, H. (1995). *Leading minds: An anatomy of leadership.* New York: Basic Books.

Gardner, H. (Ed.). (2007). *Responsibility at work: How leading professionals act (or don't act) responsibly.* San Francisco: Jossey-Bass.

Gardner, H., Csikszentmihalyi, M., & Damon, W. (2002). *Good work: When excellence and ethics meet.* New York: Basic Books.

Gogoi, P. (2005). Wal-Mart's China card. *BusinessWeek.* Retrieved October 13, 2008, from http://www.businessweek.com/bwdaily/dnflash/jul2005/nf20050726_3613_db016.htm

Goleman, D. (1995). *Emotional intelligence: Why it can be more important than IQ.* New York: Bantam Books.

Goodlad, J. (1994). *Educational renewal, better teachers, better schools.* San Francisco: Jossey-Bass.

Goodnough, A. (2001). Ad campaign to recruit teachers draws fire. *New York Times.* Retrieved October 13, 2008, from http://query.nytimes.com/gst/fullpage.html?res=9C02E2DD1030F934A25751C0A9679C8B63

Hargreaves, A. (2000). *Changing teachers, changing times: Teachers' work and culture in the postmodern age.* London: Continuum International Publishing Group.

Hargreaves, A., & Fink, D. (2004). The seven principles of sustainable leadership. *Educational Leadership, 61*(7), 8–13.

Hargreaves, A., & Fullan, M. (1998). *What's worth fighting for out there?* New York: Teachers College Press.

Harris, A. (2008). *Distributed leadership in schools: Developing the leaders of tomorrow.* London: Routledge & Falmer Press.

Hassel, B., & Steiner, L. (2004). *Stimulating the supply of new choices for families in light of NCLB: The role of the state.* Denver, CO: Education Commission of the States.

Hatch, T. (1998a). The differences in theory that matter in the practice of school improvement. *American Educational Research Journal, 35*(1), 3–31.

Hatch, T. (1998b). How community action contributes to achievement. *Educational Leadership, 55*(8), 16–19.

Hatch, T. (2001a). Incoherence in the system: Three perspectives on the implementation of multiple improvement initiatives in one district. *American Journal of Education, 109*(4), 107–137.

Hatch, T. (2001b). It takes capacity to build capacity. *Education Week, 20* (22), 44, 47.

Hatch, T. (2001c). What does it take to break the mold? *Teachers College Record, 102*(3), 561–589.

Hatch, T. (2002). When improvement programs collide. *Phi Delta Kappan, 83*(8), 626–634.

Hatch, T. (2006). *Into the classroom: Developing the scholarship of teaching and learning.* San Francisco: Jossey-Bass.

Hatch, T., & White, N. (2002). The raw materials of reform: Rethinking the knowledge of school improvement. *Journal of Educational Change, 3*(2), 117–134.

Hess, F. (1999). *Spinning wheels: The politics of urban school reform.* Washington, DC:

Brookings Institution Press.

Hess, F. (Ed.). (2005). *Urban school reform: Lessons from San Diego.* Cambridge, MA: Harvard University Press.

Hess, F. (2006). *Educational entrepreneurship: realities, challenges, possibilities.* Cambridge, MA: Harvard University Press.

Hightower, A. (2002). San Diego's big boom: Systemic instructional change in the central office and schools. In A. Hightower, M. Knapp, J. Marsh, & M. McLaughlin (Eds.), *School districts and instructional renewal* (pp. 76–93). New York: Teachers College Press.

Hightower, A., Knapp, M., Marsh, J., & McLaughlin, M. (2002). *School districts and instructional renewal.* New York: Teachers College Press.

Hill, P. (2005). The supply side of choice. *Journal of Education, 186*(2), 9–25.

Hill, P., & Celio, M. (1998). *Fixing urban schools.* Washington, DC: Brookings Institution Press.

Hirschman, A. O. (1970). *Exit, voice, and loyalty: Responses to decline in firms, organizations, and states.* Cambridge, MA: Harvard University Press.

Honig, M. (2007, April). *No small thing: School district central office bureaucracies and the implementation of new small autonomous schools initiatives.* Paper presented at the annual conference of the American Educational Research Association, Chicago.

Honig, M., & Hatch, T. (2004). Crafting coherence: How schools strategically manage multiple external demands. *Educational Researcher, 33*(8), 16–30.

Huffman, T. (2003). Wal-Mart in China: Challenges facing a foreign retailers supply chain. *China Business Review.* Retrieved October 13, 2008, from http://www.chinabusinessreview.com/public/0309/wal-mart.html

Ingersoll, R. (2003a). *Is there really a teacher shortage?* Seattle, WA: University of Washington, Center for the Study of Teaching and Research.

Ingersoll, R. (2003b). *Why do high-poverty schools have difficulty staffing their classrooms with qualified teachers?* Washington, DC: Center for American Progress.

Institute of Education Sciences. (2008). *What works clearinghouse.* Washington DC: U.S. Department of Education. Retrieved December 2, 2008, from http://ies.ed.gov/ncee/wwc/

Jennings, J. (2008). The social structure of competition in the urban educational marketplace. Paper presented at the Annual Meeting of the American Sociological Association, Boston, MA.

Kahne, J., Sporte, S., de la Torre, M., & Easton, J. (2008). Small high schools on a larger scale: The impact of school conversions in Chicago. *Educational Evaluation and Policy Analysis, 30*(3), 281–315.

Kanter, R. (2004). *Confidence: How winning streaks and losing streaks begin and end.* New York: Crown Business.

Kreader, J. (2005) *Introduction to child-care subsidy research.* New York: Child Care & Early Education Research Connections. Retrieved July 20, 2008, from http://www.childcareresearch.org/SendPdf?resourceId=7458

Lange, C., & Sletten, S. (2002). *Alternative education: A brief history and research synthesis.* Alexandria, VA: Project Forum, National Association of State Directors of Special Education.

Lave, J., & Wenger, E. (1991). *Situated cognition: Legitimate peripheral participation.* Cambridge: Cambridge University Press.

Lawler, E. (1986). *High-involvement management.* San Francisco: Jossey-Bass.

Leithwood, K., & Menzies, T. (1998). Forms and effects of school-based management: A review. *Educational Policy, 12*(3), 325–347.

Lips, D. (2008). *School choice: Policy developments and national participation estimates in 2007–2008.* Backgrounder #2102. Retrieved October 13, 2008 from http://www.heritage.org/Research/Education/bg2102.cfm

Little, J. W. (1990). The persistence of privacy: Autonomy and initiative in teachers' professional relations. *Teachers College Record, 91*(4), 509–536.

Little, J. W. (1996). The emotional contours and career trajectories of (disappointed) reform enthusiasts. *Cambridge Journal of Education 26*(3), 345–359.

Loeb, S., Bryk, T., & Hanushek, E. (2007). *Getting down to facts: School finance and governance in California.* Stanford, CA: Institute for Research, Policy, and Practice. Retrieved October 13, 2008, from http://www.stanford.edu/group/irepp/documents/GDF/GDF-Overview-Paper.pdf

Lortie, D. (1977). *Schoolteacher.* Chicago: University of Chicago Press.

Louis, S. K., & Kruse, S. (1995). *Professionalism and community perspectives on reforming urban schools.* Thousand Oaks, CA: Corwin Press.

Lui, E., & Johnson, S. M. (2006). New teachers' experiences of hiring: Late, rushed, and information-poor. *Educational Administration Quarterly, 42*, 324–360.

Malen, B., Croninger, R., Muncey, D., & Redmond-Jones, D., (2002). Reconstituting schools: "Testing" the "theory of action." *Educational Evaluation and Policy Analysis, 24*(2), 113–132.

Malen, B., & King Rice, J. (2004). A framework for assessing the impact of education reforms on school capacity: Insights from studies of high-stakes accountability initiatives. *Educational Policy, 18*(5), 631–660.

March, J. (1991). Exploration and exploitation in organizational learning. *Organization Science, 2*(1), 71–87.

Marsh, J. (2000). *Connecting districts to the policy dialogue: A review of literature on the relationship of districts with states, schools, and communities.* Seattle: University of Washington, Center for the Study of Teaching and Policy.

McDonald, J. (1996). *Redesigning school.* San Francisco: Jossey-Bass.

McDonald, J., Mohr, N., Dichter, A., & McDonald, E. (2007). *The power of protocols: An educator's guide to better practice.* New York: Teachers College Press.

McLaughlin, M. (1990). The Rand Change Agent Study Revisited: Macro Perspectives and Micro Realities. *Educational Researcher, 19* (9), 11–16.

McLaughlin, M., & Talbert J. (2001). *Professional communities and the work of high school teaching.* Chicago: University of Chicago Press.

Merriam-Webster Online Dictionary. (2007). Retrieved October 31, 2008, from http://www.merriam-webster.com

Metz, M. (1990). Real school: A universal drama amid disparate experience. In D. Mitchell & M. Goertz (Eds.), *Education politics for the new century: 20th anniversary yearbook of the politics of education association* (pp. 75–91). Philadelphia: Falmer Press.

Meyer, J., & Rowan, B. (1977). Institutionalized organizations: Formal structure as myth and ceremony. *American Journal of Sociology, 83*, 340–363.

Mintrop, H. (2003). The limits of sanctions in low-performing schools: A study of Maryland and Kentucky schools on probation. *Education Policy Analysis Archives,*

11(3). Retrieved July 23, 2008 from http://epaa.asu.edu/epaa/v11n3.html

Murphy, J. (1991). *Restructuring schools: Capturing and assessing the phenomena*. New York: Teachers College Press.

Murphy, J., & Beck, L. (1995). *School-based management as school reform: Taking stock*. Thousand Oaks, CA: Corwin Press.

National Center for Education Statistics (1999). *Condition of America's public school facilities*. Washington, DC: Institute of Educational Sciences, U.S. Department of Education. Retrieved December 2, 2008 from http://nces.ed.gov/pubs2000/2000032.pdf

National Center for Education Statistics. (2007). *Digest of education statistics: 2007*. Washington, DC: Institute of Educational Sciences, U.S. Department of Education. Retrieved October 13, 2008, from http://nces.ed.gov/programs/digest/d07/

National Center for Education Statistics. (2008). *Participation in education: Elementary and secondary education: Racial/ethnic distribution of public school students*. Washington, DC: Institute of Educational Sciences, U.S. Department of Education. Retrieved August 23, 2008, from http://nces.ed.gov/programs/coe/2008/section1/indicator05.asp

National Center for Education Statistics. (2002). *Characteristics of the 100 largest public elementary and secondary school districts in the United States: 2000–01* (NCES No. 202-351). Washington, DC: U.S. Department of Education.

National Clearinghouse for Educational Facilities. (2008). [*School construction data.*] Retrieved July 17, 2008, from http://www.edfacilities.org/cd/McGraw-Hill-Construction-Data.pdf

National Clearinghouse for English Language Acquisition (2005). *ELL demographics by state*. Retrieved on July 17, 2008, from http://www.ncela.gwu.edu/stats/3_bystate.htm

National Commission on Excellence in Education. (1983). *A nation at risk: The imperative for educational reform*. Washington, DC: U.S. Government Printing Office.

National Working Commission on Choice in K–12 Education. (2003). *School choice: Doing it the right way makes a difference*. Washington, DC: Brown Center on Education Policy, Brookings Institution.

Newmann, F. M., King, M. B., & Youngs, P. (2000). Professional development that addresses school capacity: Lessons from urban elementary schools. *American Journal of Education, 108*(4), 259–299.

Newmann, F., Smith, B., Allensworth, E., & Bryk, T. (2001). Instructional program coherence: What is it and why should it guide school improvement policy? *Educational Evaluation and Policy Analysis, 23*(4), 297–321.

Northwest Regional Educational Laboratory. (2001). *Catalog of school reform models*. Portland, OR: Northwest Regional Educational Laboratory.

O'Day, J., Goertz, M., & Floden, R. (1995). *Building capacity for education reform*. New Brunswick, NJ: Consortium for Policy Research in Education.

O'Day, J., & Smith, M. (1993). Systemic reform and educational opportunity. In S. H. Fuhrman (Ed.), *Designing coherent education policy* (pp. 250–312). San Francisco: Jossey-Bass.

Perkins, D. (1992). *Smart schools: From training memories to educating minds*. New York: Free Press.

Perry, M., Miller, B., Carlos, L., Teague, J. & Frey, S. (2001). *Aligning California's edu-*

cation reforms: Progress made and the work that remains. Palo Alto, CA: Ed Source.

Perry, M. & Teague, J. (2001). *Update on California's teacher workforce issues*. Palo Alto, CA: EdSource.

Popkewitz, T., Tachnick, B., & Wehlage, G. (1982). *The myth of education reform*. Madison: University of Wisconsin Press.

Porter, M. (1998). *Competitive advantage: Creating and sustaining superior performance*. New York: Free Press.

Porter, M. (2000). Location, competition and economic development: Local clusters in a global economy. *Economic Development Quarterly, 14*(1), 15–34.

Purkey, S., & Smith, M. (1983). Effective schools: A review. *The Elementary School Journal, 83*(4), 427–452.

Putnam, R. (2000). *Bowling alone: The collapse and revival of American community*. New York: Simon & Shuster.

Ries, A., & Trout, J. (1981). *Positioning: The battle for your mind*. New York: Warner Books.

Rowan, B. (2002). The ecology of school improvement: Notes on the school improvement industry in the United States. *Journal of Educational Change, 3*, 283–314.

Rowan, B., & Miskel, C. (1999). Institutional theory and the study of educational organizations. In J. Murphy & K. S. Louis (Eds.), *Handbook of research on educational administration* (2nd ed., pp. 359–383). San Francisco: Jossey-Bass.

Shields, P., Esch, C., Humphrey, D., Wechsler, M., Chang-Ross, C., Gallagher, H. A., Guha, R., et al. (2003). *The status of the teaching profession 2003*. Santa Cruz, CA: Center for the Future of Teaching and Learning.

Shirley, D. (2002). *Valley Interfaith and school reform: Organizing for power in South Texas*. Austin: University of Texas Press,

Smith, T., & Ingersoll, R. (2004). What are the effects of mentoring and beginning teacher induction on turnover? *American Educational Research Journal, 41*(3), 681–714.

Smylie, M., Lazarus, V., & Brownlee-Conyers, J. (1996). Instructional outcomes of school-based participative decision-making. *Educational Evaluation and Policy Analysis, 18*, 181–198.

Spillane, J. (2006). *Distributed leadership*. San Francisco: Jossey-Bass.

Spillane, J., & Diamond, J. (Eds.). (2007). *Distributed leadership in practice*. New York: Teachers College Press.

Spillane, J., & Thompson, C. (1997). Reconstructing conceptions of local capacity: The local education agency's capacity for ambitious instructional reform. *Educational Evaluation and Policy Analysis, 19*(2), 185–203.

Stoll, L. (1999). Realizing our potential: Understanding and developing capacity for lasting improvement. *School Effectiveness and School Improvement, 10*(1), 1–30.

Stoll, L., & Earl, L. (2003). Making it last: Building capacity for sustainability. In B. Davies & J. West-Burnham (Eds.), *Handbook of educational leadership and management* (pp. 491–504). London: Pearson Education.

Stoll, L., & Louis, K. S. (2007). *Professional learning communities*. London: Open University Press.

Stullich, S., Eisner, E., McCrary, J., & Roney, C. (2006). *National Assessment of Title I: Interim Report: Vol. I. Implementation of Title I*. Washington, DC: Institute of Education Sciences, U.S. Department of Education.

Texas Center for Educational Research. (2000). *The cost of teacher turnover.* Austin, TX: Texas State Board for Educator Certification.

Timar, T. (2006) *Financing K–12 education in California: A system overview.* Stanford, CA: Institute for Research, Policy, and Practice.

Tyack, D. (1974). *The one best system: A history of American urban education.* Cambridge, MA: Harvard University Press.

Tyack, D., & Cuban, L. (1995). *Tinkering toward utopia: A century of public school reform.* Cambridge: Harvard University Press.

U.S. Charter Schools. (2008). *National charter school data: 2007–2008 new school estimates.* Retrieved August 23, 2008, from http://www.uscharterschools.org/cs/r/view/uscs_rs/2347

Warren, M. (2005). Communities and schools: A new view of urban education reform. *Harvard Educational Review, 75*(2), 133–173.

Weick, K. (1976). Educational organizations as loosely coupled systems. *Administrative Science Quarterly, 21,* 1–19.

Wenger, E. (1998). *Communities of practice: Learning, meaning, and identity.* Cambridge: Cambridge University Press.

Wilson, S. (2003). *California dreaming: Reforming mathematics education.* New Haven: Yale University Press.

Wilson, S. M., Bell, C., Galosy, J., & Shouse, A. (2004). "Them that's got shall get": Re-imaging teacher recruitment, induction, and retention. In M. A. Smylie & D. Miretzky (Eds.), *Developing the teacher workforce. 103rd Yearbook of the National Society for the Study of Education, Part 1* (pp. 145–179). Chicago, IL: University of Chicago Press.

Wisconsin Department of Public Instruction. (2008). *Milwaukee parental choice program facts and figures for 2007–08.* Retrieved August 3, 2008, from http://dpi.wi.gov/sms/choice.html

Witte, J., & Thorn, C. (1996). Who chooses? Vouchers and interdistrict choice programs in Milwaukee. *American Journal of Education, 104,* 186–217.

Wohlstetter, P., Malloy, C., Smith, J., & Hentschke, G. (2004). Incentives for charter schools: Building school capacity through cross-sectoral alliances. *Educational Administration Quarterly, 40* (3), 321–365.

Wohlstetter, P., & Odden, A. (1992). Rethinking school-based management policy and research. *Educational Administration Quarterly, 28,* 529–549.

Wohlstetter, P., Smyer, R., & Mohrman, S. A. (1994). New boundaries for school-based management: The high involvement model. *Educational Evaluation and Policy Analysis, 16,* 268–286.

Index

189

About the Author

Thomas Hatch is an associate professor at Teachers College, Columbia University, and codirector of the National Center for Restructuring Education, Schools, and Teaching (NCREST). In addition to studies of large-scale school reform, his work includes research on teacher quality in pre-K–12 and higher education. He is also involved in a variety of efforts to use multimedia and the Internet to document teaching and share teachers' expertise (http://www. tc.edu/ncrest/images.htm). That work includes two digital exhibitions produced with colleagues: "Learning from the practice of veteran and novice teachers" published in the *Journal of Teacher Education* (http://www.tc.edu/ ncrest/exhibitions/learningfrompractice/) and "Making teaching public" published by *Teachers College Record* (http://www.tcrecord.org/makingteach- ingpublic/). His other books include *Into the Classroom: Developing the Scholar- ship of Teaching and Learning* (Hatch, 2006); a coedited volume of work produced by teachers examining their teaching, *Going Public with Our Teaching: An Anthology of Practice* (Hatch, Ahmed, Lieberman, Faigenbaum, Eiler White, & Pointer Mace, 2005); and *School Reform Behind the Scenes* (McDonald, Hatch, Kirby, Haynes, & Joyner, 1999). He previously served as a Senior Scholar at the Carnegie Foundation for the Advancement of Teaching where he co- directed the K–12 program of the Carnegie Academy for the Scholarship of Teaching and Learning (CASTL) and established the Carnegie Knowledge Media Laboratory. Further information and additional materials related to *Managing to Change,* including links to related resources and references, can be found at http://www.tc.edu/ncrest/hatch/managingtochange.